TRANSFORMING MULTILATERAL DIPLOMACY

TRANSFORMING MULTILATERAL DIPLOMACY

The Inside Story of the
SUSTAINABLE DEVELOPMENT GOALS

AMBASSADOR MACHARIA KAMAU
Permanent Representative of Kenya to the United Nations

PAMELA CHASEK
Professor of Political Science, Manhattan College

DAVID O'CONNOR
Former Chief of Policy and Analysis,
United Nations Division for Sustainable Development

Routledge
Taylor & Francis Group

LONDON AND NEW YORK

First published 2018
by Routledge
2 Park Square, Milton Park, Abingdon, Oxon OX14 4RN

and by Routledge
711 Third Avenue, New York, NY 10017

Routledge is an imprint of the Taylor & Francis Group, an informa business

British Library Cataloguing-in-Publication Data

A catalogue record for this book is available from the British Library

Library of Congress Cataloging-in-Publication Data

A catalog record for this book has been requested

ISBN: 978-1138-58998-8 (hbk)
ISBN: 978-0-8133-5086-8 (pbk)
ISBN: 978-0-8133-5088-2 (ebk)

Typeset in Minion Pro
by Servis Filmsetting Ltd, Stockport, Cheshire

CONTENTS

ILLUSTRATIONS

FIGURES

PHOTOS

ACRONYMS

AAAA	Addis Ababa Action Agenda
ALBA	Bolivarian Alliance for the Peoples of Our America
AOSIS	Alliance of Small Island States
BRICS	Brazil, Russia, India, China, and South Africa
CBD	Convention on Biological Diversity
CBDR	common but differentiated responsibilities
CSD	Commission on Sustainable Development
CSOs	civil society organizations
DESA	UN Department of Economic and Social Affairs
DSD	UN Division for Sustainable Development
ECOSOC	Economic and Social Council
EU	European Union
FfD	Financing for Development
G-77	Group of 77
GDP	gross domestic product
GRULAC	Group of Latin American and Caribbean Countries
HLPF	High-Level Political Forum on Sustainable Development
IGN	Intergovernmental Negotiations on the Post-2015 Development Agenda
ILO	International Labour Organization
IMF	International Monetary Fund
IPCC	Intergovernmental Panel on Climate Change
LDCs	least-developed countries
LDNW	land-degradation–neutral world
LGBT	lesbian, gay, bisexual, transgender
MDGs	Millennium Development Goals
MOI	means of implementation
NCDs	noncommunicable diseases

NGOs	nongovernmental organizations
NIEO	New International Economic Order
ODA	official development assistance
OECD	Organization for Economic Cooperation and Development
OWG	Open Working Group on Sustainable Development Goals
Rio+20	United Nations Conference on Sustainable Development
SCP	sustainable consumption and production
SDGs	Sustainable Development Goals
SDSN	Sustainable Development Solutions Network
SIDS	small island developing states
STI	science, technology, and innovation
TST	Technical Support Team
UHC	universal health care
UN	United Nations
UNCCD	United Nations Convention to Combat Desertification
UNCLOS	United Nations Convention on the Law of the Sea
UNCSD	United Nations Conference on Sustainable Development
UNCTAD	United Nations Conference on Trade and Development
UNDP	United Nations Development Programme
UNEP	United Nations Environment Programme
UNFCCC	UN Framework Convention on Climate Change
UNICEF	United Nations Children's Fund
VNR	voluntary national review
WEOG	Western European and Others Group
WHO	World Health Organization
WTO	World Trade Organization

PREFACE

The United Nations system is made up of more than fifty organizations and agencies that are legislated, administered, and managed through a labyrinth of institutional structures that include the United Nations Secretariat, under the Secretary-General; specialized and technical agencies, which have their governing bodies; and the General Assembly, the premier decision-making body of the entire global system, with its myriad subsidiary councils and entities.

Navigating this dense maze of legislative, administrative, and institutional systems is one of the most confounding and complex undertakings known to modern bureaucratic and institutional engagement.

Most of what we have come to accept as the body of international norms and legislation that govern our global system of cooperation, humanitarian support, and peace and security is negotiated, endorsed, legislated, and enforced through this system of organizations, agencies, councils, and offices.

Mastering the functions and operations of this global multilateral system takes years, if not decades, of engagement and practice. For many ambassadors and technical officers arriving at United Nations Headquarters in New York, the nerve center of this international system, the task of engaging the system and its executives, technocrats, organizations, institutions, and offices can be daunting and at times impossible.

This book documents one of the greatest twin outcomes of the cooperative work done by the United Nations in recent history: the creation of the Sustainable Development Goals and the 2030 Agenda for Sustainable Development. The three-and-a-half-year journey of the negotiation of these goals—goals that will guide international cooperation in sustainable development—involved and touched on virtually every office, organization, agency, and institution of the United Nations. More remarkably, it involved the direct participation of negotiators and the concurrence of every country in the world! This was unprecedented.

The complexity of the task and the amount of time it took to get it done have left a deep impression on the international system as well as on the ambassadors, negotiators, and officers who were involved. Many people in government, nongovernmental organizations, and the private sector have wondered how this feat was achieved. How did something that seemed impossible, and even ludicrous to some, come to fruition through negotiators and technocrats from all over the world brought together by the United Nations system?

This book tells that story. It is meant for the lay reader who may have an interest in how complex organizations work, how modern multilateral negotiations are carried out, and the inner mechanics of how the United Nations system works. It is also meant for ambassadors, newly arrived in New York, who are trying to understand and navigate the system and its archaic operations and traditions, but, probably most importantly, it is also for the student, the young professional seeking to understand the international multilateral system and hopefully become a part of it with a view to making it better and more productive for the world's people, for a better planet, and for global peace and prosperity.

Ambassador Macharia Kamau

ACKNOWLEDGMENTS

Writing a book that is part history, part personal reflection, and part textbook is no easy feat. Beginning with our earlier conversations on how to structure this book in a way that would be engaging and approachable to students and diplomats alike, we knew that we were embarking on an exciting journey that would tell the story of the sustainable development goals through the collective eyes of a diplomat, a member of the UN Secretariat, and an academic observer. We hope that we have enabled a greater understanding of what happens inside the United Nations, who is involved, what they do, why they do it, and how an outcome evolves. We also hope that we have been able to show how the work of UN multilateral negotiations affects people, planet, peace, prosperity, and partnerships.

This book has been made possible by the hard work of the representatives of UN member states, international organizations, civil society and other stakeholders, and the UN Division for Sustainable Development Secretariat, who dedicated many hours to the creation of the Sustainable Development Goals from 2011 to 2015.

We couldn't have written this book without the help of many people who shared their personal experiences with us along the way. Special thanks go out to Tobias Ogweno, Nikhil Seth, Csaba Kőrösi, David Donoghue, Amit Narang, Farrukh Khan, Stephan Contius, Abdullah Tawleh, Elizabeth Cousens, Louise Kantrow, and especially Paula Caballero Gómez—there would not be SDGs or this book without her vision. We also want to thank Sam Kutesa and Amina Mohammed for writing the forewords for this book and for their leadership throughout the process.

We also need to thank the members of the *Earth Negotiations Bulletin* team who covered the Open Working Group on Sustainable Development Goals and the intergovernmental negotiations on the post-2015 development agenda, especially Faye Leone, Ana-Maria Lebădă, Nathalie Risse, Lynn Wagner, Kate Offerdahl, Joanna Dafoe, and Delia Paul. Their work helped to keep our memories based on reality.

Thanks go out to the Kenyan Mission to the United Nations, especially Grace Mbabu and Mumbi-Michelle Kimani, for all of their logistical and moral support.

We also want to thank our editors, Katie Moore and James Sherman, and everyone at Westview Press for their support and positive attitude throughout this process. We also want to thank all of the peer reviewers who gave us positive feedback and helpful suggestions.

Finally, Pamela Chasek thanks her family—Kimo, Sam, and Kai Goree and Arlene and Marvin Chasek—for all of their patience, support, and love.

And for the many years that the SDG and 2030 agenda process took away from what could have been quality time with his family, Macharia Kamau begs their indulgence and understanding.

David O'Connor shares the sentiments of the other two authors. He thanks his family—Tu Quyen and Juliet—for all the support and inspiratioin they have provided during the negotiations. He is eternally grateful to them. He also thanks his colleagues in the UN Division for Sustainable Development who worked so tirelessly and professionally as a team throughout

FOREWORDS

I N PLANNING TO take up the stewardship of the General Assembly as president, on behalf of Africa, I was acutely aware that I would have two major concerns during my tenure. First, the United Nations was about to celebrate its seventieth birthday, and thus the United Nations was at a crossroads: a changing world with new and emerging economies, rapidly evolving global power relations, and fluid social developments across the globe, which meant that the United Nations had to revisit its relationship with its member states in order to chart its way forward for the next seventy years.

Charting this way forward was going to happen on two levels: first, in regard to the United Nations' development agenda as well as the United Nations' stewardship, particularly its impact on least-developed countries (LDCs). The Millennium Development Goals had run their course, and although highly impactful, they had left huge challenges in their wake. Moreover, new and emerging social, economic, and environmental challenges had arisen that required a new approach to the United Nations' development work.

Second, as a long-serving minister of foreign affairs of Uganda, I was also acutely aware of the persistent peace and security challenges faced by many African countries. Therefore, it was my deep desire to ensure that my tenure as president of the General Assembly had a positive and lasting impact on peace and security on our continent.

These two concerns, development and peace and security, framed my year as president of the General Assembly and dominated my agenda for the work of the General Assembly in 2015.

Attending to the first challenge of the United Nations Development Agenda had already started in earnest at the United Nations Conference on Sustainable Development (Rio +20), where the world had adopted a far-sighted and comprehensive vision for sustainable development, known as the "The Future We Want." As an outcome of this conference, the member states agreed to work through an Open Working Group (OWG) to develop a new set of goals for sustainable development, which would be called the Sustainable Development Goals (SDGs). The success of this group would determine the future agenda of the United Nations' development work and frame its relationship with its member states for the next fifteen years. The OWG was a resounding success, and the SDGs were developed and adopted.

It was during the OWG that the great work done by Ambassador Macharia Kamau in providing leadership for the OWG became recognized. Therefore, in preparing for my year as president of the General Assembly and realizing that the first expected deliverable of my tenure would be the production of the 2030 Agenda for Sustainable Development (with the SDGs at its core), I was cognizant that for the member states to have success in developing the 2030 Agenda, I needed continuity, dedication, determination, and a diplomat of high intelligence and experience at the helm of negotiations for the future agenda.

I never hesitated in recognizing the work and dedication of Ambassador Kamau. Not only is he a distinguished diplomat, but he is also incredibly passionate about the peoples of this world and future generations. I believe that it was this passion that enabled him to withstand the various pressures and obstacles that followed. It was only logical that I would tap him to provide leadership, together with Ambassador David Donoghue of Ireland, for the way forward. Ambassador Kamau and his co-facilitator led and guided the global negotiations to great success.

The world is indebted to Ambassador Kamau for his steadfast leadership on the SDGs and the 2030 Agenda. He worked on both processes for more than three years. It took an immense amount of personal sacrifice to steer the negotiations to a successful conclusion. Without his leadership, the world would not have the most transformative agenda of our time for the benefit of the people, the planet, and the prosperity of our world.

This book provides a detailed and rigorous analysis of the challenges and complexities of modern international, multilateral negotiations. I am proud of Ambassador Kamau's work; I am also proud of him as an African, a world citizen, and a global diplomat. The legacy of his work will remain with us for years to come.

Hon. Sam K. Kutesa (MP), Minister of Foreign Affairs, Uganda
President of the 69th General Assembly

* * *

IN JUNE 2012 UN Secretary-General Ban Ki-moon appointed me as his special adviser on Post-2015 Development Planning. When we embarked on this three-year journey, it was with the understanding that the international community had a unique opportunity to integrate economic growth, social justice, and environmental concerns by putting sustainable development at the heart of a bold yet practical universal agenda. Although no one could have predicted that the result would be a universal set of seventeen Sustainable Development Goals (SDGs) and 169 targets as part of the comprehensive 2030 Agenda for Sustainable Development, we recognized that the post-2015 development agenda had to lead to peaceful, just, and inclusive societies that are free from fear and violence.

The years leading up to the adoption of the 2030 Agenda for Sustainable Development were hectic. We had many consultations and conversations to find out what people at every level of society in regions, cities, towns, and villages wanted to see in the SDGs. We questioned representatives of all sectors—political, economic, financial, humanitarian, civic, scientific, and industrial, to name but a few. We sought the views of people of all ages, all socioeconomic levels, and all walks of life, in more than one hundred countries. We involved tens of millions of people, of whom about 70 percent were under thirty years of age, and at least eight million of these people were contacted through social media.

Elaborating the SDGs and defining the 2030 Agenda was a daunting yet inspiring and historic task for the United Nations and its member states. During this period I worked very closely with member states, eminent persons, business, civil society, parliamentarians, local authorities, and academia. This unprecedented open, inclusive, and transparent effort led to the collective realization that business as usual would not work for achieving the future we want and ensuring that no one is left behind. This book does an excellent job of charting this journey with a focus on the Open Working Group on Sustainable Development Goals, which had the responsibility to draft the SDGs and targets in an open and inclusive manner.

The co-chairs, Ambassador Macharia Kamau and Ambassador Csaba Kőrösi, skillfully and successfully guided the deliberations. Subsequently, Kamau and Ambassador David Donoghue shepherded the process that resulted in the formulation of the overarching 2030 Agenda. It was a humbling experience and my utmost pleasure to collaborate with these distinguished diplomats.

In the spirit of the transparent and collaborative undertaking that led to the 2030 Agenda and the accompanying SDGs, this book effectively opens up the inner workings of the United Nations, explains the broader context in which the SDGs were negotiated and how that influenced the outcome, and also engages people in the agenda's implementation at the international, regional, national, and local levels.

Each of these goals feels like one of my children. Like a family, the goals are all different but interrelated, and each depends on the others. Together, they are a bold and transformative blueprint for a world of peace and prosperity where no one is left behind. In practice, that means ending poverty and hunger, providing opportunities for all to fulfill their potential, and protecting our home, the planet. These are the essential ingredients for peaceful, just, and inclusive societies that are free from fear and violence.

The world today stands at the threshold of significant opportunity. Together we can realize our quest for dignity, peace, prosperity, justice, sustainability, and an end to poverty.

Amina J. Mohammed
Deputy Secretary-General, United Nations

Former Minister of Environment, Nigeria

Former Special Adviser to the UN Secretary-General
on Post-2015 Development Planning

1

SETTING THE STAGE

The new agenda is a promise by leaders to all people everywhere. It is an agenda for people, to end poverty in all its forms—an agenda for the planet, our common home.

—BAN KI-MOON, UN SECRETARY-GENERAL[1]

The lessons learnt from the implementation of [the] Millennium Development Goals show that much can be achieved when the world finds focus around a shared vision and common goals. The new agenda we adopt today is an ambitious plan for collective action to transform the fate of humanity, by lifting all people out of poverty, while remaining in harmony with our planet.

—UHURU KENYATTA, PRESIDENT OF THE REPUBLIC OF KENYA[2]

There really were moments when I thought the thing [the Sustainable Development Goals project] was going to collapse because it was so inclusive, and views were so divergent and everyone felt so strongly about what they wanted to see [in the goals]. But in the end a common agenda emerged.

—PHUMZILE MLAMBO-NGCUKA, EXECUTIVE DIRECTOR, UN WOMEN[3]

In September 2015 the United Nations made history. After months of negotiations, all 193 member states formally adopted "Transforming Our World: The 2030 Agenda for Sustainable Development," including seventeen universal sustainable development goals (SDGs). The event made news around the world, from the *New York Times* and the *Guardian* to the *Indian Express* and Kenya's *Daily Nation*. The *Financial Times* published a special report on the SDGs. Even Pope Francis came to New York and addressed the General Assembly, noting that in many ways his recently released encyclical, *Laudato Si,* embodied the integrated and indivisible nature of the sustainable development agenda.[4]

Yet three years earlier, no one thought that a set of universal sustainable development goals could be negotiated using a broad-based, consultative process that involved not only UN member states but also representatives from civil society; the private sector; UN agencies, programs, and funds; and other nonstate actors. At a point in history when many were questioning the future of UN multilateralism—multiple countries working together on a given issue—and member states were increasingly failing to reach consensus on key decisions, the outcome of these negotiations was not only considered to be a major accomplishment but also gave both the United Nations and multilateralism a new lease on life.

WHAT ARE THE
SUSTAINABLE DEVELOPMENT GOALS?

The Sustainable Development Goals are a set of seventeen goals and 169 targets that form the heart of the United Nations' post-2015 sustainable development agenda. The SDGs build on both the Millennium Development Goals (MDGs), which were adopted by the United Nations in 2000 and then expired in 2015, and the series of sustainable development summits that began with the UN Conference on the Human Environment in Stockholm, Sweden, in 1972 and concluded with the UN Conference on Sustainable Development in Rio de Janeiro, Brazil, in 2012 (see Box 1.1).

At the UN Millennium Summit in September 2000, world leaders adopted the UN Millennium Declaration, which committed their nations to a new global partnership to reduce extreme poverty. The United Nations then set out a series of time-limited targets that became known as the

■ **Box 1.1.**

The Sustainable Development Goals

1. End poverty in all its forms everywhere.

2. End hunger, achieve food security and improved nutrition and promote sustainable agriculture.

3. Ensure healthy lives and promote well-being for all at all ages.

4. Ensure inclusive and equitable quality education and promote lifelong learning opportunities for all.

5. Achieve gender equality and empower all women and girls.

6. Ensure availability and sustainable management of water and sanitation for all.

7. Ensure access to affordable, reliable, sustainable and modern energy for all.

8. Promote sustained, inclusive and sustainable economic growth, full and productive employment and decent work for all.

9. Build resilient infrastructure, promote inclusive and sustainable industrialization and foster innovation.

10. Reduce inequality within and among countries.

11. Make cities and human settlements inclusive, safe, resilient and sustainable.

12. Ensure sustainable consumption and production patterns.

13. Take urgent action to combat climate change and its impacts (taking note of agreements made by the UNFCCC forum).

14. Conserve and sustainably use the oceans, seas and marine resources for sustainable development.

15. Protect, restore and promote sustainable use of terrestrial ecosystems, sustainably manage forests, combat desertification and halt and reverse land degradation and halt biodiversity loss.

16. Promote peaceful and inclusive societies for sustainable development, provide access to justice for all and build effective, accountable and inclusive institutions at all levels.

17. Strengthen the means of implementation and revitalize the global partnership for sustainable development.

SOURCE: United Nations, *Transforming Our World: The 2030 Agenda for Sustainable Development,* 2015, https://sustainabledevelopment.un.org/post2015/transforming ourworld.

Millennium Development Goals. The eight MDGs, which included halving extreme poverty, halting the spread of HIV/AIDS, and providing universal primary education, all by the target date of 2015, formed a blueprint for development and galvanized unprecedented efforts to meet the needs of the world's poorest people. (See Chapter 2 for more about the MDGs.)

During a high-level meeting of the UN General Assembly in 2010, governments called not only for accelerating progress towards achieving the MDGs but also for thinking about ways to advance the UN development agenda beyond 2015. At the same time, preparations were under way for the United Nations Conference on Sustainable Development (Rio+20), which was convening in Brazil in June 2012, twenty years after the 1992 Rio Earth Summit and forty years after the very first such UN conference— the UN Conference on the Human Environment. The idea to develop a new set of successor goals to the MDGs that would be applicable to all countries emerged during the preparations for Rio+20. Colombia proposed that one outcome from the conference could be the development of a set of SDGs that could replace the MDGs. The SDGs concept continued to evolve, and in the Rio+20 outcome document, "The Future We Want," governments agreed to develop a set of "goals to be agreed by the General Assembly."[5] These goals were supposed to help provide a "concrete approach that delivers means for measuring—in accordance with the contexts and priorities of each country—both advances as well as bottlenecks in efforts to balance sustained socioeconomic growth with the sustainable use of natural resources and the conservation of ecosystem services."[6] Many agreed that the MDGs demonstrated the value of setting common goals for bringing the international community to work together.

What makes the SDGs special? First, the new goals are universal. The SDGs are the core of an agenda that recognizes shared national and global challenges and offers a much-needed paradigm shift away from outdated global development assumptions of the past. In other words, these goals are not just to be achieved by developing countries with financial support from the industrialized countries. They are to be achieved by *all* countries.

Second, unlike the MDGs, which were crafted by a group of UN experts under the guidance of the Secretary-General, the SDGs resulted from a transparent and inclusive process involving thousands of participants from governments, intergovernmental organizations, the business community, civil society, and nongovernmental organizations (NGOs). As a result, the ideas that informed the discussions and the process of shaping the SDGs were more diverse than those in earlier efforts such as the MDGs.

Third, the seventeen SDGs and 169 targets represent a broader agenda than did the MDGs. The SDGs not only seek to end poverty and hunger but also to encompass the broader sustainable development agenda by promoting inclusive economic growth, protecting the environment, and promoting social inclusion. Furthermore, the SDGs expand the sustainable development agenda to include the need for peaceful and inclusive societies, access to justice for all, and effective, accountable, and inclusive institutions at all levels.

Fourth, the SDGs are interconnected; success in one will involve tackling issues more commonly associated with others. And, as often repeated throughout the negotiations, the SDGs are supposed to ensure that no country or person is left behind.

The SDGs were negotiated by the Open Working Group (OWG), which was established by the UN General Assembly in early 2013. The OWG met for a total of thirteen sessions between March 2013 and July 2014, when it adopted the SDGs and the targets. Following the conclusion of the OWG's efforts, a new process was established to reach final agreement on the SDGs and the broader post-2015 or post-MDGs development agenda. These negotiations began in January 2015 and concluded in early August 2015 with

PHOTO 1.1. Youth delegates pose with their favorite Sustainable Development Goals, which represent a much broader agenda than the Millennium Development Goals. *Photo by IISD/Kiara Worth (enb.iisd.org)*

the provisional adoption of "Transforming Our World: The 2030 Agenda for Sustainable Development." The agenda, with the SDGs and targets as the cornerstone, also contains a declaration and sections on means of implementation, and follow-up and review.[7] This book tells the story of these negotiations, what was at stake, and how this unique process restored faith in multilateralism and has opened the door to changing the way that UN negotiations are conducted.

TIME FOR A CHANGE

The negotiation and successful adoption of the 2030 Agenda came at a time when many were questioning the United Nations' role in economic and social development. If the second half of the twentieth century was an age of coming together into a new, post–World War II system of multilateral institutions, the early twenty-first century looked quite the opposite. The gap between the rich and the poor within and between countries remained wide. And even China's export-led development model, which accounted for the vast majority of people lifted out of extreme poverty globally, had proven to be environmentally unsustainable and had still left tens of millions in China below the absolute poverty line of $1.95 per day.[8] Many experts realized that existing instruments of development policy meant to achieve the long-standing development goal of lifting everyone out of poverty were not working.[9] The time was ripe to rethink the existing approaches to development policy, which had not eradicated the most extreme poverty around the world. Existing development approaches were also wreaking a heavy toll on the environment and on people's health, most dramatically illustrated by the abysmal air quality in many megacities of Asia. As the concept of sustainable development became more widely accepted, people increasingly understood that economic and social development could not take place indefinitely without taking into consideration the natural resource base and the environment. At the same time, it became apparent that poverty eradication is a necessary and fundamental requirement for environmentally and socially sustainable development.

Concepts of sustainability and sustainable development are appealing because they hold out the promise of reconciling divergent views about the relationship among economic development, social development, and the health of the natural environment. Yet, although one can argue that removing the tension between ecology and economy is the central goal of sustainable development, there is little agreement on what sustainable development actually means. Sustainable development has a multiplicity of definitions. Generally, it implies that it is possible to achieve sound environmental planning without sacrificing economic and social improvement.[10] Some definitions emphasize sustainability and focus on the protection and conservation of living and nonliving resources. Other definitions emphasize development, targeting changes in technology as a way to reconcile growth and environmental protection. Still others insist that sustainable development is a contradiction in terms, for development as it is now practiced is essentially unsustainable.[11] Within the UN system, the most common definition is that of the 1987 Brundtland Commission: "development that meets the needs of the present without compromising the ability of future generations to meet their own needs."[12]

Thus, if development is to be genuinely sustainable, policy makers need to substantially modify their strategies and their assumptions. For many years the predominant paradigm was "grow now, clean up later." Export-led industrial and agricultural development depleted not just nonrenewable resources (oil, gas, coal, minerals) but also renewable resources through land degradation, water and air pollution, overfishing, and deforestation. However, the failure to make the shift to more sustainable development and actually deliver on the hopes that many people around the world have attached to the idea of sustainable development has become increasingly evident. In part, these difficulties reflect political problems grounded in questions of financial resources, equity, and competition with other issues, such as terrorism and war, for the attention of decision makers. They also reflect differing views about what should be developed, what should be sustained, and over what period.[13]

While governments and members of civil society were grappling with the operationalization of sustainable development, UN multilateralism was suffering. On the surface, UN multilateral negotiations appeared to be flourishing. In the twenty years between the 1992 Earth Summit and the 2012 Rio+20 conference, the sustainable development negotiating calendar grew in terms of the number of meetings, the number of participants, and the complexity of the issues. The number of UN member states grew from 166 to 193, and each year more participants from civil society, the business community, and intergovernmental organizations joined the discussions. However, as the number of meetings and the number of participants grew, the traditional consensus decision-making model began to break down.

Most decisions, resolutions, declarations, and treaties adopted at the United Nations result from a complex series of multilateral negotiations often based on consensus decision making—a group decision-making process where group members develop, and agree to support, a decision in the best interest of the whole. Trying to achieve consensus among 193 countries with different interests and priorities was becoming increasingly difficult. The traditional way of viewing negotiations in a North-South or Cold War frame of reference was no longer working because of the complexity and diversification of interests within groups of countries. Traditional large coalitions, including the 134-member Group of 77, were less unified, and new, smaller coalitions emerged. For example, during the negotiations on climate change, small island developing states facing dire consequences caused by climate change broke away from the Group of 77, whose oil-producing members often dominated the group's position. The least-developed countries found their priorities to be quite different from those of the large industrializing countries. As a result, more and more countries were not always willing to go along with the consensus.

Technology also increased the complexity and challenges of multilateral negotiations. On the one hand, the use of e-mail, laptops, smartphones, and other technology allows delegations to refer to documents, consult websites, e-mail colleagues, record impressions of meetings, and transcribe key exchanges. However, technology is a double-edged sword. Technological advances mean that more can be done in less time, and this has heightened, rather than alleviated, the stress of negotiations. The ease with which proposals can be submitted seems to have discouraged restraint, with an ever-greater volume of proposals reaching the chairs and secretariats.[14] Although the point of consensus decision making is to allow all participants to have a hand in crafting the outcome so they will all have a stake in its successful implementation, the reality could be in line with the old proverb: "Too many cooks spoil the broth."

A QUICK GUIDE TO UN NEGOTIATIONS

So how do UN sustainable development negotiations usually work? Multilateral negotiations—negotiation by three or more parties over one or more issues—are the process through which UN member states achieve agreement on issues of global concern.[15] Within the UN system, a multilateral negotiating process on sustainable development issues usually starts when governments propose, individually or collectively, that a particular issue or set of issues needs to be addressed. The participating governments discuss the issue and negotiate the written language of a draft agreement, which can take a variety of formats. The vast majority of UN decisions appear as resolutions, which include background paragraphs in a preamble followed by either a list of operative paragraphs or agreements on future actions. Other outcomes include declarations, which are statements conveying a high level of political concern, such as the 1992 Rio Declaration on Environment and Development; programs of action, which call upon governments to take a series of actions voluntarily, such as Agenda 21 or "The Future We Want"; and complex and legally binding treaties, which may require countries to make changes to their own domestic laws, such as the UN Framework Convention on Climate Change and the Convention on Biological Diversity.[16]

In the UN General Assembly, negotiations on different issues are organized around the committee structure (see Box 1.2). Member states that have initial ideas about an issue of concern will propose a resolution in the General Assembly plenary or one of its six committees. The first challenge is to describe the issue, which, in some cases, could take years. The second phase is the conferencing process, through which member states build a global consensus around the issue and then begin to define what the global action will be. Once the committee agrees on a draft resolution, it is forwarded to the General Assembly plenary for formal adoption.

Whatever format a decision takes, it starts as a draft text, which is prepared based on advance inputs from governments. The initial draft can be prepared by the Secretariat (although usually not), the chair of the negotiations, a group of delegations such as the European Union (EU) or the Group of 77 and China (G-77/China), an individual delegate or country, or even a person or persons appointed for the task. The draft text then becomes the focus of discussion to get reactions from other governments. In the General Assembly, member states usually look to the G-77 to draft initial resolutions because then at least two-thirds of the members are already in general or at least loose agreement. The G-77 chair is perhaps the second-most-important multilateral post after the president of the General Assembly because of this power. The chair of the G-77 is elected for a calendar year and tends to rotate among the three G-77 regions: Asia, Africa, and Latin America/Caribbean. The G-77 chair controls the drafting of new resolutions, usually by farming them out to key country proponents of each issue on the agenda. The G-77 chair is also consulted on who will chair each of the General Assembly committees. The committee chairs have the power to decide how each resolution will be negotiated in their

■ **Box 1.2.**

General Assembly Committee Structure

The UN General Assembly has a large number of issues to consider each year, so it allocates most agenda items among its six main committees, which discuss them, negotiate draft resolutions and decisions, and then present them to a plenary meeting of the Assembly for consideration. Some issues are considered only in the General Assembly plenary. Here are the six main committees:

- First Committee: Disarmament and International Security Committee
- Second Committee: Economic and Financial Committee
- Third Committee: Social, Humanitarian and Cultural Committee
- Fourth Committee: Special Political and Decolonization Committee
- Fifth Committee: Administrative and Budgetary Committee
- Sixth Committee: Legal Committee

SOURCE: United Nations, "Main Committees," www.un.org/ga/maincommittees .shtml.

committees, who will take the lead, who will participate, and who will moderate contact groups (informal negotiating groups).

UN negotiations usually take place in two sessions each day, from 10:00 A.M. to 1:00 P.M. and from 3:00 to 6:00 P.M. If necessary, evening sessions may be scheduled. It is not uncommon for the final sessions to be extended, possibly through the night, to complete negotiations. There are two different types of sessions: open and closed. Open sessions, referred to as "formal" sessions, are open to everyone with proper accreditation, including NGOs and the media. These are often referred to as plenary sessions, where member states make individual statements on the issue under discussion.[17]

During these sessions, formal decisions are also taken, including adoption of resolutions, programs of action, declarations, and treaties.

When governments reach the point that they need to find consensus on particularly contentious topics, they may break into informal sessions, often called working groups. These can be closed to everyone except delegates and Secretariat staff, although NGOs and others may be allowed to attend as observers at the discretion of the chair. During these meetings, delegates can speak and debate among themselves and address sensitive issues. If delegates are negotiating a particularly long document, such as a treaty or a program of action, they may break into a number of informal working groups, with each working on a specific issue or section of the text.[18] The United Nations tries to ensure that only two working groups meet at any given time to avoid putting smaller delegations at a disadvantage. However, as has been the case in a number of processes, especially climate change negotiations, more than two groups may meet concurrently.

In some cases, governments form contact groups or hold "informal informals," which are strictly off-limits to anyone except a core group of delegates. These groups meet outside the main negotiating rooms and bring together only those governments that have a strong interest in a particular issue that has caused disagreement. Towards the end of complicated negotiations, when the time pressure is greatest, delegates may huddle, either in or across negotiating groups, to hammer out last-minute details. Truly sticky issues often end up being tackled by measures such as the use of a facilitator, an extended bureau (chairs, vice chairs, and invited heads of delegation), or a "friends of the chair" group (participants invited by the chair). The chair, working with a handful of governments on a particularly contentious subject, may have to use all of his or her powers of persuasion or creative suggestions on new language to achieve consensus.[19]

During contact group or working group meetings, delegates often review the text from beginning to end, identify those passages that they can or cannot easily accept, and offer amendments. As the areas of agreement and disagreement become clear, a revised draft text is prepared denoting areas of disagreement, usually in square brackets. Delegates continue to meet in a succession of additional sessions, under the leadership of a chair or facilitator, where they narrow down their differences, eliminating the brackets as portions of the text are agreed upon. Delegates often check back and forth with their ambassadors or officials in their national capitals when they need to seek guidance on how far they may compromise. As a result, delegates sometimes agree to language *ad referendum* (for further consideration by those having the authority to make a final decision) until they hear back from their capital with final approval.[20]

The third phase is the outcome: a resolution, a declaration, a program of action, or a legally binding instrument (treaty). Some of these processes can take years, such as climate change negotiations, whereas UN General Assembly resolutions may take as little as four to eight weeks. So as negotiations near their conclusion, there may be some give-and-take or trade-offs as delegates consider the balance of elements in the final package and consider whether they can let go of some proposals in order to retain others. When the delegates finally reach agreement on the exact wording of the entire text, they officially adopt it.[21] In most UN processes, member states have the ability to vote for or against the proposal or to abstain. However, this is quite rare in sustainable development negotiations, where member states usually adopt agreements by consensus, meaning that everyone can accept the outcome.

The decision made in Rio in 2012 to negotiate a set of sustainable development goals introduced a different decision-making procedure for a new intergovernmental response to sustainable development challenges.

THE JOURNEY AHEAD

This book looks at the SDGs and the 2030 Agenda for Sustainable Development and examines how they changed the way that UN multilateral sustainable development negotiations are conducted. We tell the story of the people, issues, negotiations, and paradigm shift that began with the UN Conference on Sustainable Development in Rio in June 2012 and concluded three years and three months later at the UN Sustainable Development Summit in September 2015. During this process the international community essentially created a new development paradigm and set in place the first intergovernmentally negotiated set of sustainable development goals, which will guide environment and development policy and practice by the United Nations, national and local governments, the private sector, and civil society until 2030.

To understand just how much the negotiation of the SDGs changed the UN system, it is first necessary to look back at the changes that took place in the international political economy at the beginning of the twenty-first century. Chapter 2 will begin to tell the story of challenges, crises, and change that characterized the tumultuous first decade and a half of the new millennium.

In Chapter 3 we will look at the establishment of the UN General Assembly's Open Working Group on Sustainable Development Goals. This chapter will examine how the UN General Assembly chose to put into action the language in the Rio+20 outcome document, "The Future We Want," setting forth the mandate for the elaboration of the goals. In Chapter 4 our story continues through the first eight meetings of the OWG, from March 2013 to February 2014. These meetings formed the "stocktaking" portion of the process, where delegates learned about the issues through a series of seminars and discussions. This chapter will look not only at these meetings but also at how they dislodged delegates from their twentieth-century work methods and understandings of sustainable development.

In Chapter 5 we take a step back and analyze the cast of characters participating in the OWG. We introduce them and explain their interests and tactics in the negotiations that followed. In terms of negotiation theory, this chapter will help readers understand the negotiating tactics, vested interests, coalition building, trade-offs, and challenges faced by the co-chairs. This chapter will also put the issues discussed in Chapter 4 into the context of the different groups that advocated for the old and the new. Governments were not the only actors. NGOs and coalitions of civil society members, international organizations, and the business community all participated and influenced the process.

In Chapter 6 we turn to the negotiations themselves and tell the inside story of the OWG during the last five meetings (March to July 2014), where the goals and targets were elaborated. Here we will focus primarily on the co-chairs' leadership, their strategies, and their relationship with the participants in the deliberations of the OWG.

The seventeen goals did not all emerge in the same way, so in Chapter 7 we focus on the negotiations and drama surrounding the goals themselves, with particular emphasis on some of the more difficult negotiations, and describe the key players and outcomes to achieve a better understanding of how agreement was reached on each goal. Immediately after the goals were adopted in 2014, a new process began to put together the rest of the 2030 development agenda. Chapter 8 examines this process, which started in January 2015 and concluded in August 2015. Chapter 9 uses the 2015 Sustainable Development Summit as its starting point and reviews the launch of the goals both within and outside the United Nations and the initial efforts by multiple stakeholders to implement the goals. Finally, Chapter 10 looks at the lessons learned from the SDGs and their negotiation and how this process changed the United Nations, multilateralism, and sustainable development.

2

MULTILATERALISM:
Complexity and Intrigues

The perfect storm of weather disruptions, biodiversity collapse, social unrest and the rise of inequality together with
persistent economic crises had left the world on edge.

—AMBASSADOR MACHARIA KAMAU

Although multilateralism had become a norm of diplomatic practice and a
fundamental feature of international organizations in the post–World War
II era, by the beginning of the twenty-first century its utility was being
questioned. Was it becoming too unwieldy and ineffective? With 193 UN
member states, the rise of globalization, and the increasing importance of
nonstate actors (including nongovernmental organizations [NGOs], community groups, religious groups, and the business community), the conventional understanding of multilateralism had to be revised to reflect the
dramatically changed political, economic, and social landscape.[1] Initially,
the discussion focused on how to make the existing multilateral system,
especially the United Nations, work within the rapidly changing international environment. This evolved into a broader debate about the nature
and direction of globalization and the implications of global change in the
twenty-first century.

The greater number of players has complicated multilateral diplomacy
and negotiations aimed at finding common ground to reach agreement on
collective action, norms, or rules.[2] This chapter looks at the challenge of
managing these complexities during the 1990s and early 2000s.

TWENTY-FIRST-CENTURY CHALLENGES
TO MULTILATERALISM

In September 1990 US President George H. W. Bush proclaimed a "new world order," following the multilateral response to Iraq's invasion of Kuwait, which gave hope that the post-Cold War period would see the realization of the multilateralism that the UN had promised but had failed to live up to during its first forty-five years. As President Bush said,

> We stand today at a unique and extraordinary moment. The crisis in the Persian Gulf, as grave as it is, also offers a rare opportunity to move toward an historic period of cooperation. Out of these troubled times, our fifth objective—a new world order—can emerge: a new era—freer from the threat of terror, stronger in the pursuit of justice, and more secure in the quest for peace. An era in which the nations of the world, East and West, North and South, can prosper and live in harmony.[3]

Although the unprecedented cooperation among the UN Security Council, the North Atlantic Treaty Organization (NATO), and numerous states and NGOs restored Kuwait's sovereignty, the new world order did not result in a more secure world. Both the US role as sole superpower and the UN role in establishing this new world order were weakened as a result of terrorism, violent ethno-political conflicts, the rise of separatist movements, and economic dislocation that destabilized the world order. The US decision to go to war in Iraq in 2003 without the explicit authority of the UN Security Council also contributed to a loss of faith in the system. As then UN Secretary-General Kofi Annan observed in November 2003, "The past year has shaken the foundations of collective security and undermined confidence in the possibility of collective responses to our common problems and challenges. It has also brought to the fore deep divergences of opinion on the range and nature of the challenges we face, and are likely to face in the future."[4]

At its outset, the twenty-first century witnessed a global gridlock in both multilateral negotiations and the understanding of how to tackle issues resulting from globalization and wide inequalities within and between countries. Many were concerned that the United Nations and other international organizations no longer had the confidence of their members to deal with multiple challenges: threats to security, widespread poverty and hunger, financial and economic crises, climate change, organized crime, drug trafficking, and terrorism. All of these problems remained pervasive despite attempts at multilateral solutions. Meanwhile, the emergence of new global players such as the BRICS (Brazil, Russia, India, China, and South Africa) shifted the balance of power in international governance. Nonstate actors were playing a larger role in solving global problems. In sum, the existing multilateral governance system appeared to be outdated in terms of both the distribution of power among the states and its essentially state-based nature.[5]

REBALANCING ECONOMIC AND POLITICAL POWER

There is no doubt that the Cold War shaped post–World War II multilateralism and the first four decades of the United Nations. But as the Soviet Union disintegrated and the East-West conflict no longer dominated UN discourse, there was a resurgence of North-South (developed versus developing country) antagonism beginning with the UN Conference on Environment and Development (UNCED, or Earth Summit) in 1992. However, to understand this North-South conflict, some historical perspective is needed.

In the early 1960s, developing countries at the United Nations Conference on Trade and Development (UNCTAD) formed a coalition that became known as the Group of 77 (G-77). Encouraged by a surge in commodity prices and the successful manipulation of oil supplies in the early 1970s by the Organization of Petroleum Exporting Countries (OPEC), developing countries attempted to restructure the global economic system and push for a new international economic order (NIEO). This aspiration grew out of the neo-Marxist political economy theory known as dependency theory, which argued that the international trading system was condemning the "periphery"—developing countries in Africa, Asia, and Latin America—to poverty, exploitation, and dependency. Among other measures, the NIEO specifically called for a system of price supports for a number of key developing-country commodity exports, technology transfer, and the negotiated redeployment of some developed-country industries to developing nations.[6]

After the late 1970s, however, the NIEO faded from the global political agenda as economic trends turned against the South. Some officials in the North consequently felt that they could disregard southern demands for change. Yet, although some in the North might have considered the NIEO agenda "discredited,"[7] it remained unfinished business for much of the South and was still considered a goal "very much worth pursuing."[8] Thirty years later, the conflict between the developing countries of the South and the rich industrialized countries of the North remained, and with the end of the Cold War this confrontation moved front and center.

In the 1980s commodity prices, debt, and trade issues shaped the economic picture in developing countries. Falling prices devastated the economies of countries heavily dependent on commodity exports. Between 1980 and 1991, the price of a weighted index of thirty-three primary commodities exported by developing countries, not including energy, declined by 46 percent.[9] Meanwhile, heavy debt burdens, taken on at a time when commodity prices were high and northern banks were freely lending dollars from Arab oil revenues, siphoned off much of the foreign exchange of many developing countries. By 1995, the total external debt of the least-developed countries was $136 billion, a sum that represented 112.7 percent of their gross national product that year.[10] In 1996 the World Bank and the International Monetary Fund (IMF) responded by launching the Heavily Indebted Poor Countries (HIPC) Initiative with the aim of ensuring that no poor country would face a debt burden that it could not manage.[11]

The World Commission on Environment and Development (also called the Brundtland Commission after its chair, Norway's Gro Harlem Brundtland) echoed some elements of the NIEO in its 1987 report, *Our Common Future*. Recognizing "an accelerating ecological interdependence among nations,"[12] the Brundtland Commission emphasized the link between economic development and the environment, and identified poverty eradication as a necessary and fundamental requirement for environmentally sustainable development. The report noted that the goals of economic and social development must be defined in terms of sustainability in all countries: developed or developing, market oriented or centrally planned.[13] It also determined that a series of rapid transitions and policy changes would be required, including keeping population levels in harmony with the ecosystem, reducing mass poverty, increasing equity within and between nations, increasing efficiency in the use of energy and other resources, reorienting technology, and merging environment and economics in decision making.[14]

During the negotiations on Agenda 21, the program of action adopted at the Earth Summit in 1992, concepts from the NIEO also resurfaced. The Earth Summit was the first major UN conference to take place amid the geopolitical transformation that resulted from the end of the Cold War. The vast economic requirements of handling the transformation of the former communist countries to a market economy became a serious barrier to the Western European countries' willingness and ability to accommodate developing countries when they requested new and additional financial resources for sustainable development.[15] Despite the question of political will, this became the underlying "bargain" in Rio: the developing countries would undertake more environmentally sustainable forms of development in exchange for new and additional financial resources and technology transfer on preferential and concessional terms from the industrialized countries.

In spite of its inclusion in Agenda 21, the underlying bargain was not honored. Within a year of the Earth Summit, official development assistance (ODA) levels fell, sending a negative political signal as the Commission on Sustainable Development (CSD), the body charged with monitoring the implementation of Agenda 21, embarked on its work. ODA flows fell from $79.3 billion in 1992 to $71 billion in 2000.[16] The Rio promise of a global partnership between industrialized and developing countries did not materialize.

But the global economy continued to change. By 2004, industrialized countries' share of global gross domestic product (GDP) was dropping,[17] and their share of exports declined from 73 to 59 percent of the global total.[18] The revolution in information technology, trade liberalization, economic reforms, the accession of China into the World Trade Organization (WTO), and the increased movement of capital and technology from developed to developing countries spurred unprecedented growth in the global economy.[19] Although this economic growth reached practically every region of the world, a handful of large developing countries—led by

China, India, and Brazil—accounted for a major share of global growth. Other emerging economies, such as Indonesia, Mexico, Russia, Turkey, and Vietnam, also grew at a rapid pace. This enabled developing countries to expand their share of global GDP by 2012, suggesting that the world's economic balance of power was shifting away from the United States and Europe toward Asia and Latin America.[20] (See Figure 2.1.)

■ **Figure 2.1**

Change in GDP Distribution 1992–2012

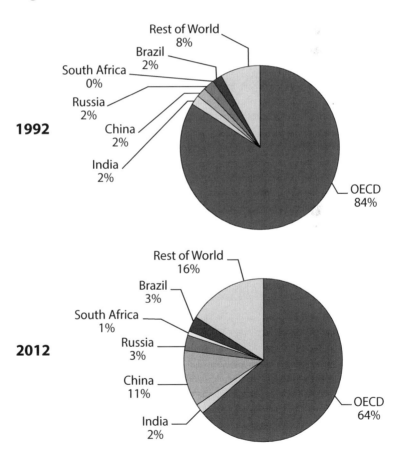

SOURCE: World Bank, http://databank.worldbank.org.

North-South economic issues echoed in debates both inside the United Nations and in the Bretton Woods institutions (World Bank and International Monetary Fund [IMF]), the World Trade Organization, and the regional development banks. It was becoming clear that the socioeconomic situations in different countries were changing the nature of both negotiations and the prevailing models of economic development. No longer could multilateralism be simplified as just "East-West" or "North-South" negotiations. The "multi" had gained new significance and was changing the way the UN system and its member states were operating. There was no more business as usual.

THE MILLENNIUM DEVELOPMENT GOALS

In 2000 a momentous turn of the calendar offered the UN system and world leaders the opportunity to revise the terms of global cooperation. Although the United Nations had a mixed track record in supporting economic and social development during the twentieth century, the fact that it had nearly universal membership gave it the legitimacy to convene the global conversation. Moreover, UN Secretary-General Kofi Annan was at the height of his influence, and his perceived moral leadership was pivotal to reframing debates around a new spirit of partnership. That spirit gave rise to the MDGs.[21]

Creating the MDGs

In September 2000 the UN Millennium Summit adopted the Millennium Declaration, committing world leaders to combat poverty, hunger, disease, illiteracy, discrimination against women, and environmental degradation. The text distilled a wide-ranging global agenda down to a relatively pithy framework of global priorities.[22] The aim was a results-oriented approach to global collaboration that put people at the center.[23]

The Millennium Declaration was a response to many of the world's foremost development challenges as they appeared in 2000. The policy orthodoxy that had focused on development through macroeconomic fundamentals had achieved only limited results. The Asian financial crisis of 1997–1998 had sent shock waves around the globe, and Latin America was recovering from its own series of economic crises. Post–Cold War ODA

budgets were in decline. Many Eastern European and Central Asian countries were struggling to regain their economic footing in the post-Commu-
nist era. Sub-Saharan Africa had suffered two "lost decades" of economic
growth while the HIV/AIDS pandemic infected twenty-five million people
without a global treatment effort. Many people viewed globalization as a
force imposing the will of rich corporate interests against the needs of the
disempowered poor.[24] Tensions culminated in the December 1999 "Battle
in Seattle," where antiglobalization street protests forced the midstream
abandonment of the third WTO ministerial meeting.

After the Millennium Summit, the UN General Assembly adopted Resolution 55/162 to mandate the Secretary-General to prepare a long-term
road map towards implementation of the Millennium Declaration.[25] The
drafting process was led by Mark Malloch-Brown, head of the United Nations Development Programme (UNDP). The resulting September 2001
report was the first document to include the term "Millennium Development Goals" as a specific package of goals and targets.[26]

The eight MDGs (see Box 2.1) were extracted from a wide array of
global conferences held in the 1990s, where many international goals and
targets were established. These conferences included the following:

- World Conference on Education for All (Jomtien,
  Thailand, 1990)
- World Summit for Children (New York, 1990)
- UN Conference on Environment and Development
  (Rio de Janeiro, 1992)
- International Conference on Population and Development
  (Cairo, 1994)
- World Summit on Social Development (Copenhagen, 1995)
- Fourth World Conference on Women (Beijing, 1995)

Although the MDGs did not garner initial support, especially from
NGOs and some developing countries, over their fifteen-year life span they
became the world's central reference point for development cooperation.
In the post-Cold War period, as Mark Malloch-Brown stated, "Nothing
had replaced geopolitical competition for influence as a rationale for

■ **Box 2.1.**

The Millennium Development Goals

By 2015, all UN member states have pledged to:

1. Eradicate extreme poverty and hunger

2. Achieve universal primary education

3. Promote gender equality and empower women

4. Reduce child mortality

5. Improve maternal health

6. Combat HIV/AIDS, malaria and other diseases

7. Ensure environmental sustainability

8. Develop a global partnership for development

SOURCE: United Nations, "Millennium Development Goals," www.un.org /millenniumgoals.

development assistance. And the development community itself was divided by disputes over means." The MDGs led to a "realignment of development efforts" and "the birth of major new funding pools."[27]

Economic Crisis and Change

Following the introduction of the MDGs, total official development assistance rose from $71 billion in 2000 to $124 billion in 2014.[28] The goals gave the international community something tangible to rally around and signaled what could be done with a set of goals. The MDGs provided individual countries with a universal scorecard against which to measure and compare gains. Yet at the same time, the world was changing, and the implementation of the MDGs, despite significant progress made by many countries, proved insufficient to confront the challenges facing humanity and the planet.[29] So what happened?

First, there was a shake-up in the global economy triggered by the 2008 global financial crisis. For years, globalization had been characterized by "free market" ideology and financial deregulation. However, the result was financial speculation, an economic structure with an outsized financial sector, and, in many countries, growing inequality.[30] This all came to a head in September 2008 with the collapse of Lehman Brothers, a sprawling global bank whose failure almost brought down the world's financial system. The crisis, which actually began in 2007 when sky-high home prices in the United States turned decisively downward, spread first through the US financial sector and then to financial markets overseas. In the United States the crisis affected the entire investment banking industry, the biggest insurance company, two enterprises chartered by the US government to aid mortgage lending, the largest mortgage lender, the largest savings and loan, and two of the largest commercial banks. The financial sector was not the only one affected. Many companies and the US auto industry suffered heavily. Banks stopped making the loans that most businesses needed to regulate their cash flows. Stock markets around the world plunged. The Dow Jones Industrial Average lost 33.8 percent of its value in 2008, and by the end of the year a deep recession had enveloped most of the globe.[31]

The 2008 financial crisis had multiple causes, including financiers who claimed to have found a way to banish risk when in fact they had simply lost track of it, as well as central bankers and other regulators that tolerated this recklessness. The macroeconomic backdrop was also important. Years of low inflation and stable growth fostered complacency and risk taking. A "savings glut" in Asia pushed down global interest rates. Some research also implicates European banks, which borrowed greedily in US money markets before the crisis and used the funds to buy dodgy securities.[32] In Europe the creation of the euro prompted an extraordinary expansion of the financial sector both within the euro zone and in nearby banking hubs such as London and Switzerland. Southern European economies racked up huge current-account deficits in the first decade of the euro while countries in northern Europe ran offsetting surpluses. The imbalances were financed by credit flows from the euro-zone core to the overheated housing markets of countries such as Spain and Ireland.[33] All these factors came together to foster a surge of debt in what seemed to have become a less risky world. In the midst of the crisis, the problems of growing inequalities and rising unemployment resurfaced on the global agenda, challenging the predominant economic model and calling for a stronger state presence in the economy and more-robust public policies.[34]

At the same time, the developing world had unprecedented growth rates. Following China's accession to the WTO in 2001, the Chinese economy grew rapidly. China's GDP growth rate averaged 10.5 percent annually from 2001 to 2011, almost quadrupling the size of the Chinese economy from $1.3 trillion to $4.98 trillion, upgrading its ranking from the sixth-largest to the second-largest economy. Imports increased by nearly fivefold during this period. Household income increased from about $800 to $3,300, and more than 200 million Chinese were successfully lifted out of poverty.[35]

China's economic growth had ripple effects around the world. In 2010 China became the largest import destination for Australia, Brazil, Japan, and South Africa, the second largest for the European Union (EU), and the third largest for the United States. Between 2000 and 2009, China's imports from the least-developed countries (LDCs) increased 24 percent annually. Beginning in 2008, China had become the largest export destination of the LDCs. At the same time, under the "going global" strategy, China's accumulated overseas investment reached $300 billion. These outward investments brought new jobs, greater production capacity, and up-to-date technologies to many developing countries.[36]

So while the developed world was mired in the financial crisis, a number of emerging economies, led by China, Brazil, Indonesia, and India, came into their own not only financially but also as countries that could believe in themselves. Following the Asian financial crisis of 1997–1998, many countries learned the hard lesson that they needed a cushion of foreign exchange reserves against a possible future banking crisis. Therefore, when the 2008 crisis hit at the epicenter of the world financial system, it was these countries that could step in. They had foreign exchange reserves that they could use to stimulate their own economies. In fact, had it not been for the emerging economies, the crisis would have been much more severe. These countries developed a sense of confidence that hadn't been seen for centuries.

Meanwhile, Africa was rising. The cycle of the postcolonial malaise of poor governance, corrupt politicians, and civil wars was ending for many countries. In fact, most African countries were on an upward trajectory, although there were still some bogged down by civil conflict. This marked a real shift in the geopolitical relations of countries; by 2012, rather than allowing the North to set the agenda, the voices of the South were getting stronger and put the development debate in a new context.

The financial crisis upended the decades-old perception that the northern "developed" countries had resources that were available as ODA to assist developing countries in their economic and social development and finance the implementation of the MDGs. Suddenly the underlying premise of international cooperation was shaken to its core as developed countries found themselves financially strapped in ways that had not happened since World War II. This came as a major shock, not only to the countries themselves, but also to the international development framework, which relied on the generosity of northern industrialized states and was predicated on their wealth.

The Impact of the MDGs

As the MDG era was coming to a close, even though many of the goals had not been met, there was still significant progress to report. Extreme poverty declined significantly: in 1990 nearly half the population in the developing world lived on less than $1.25 per day, but by 2015 that had dropped to 14 percent. The proportion of undernourished people in the developing regions fell by almost half, from 23.3 percent in 1990 to 12.9 percent in 2015. The primary school enrollment rate reached 91 percent in 2015, up from 83 percent in 2000, and many more girls were in school. The global under-five mortality rate declined by more than half, the maternal mortality ratio declined by 45 percent, and new HIV infections fell by approximately 40 percent between 2000 and 2013, from an estimated 3.5 million cases to 2.1 million.[37]

Yet progress was uneven across regions and countries, leaving significant gaps. Millions of people were left behind, especially the poorest and those disadvantaged because of their sex, age, disability, ethnicity, or geographic location. In 2015 about 800 million people still lived in extreme poverty. Over 160 million children under age five had inadequate height for their age caused by insufficient nutrition. Despite gains, 57 million children of primary school age were not in school. Each day, about 16,000 children died before their fifth birthday, mostly from preventable causes. The maternal mortality ratio in the developing regions was fourteen times higher than in the developed regions. One in three people (2.4 billion) still used unimproved sanitation facilities, including 946 million people who still practiced open defecation. More than 880 million people were estimated to be living in slum-like conditions in the developing world's cities.[38]

Thus, although the MDGs helped to lift more than one billion people out of extreme poverty, made inroads against hunger, enabled more girls to attend school, helped in combating communicable diseases, and demonstrated the value of setting ambitious goals, these shortcomings could not be ignored.

THE NEED FOR A PARADIGM SHIFT

The MDGs were noble but limited from the start. They left out many factors that contribute to global poverty, including war and political instability, discrimination and social inequality, vulnerability to natural disasters, rule of law, and corruption. They were primarily a social development agenda, focused on health and education, with the overall goal of reducing extreme poverty. The environmental causes of poverty were almost an afterthought. As former UNDP administrator Mark Malloch-Brown commented, "The document had gone to the printing presses as I passed the head of the UN's environmental programme . . . and a terrible swearword crossed my mind when I realised we'd forgotten an environmental goal . . . we raced back to put in the sustainable development goal."[39] These items that were left out should not have been treated as mere afterthoughts or add-ons, notes Dan Smith, director of the Stockholm International Peace Research Institute.[40] They are some of the fundamental, determinative considerations of development.

At the same time, science was advancing, and other problems that were challenging the world were becoming more severe, including climate change, biodiversity loss, noncommunicable diseases such as cancer, chemicals, and pollution. The 2007 Fourth Assessment Report of the

Intergovernmental Panel on Climate Change (IPCC) stated that "warming of the climate system is unequivocal" and that "most of the observed increase in global average temperatures since the mid-20th century is very likely due to the observed increase in anthropogenic greenhouse gas concentrations."[41] The UN Environment Programme's 2012 *Global Chemicals Outlook* found that coordinated action by governments and industry would be urgently needed to reduce the growing risks to human health and the environment posed by the unsustainable management of chemicals worldwide.[42] In 2005 the Millennium Ecosystem Assessment found that human actions were rapidly depleting the Earth's natural resources and putting such strain on the environment that the ability of the planet's ecosystems to sustain future generations could no longer be taken for granted.[43] These and other reports resulted in an emerging global consensus that business as usual was not acceptable.

The international community had to do something dramatically different: not just fix a few pieces of the puzzle as the MDGs did but also look at the bigger picture because something was fundamentally wrong with the way that the world was being managed. On the economic side, the 2008 financial crisis had made it clear that the management of national and global economies was problematic. On the development side, poverty was still entrenched in parts of the world. Massive numbers of new jobs were needed to employ large youth populations in South Asia and Africa. In China, with its breakneck economic growth, pollution was out of control. According to the World Health Organization, noncommunicable diseases such as diabetes, obesity, heart disease, and cancer caused 36 million of the 57 million global deaths (63 percent) in 2008, and national health systems were not able to effectively respond.[44]

At the same time, the United Nations itself was being called into question. It seemed to have reached its pinnacle of influence with the MDGs in 2000. In the following years, deep failures in the United Nations' performance on both peace and security and sustainable development began to show the limits of the UN system. As the 2006 report of the Secretary-General's High-Level Panel on UN System-Wide Coherence in the Areas of Development, Humanitarian Assistance, and the Environment stated,

We know that the UN has been seen by some to fail in delivering some of the vision and mission we expect from it. There are many reasons why the UN has become fragmented and weak: from a lack of buy-in and mixed messages from member states between capitals and representatives in various bodies, to a proliferation of agencies, mandates and offices, creating duplication and dulling the focus on outcomes, with moribund entities never discontinued. Even when mandates intersect UN entities tend to operate alone with little synergy and coordination between them. The UN system now encompasses 17 specialized agencies and related organisations, 14 funds and programmes, 17 departments and offices of the UN Secretariat, 5 regional commissions, 5 research and training institutes and a plethora of regional and country level structures. The loss of cohesion prevents the UN from being more than the sum of its parts.[45]

The report also said that work on development and environment is often hindered by inefficient and ineffective governance and unpredictable funding. Cooperation between organizations has been hindered by competition for funding, mission creep, and outdated business practices.[46] The UN development agencies, funds, and programs have seemed to lack accountability. These weaknesses, combined with economic realities and the shortcomings of the MDGs, demanded a new development paradigm.

THE TIPPING POINT:
RIO+20 AND THE BIRTH OF THE SDGS

Partly in response to these mounting global environmental and economic challenges, there were calls for another global sustainable development conference. In September 2007, in his address to the 62nd session of the UN General Assembly, Brazilian President Luiz Inácio Lula da Silva proposed holding a new sustainable development conference in 2012 in Brazil to review what had been achieved since the 1992 Earth Summit and set a new agenda.[47] It took two years before the General Assembly was able to adopt a resolution to this effect. Although the G-77 and China were supportive, some developed countries, including the United States, argued that another conference could detract valuable attention from efforts to fulfill existing commitments.[48] In 2009 the General Assembly agreed to organize this conference, to be held on the twentieth anniversary of the Earth Summit. Its objective, as set forth in Resolution 64/236, was to secure renewed political commitment for sustainable development, assess the progress to date and the remaining gaps in the implementation of the outcomes of the major summits on sustainable development, and address new and emerging challenges.[49]

The resolution also called on the conference to focus on two themes: (1) green economy in the context of sustainable development and poverty eradication and (2) the institutional framework for sustainable development. Achim Steiner, executive director of the United Nations Environment Programme (UNEP), and the EU, with some support from Brazil, shared the view that the green economy should be one of the main themes of the conference to renew political commitment towards this "key issue of sustainable development" and define new initiatives. Steiner had been pushing for greater support for the Green Economy Initiative, a $4 million UNEP-backed initiative launched in October 2008, which focused on valuing nature's services and mainstreaming them into national and international accounts, generating employment through green jobs, and developing instruments and market signals able to accelerate a transition to a green economy.[50] Meanwhile, the French had been pushing for decisive progress on international environmental governance. Norway and others agreed that a high-level conference could provide the necessary political momentum to address the governance challenges, including fragmentation, overlap, lack of coherence, multiple and costly administrative entities, and insufficient funding for environmental and sustainable development action.

The Ghosts of Copenhagen

When the preparatory process for Rio+20 (officially known as the UN Conference on Sustainable Development, or UNCSD) began in May 2010, delegates were haunted by the failure to reach agreement on a new climate change agreement at the Copenhagen Climate Conference six months earlier—a debacle that contributed to concerns about the purported failure of multilateralism. Copenhagen was a classic example of how the twentieth-century negotiation system had run its course.

In 2009 the United Nations was in the habit of building hype for global conferences. Secretary-General Ban Ki-moon had even launched a campaign for parties to the UN Framework Convention on Climate Change (UNFCCC) to "Seal the Deal" in Copenhagen. By inviting world leaders to actually come to a UNFCCC Conference of the Parties, whose high-level segment was usually attended by ministers, the United Nations and the host country, Denmark, had raised the stakes for this meeting. With the Kyoto Protocol set to expire in 2012, many believed that parties had to adopt a new agreement in 2009 to allow the necessary time for countries to ratify the agreement so it could enter into force in 2012, thereby avoiding a vacuum. However, the time was not ripe in Copenhagen for a deal, and the final round of negotiations was conducted with such a lack of organization and transparency that many countries and observers cried foul.

After months of negotiations leading up to Copenhagen, governments had fallen short. With no negotiated agreement in sight, halfway through the conference the Danish presidency announced that it intended to table a new text of a possible Copenhagen outcome—a step that many had already anticipated or feared. In the corridors, many were outraged at what they described as an attempt to sideline the work that was already done.

In the eyes of many developing countries, the supposed deal in Copenhagen had been precooked so that parties would be served up a deal by the United Nations, working with a number of northern countries and consulting a few southern countries to give it some legitimacy. In fact, by the time delegates arrived in Copenhagen, the perception of some large developing countries with emerging economies was that developed countries were aiming to slow their development, using climate change and green economy as the tools.

Negotiations moved behind closed doors, with only a few "friends of the chair" (members of a contact group convened by the presiding officer) at the highest political level invited to attend. In the meantime, the other 115 presidents and prime ministers were sitting around waiting for the "smoke to come out of the chimney," noted one delegate, comparing the "secret" meetings to a papal conclave. A tired and bewildered Kenyan

President Mwai Kibaki spoke for many in the final hours of the conference when he wondered "Why am I here? To rubber stamp what? We will not accept this." There was a groundswell of discontent, and late Friday evening, hours after the conference was supposed to have concluded, the chosen few countries that had been taken into the confidence of the Danish presidency emerged with the Copenhagen Accord. US President Barack Obama immediately announced the results before his quick departure back to Washington because of an impending snowstorm, and this was widely reported by the media. In fact, many delegates first learned about the Copenhagen Accord on the Internet, and draft versions of the text were also leaked through the media long before the official UNFCCC document was produced. Most media reports alluded to a deal crafted by a small number of countries. Many close to the process despaired, arguing that announcing an agreement reached by a small group of countries was not democratic or diplomatic. "We are at the United Nations and everyone has to agree before you can report that agreement has been reached," commented one developing-country negotiator.[51]

During the closing plenary, which lasted nearly thirteen hours, lengthy and what many characterized as "acrimonious" discussions ensued on the transparency of the process that had led to the conclusion of the Copenhagen Accord and on whether it should be adopted. Some developing countries opposed the accord, which was reached during what they described as an "untransparent" and "undemocratic" negotiating process. During informal negotiations facilitated by UN Secretary-General Ban Ki-moon through the night and early morning, parties agreed to adopt a decision whereby the parties would "take note" of the Copenhagen Accord, which was attached to the decision as an unofficial document. This is the lowest form of recognition given to any outcome by a UN negotiation process, other than outright rejection.[52]

Although the actual text of the Copenhagen Accord[53] was in fact aspirational and guided subsequent negotiations that led to the 2015 Paris Agreement, it was the negotiating process that led to the refusal of many to adopt the text. Delegates left Copenhagen with an accord that had no official status, leaving in question any agreement on the billions of dollars needed for climate change adaptation and on commitments to greenhouse gas

PHOTO 2.1. *Left to right:* Indian Prime Minister Manmohan Singh, US President Barack Obama, Danish Foreign Minister Per Stig Møller, and Israeli President Shimon Peres consulting at the 2009 Copenhagen Climate Change Conference. *Photo by IISD/Leila Mead (enb.iisd.org)*

emissions mitigation. The negotiating methods had failed them. The use of contact groups, the appearance of a secret host-country text that had not been negotiated, and the announcement of an agreement that most delegations were unaware of doomed the outcome. Delegations came out of Copenhagen with no trust in the negotiating process, one another, or the UN system. These "ghosts of Copenhagen" loomed large over the preparatory process for Rio+20.

From the Preparatory Process to Rio

Six months after Copenhagen, the Preparatory Committee (PrepCom) for Rio+20 began its work. A prepcom, led by its elected co-chairs and bureau (vice chairs), prepares for a global conference by guiding delegates through the process of drafting the outcome document and/or political declaration that will be adopted at the conference. This work can often take months or years, depending on the nature of the conference and the time needed to complete the necessary negotiations.

The Rio+20 PrepCom, which held three formal sessions and six inter-sessional meetings from May 2010 through June 2012, was immediately affected by the lack of coherence of the themes for the conference. It became the challenge of the PrepCom co-chairs, John Ashe, permanent representative of Antigua and Barbuda to the United Nations, and, initially, Park In-kook, permanent representative of the Republic of Korea. In December 2011, Park was replaced by Kim Sook, who had taken over as permanent representative of the Republic of Korea in July 2011. The process was laborious and was laden with suspicion and misgivings. Discussions on the green economy proved to be the most difficult and were clearly influenced by the distrust about the motives of the Europeans that remained after Copenhagen.

Many developed countries, led by the EU, viewed a green economy as critical to achieving sustainable development. Many echoed UNEP's 2011 publication, *Towards a Green Economy: Pathways to Sustainable Development and Poverty Eradication,* and argued that the money being invested in a "brown economy" (powered by fossil fuels) should instead be invested in a green economy (powered by renewable energy).[54] Others were not convinced. One group of Latin American countries, known as the Bolivarian Alliance for the Peoples of Our America (ALBA),[55] expressed concern that the concept of the green economy was an attempt to extend capitalism into the environmental arena, in which nature is seen as "capital" for producing tradable environmental goods and services that should then be valued in monetary terms and assigned a price so that they can be used to obtain profits. They rejected any attempt to privatize, monetize, or commercialize nature, for it would go against their ethical principles.[56]

Another concern for the developing world was that the concept could be used by industrialized countries to impose restrictions on trade or ODA, or be the thin end of a wedge that would usher in trade protectionism. Many newly industrialized countries, including the BRICS, didn't want to lose their economic advantage by having to switch from existing brown industries to green industries. Some saw this as a European ploy to discredit the brown economy and push for policies that would give European green technology producers an advantage. Others were concerned that green economy would replace "sustainable development" and that, if so, the third pillar, social development, could be downplayed or lost.

The issue of sustainable development governance also proved divisive. In the debate on the institutional framework for sustainable development, the environmental dimension was the subject of particular attention. There was general agreement that the international environmental governance system was not adequately fulfilling its objectives and functions, that environmental governance reform should be addressed in the broader context of environmental sustainability and sustainable development, and that the status quo was not an option.

However, many developing countries wanted to talk less about frameworks and more about industrialized countries' "broken promises" and unmet commitments with regard to financing sustainable development initiatives dating back to the 1992 Earth Summit.[57] On the other hand, some governments and NGOs hoped that these discussions would provide the impetus for substantial reform of UNEP. Among this group there were two main camps: institutional reformists that wanted to improve the system of treaty regimes and international institutions and those that believed far deeper changes, such as the creation of a UN environment organization, were necessary. French President Jacques Chirac took the lead of this latter camp, arguing, "This United Nations Environment Organization will act as the world's ecological conscience. It will carry out impartial and scientific assessment of environmental dangers. It will have policy-making terms of reference giving it the legitimacy to implement action jointly decided. It will lend greater weight and greater cohesion to our collective endeavors."[58]

Among some Africans, there was a deeply held suspicion that UNEP, the first UN body headquartered in a developing country, was being carved up into different divisions being housed in Paris and Geneva. Some were afraid that only an empty shell would remain at the headquarters in Nairobi. Asians and Latin Americans had a slight ambivalence toward UNEP, which they said was dominated by European ideas such as the green economy.

PHOTO 2.2. United Nations Conference on Sustainable Development Preparatory Committee Co-chairs John Ashe (left), Antigua and Barbuda, and Kim Sook (right), Republic of Korea. *Photo by IISD/Leila Mead (enb.iisd.org)*

The PrepCom co-chairs were confronted with a difficult challenge. First, they did not share a common vision for the outcome document. Each co-chair went into the process as a representative of his respective bloc. Thus, they tried to ensure that each bloc's priorities were included rather than try to craft compromises. This was further complicated by the fact that neither co-chair represented a bloc with united positions. John Ashe was a seasoned diplomat with twenty years of UN experience, but as a member of the G-77 he was having trouble because the Latin Americans refused to compromise on the green economy, among other key components of the document. The lack of a united developing-country position on this issue resulted in far more proposals to change the text and far fewer opportunities for Ashe to guide the process. Kim Sook, representing the developed countries, also had to contend with a split in positions among those countries. For example, even though the Western Europeans were promoting the green economy, the Eastern Europeans were still transitioning from brown economies, and the United States and Australia were still heavily reliant on oil and coal. They diverged on governance questions, including whether UNEP should have universal membership and be upgraded to agency status. On finance questions the EU countries were amenable to increasing sustainable development funding, but the United States and Japan were not.

Second, the co-chairs did not have the trust of the delegations. The G-77 insisted that every amendment be visible and did not allow the co-chairs to engage in any "editing" of the text, fearing that their hard-fought amendments would disappear. The fear of backroom deals and secret compromise texts, similar to what happened in Copenhagen, loomed over the process.

In addition, the working methods were no longer effective. The co-chairs and the Secretariat had produced a draft outcome document at the end of 2011. As negotiations on this document began in 2012, the process began to spin out of control. After sessions in January and March, which were devoted to a first "reading," the draft had ballooned from nineteen pages to more than two hundred once all proposed amendments were added.[59] The text was projected on big screens in front of the room, and as delegates suggested amendments or alternative proposals, a member of the Secretariat typed the text in for all to see, with each country's name appended to its proposals. This built a sense of ownership into each proposal and created a dynamic where if a country agreed to delete its text, it was seen as capitulation. The document kept growing, and compromise became more and more difficult with each passing day. Twenty-four days of formal negotiations, including many late-night or all-night sessions, took place between January and June 2012, along with countless days of informal consultations among delegations and with the co-chairs.

The problem of informal drafting groups also affected the negotiations until the last day. The unintentionally but aptly named "splinter groups" proliferated to more than twenty, with each group negotiating a different part of the outcome document. This precluded participation of small delegations with only one or two delegates who couldn't actively take part in so many small groups. The inability of many delegates to attend all of the groups and the dearth of strong facilitators resulted in confusion on what

PHOTO 2.3. The Rio+20 negotiating text was projected on large screens at the front of the room while the Secretariat entered amendments during the PrepCom. *Photo by IISD/Leila Mead (enb.iisd.org)*

had actually been discussed and agreed. In several instances during the closing hours, delegations asked to re-bracket ostensibly agreed-upon passages, just to be on the safe side. One longtime participant commented that an unexpected factor—information technology—had hit the preparatory process with a vengeance: instant communication led to "excessive" twenty-four-hour control from capitals, sapping negotiators' initiative and slowing down negotiations.[60]

By the end of the final meeting in New York on June 2, 2012, only seventy paragraphs had been agreed upon, with 259 paragraphs still bracketed (under negotiation). Many attendees were frustrated, with some delegates convinced that the preparatory process, through a confluence of circumstances, had been flawed from the start. They complained (albeit unfairly in some instances) that it lacked strong leadership from the co-chairs and the Secretariat. Many delegates were not happy with the organization of work, the uneven chairing styles, and the modest role of the PrepCom's bureau, whose members seemed reluctant to wield authority to spur on negotiations and compromise during much of the negotiations. The disorder anesthetized the sense of urgency, with some delegations acting as if they had months to go, yet time was quickly running out.[61]

Enter the Sustainable Development Goals

During the difficult preparatory process, a new proposal emerged. Paula Caballero Gómez, then director of Economic, Social and Environmental Affairs for Colombia's Ministry of Foreign Affairs, was concerned that neither conference theme was particularly compelling for a broad audience. Most importantly, she said, "Neither had the potential for incentivizing the deep transformations at scale so urgently needed on a planet that is breaching so many boundaries all at once, while remaining stubbornly inequitable at many levels."[62] With the support of her foreign minister, Caballero proposed that another outcome should emerge from the conference—a more concrete option—which could be the development of a set of sustainable development goals.

To introduce her idea, Caballero circulated a draft proposal at a preparatory meeting hosted by Indonesia, in mid-2011 in the city of Solo, held to discuss the institutional framework for sustainable development in advance of the Rio+20 negotiations. This meeting was the first time that the SDGs were presented at a UN event. She also held a number of informal meetings with small groups of delegations from the five UN regional groups (Africa, Asia-Pacific, Central and Eastern Europe, Latin America and the Caribbean, and Western Europe and Others) between May and September 2011. The proposal was met with friendly skepticism, but this did not deter Caballero. In November 2011, Colombia, with support from Guatemala, formally submitted a proposal to the UNCSD Secretariat to be included in the first compilation draft outcome document for Rio+20:

The international community urgently needs benchmarks so that it can harness and catalyse multidimensional and multisectoral approaches to addressing critical global challenges. Accordingly, Colombia has proposed, together with Guatemala, that one of the

PHOTO 2.4. *Left to right:* Farrukh Khan, Pakistan; Hugo Schally, EU; Paula Caballero Gómez, Colombia; and Franz Perrez, Switzerland, discussing the SDG proposal at the March 2012 PrepCom meeting for the Rio+20 conference. *Photo by IISD/Leila Mead (enb.iisd.org)*

outcomes of the Rio Conference to be held in June 2012 should be the adoption of a set of Sustainable Development Goals, modelled on the Millennium Development Goals (MDGs), to help define the post-2015 framework.[63]

Although the Colombian and Guatemalan proposal was included in the initial draft of the outcome document, it did not have universal support. Early supporters included Kitty van der Heijden of the Netherlands, Farrukh Khan of Pakistan, Jimena Leiva of Guatemala, Chris Whaley of the United Kingdom, Victor Muñoz of Peru, Majid Hasan Alsuwaidi of the United Arab Emirates, Yeshey Dorji of Bhutan, Franz Perrez of Switzerland, Damaso Luna of Mexico, Marianne Loe of Norway, and Anders Wallenberg of Sweden, according to Caballero.[64] But as the preparatory process moved forward, the SDGs gained traction.

Consultations continued on the SDGs when the PrepCom reconvened in Rio on June 13, 2012, for one week before heads of state and government were due to arrive for the conference. The process that would be used to elaborate the goals had become the subject of much debate. The EU and the US wanted a technical working group appointed by the Secretary-General. For many in the G-77 and China, a technical working group meant a working group comprising experts and negotiators with significant political oversight and consistent with UN General Assembly rules. This would have meant a political body, negotiated by the established groups, including G-77 and China, and the EU. Caballero feared that this would have meant a replay of the political wrangling that characterized the Rio+20 negotiations.

Caballero and others instead "envisaged a technical body that could bring in experts on the daunting array of issues and themes that would need to be addressed, and that would submit its technical (and therefore hopefully structured, evidence-based) recommendations" for approval to the UN General Assembly.[65] The proponents wanted the group to be "open," inclusive, and transparent (unlike the closed process that elaborated the MDGs), but not to turn into a traditional negotiating process open to the participation of all 193 member states, in an effort to keep discussions from quickly devolving into bloc-to-bloc or North-South negotiations. After a few days of difficult discussions, a small group of G-77 and China negotiators met and after many hours finally reached agreement on the concept of an "open working group," with the understanding that its work would be fully transparent. It would deliberate in an open space so that all delegations that wanted to sit in could do so, and its deliberations would be transmitted via the Internet so anyone in the world could listen in.[66]

The next task was to sell the idea to all of the countries and reach agreement on the composition of the group. After some discussion the G-77 negotiators concluded that as a starting point, the text could call for a total of thirty representatives—six members from each of the five UN regional groups. Thirty seemed sensible because the G-77 assumed that in the ensuing negotiations the number would spiral upwards, closer to sixty or more. What they did not know was that Brazil, as host country, would essentially present a "take-it-or-leave-it-text" that was not open for negotiation. And it is for this reason that the Open Working Group (OWG) had thirty seats.[67]

In the end, the text on the SDGs was adopted along with the rest of the Rio+20 outcome document, "The Future We Want." The final agreed-upon text of paragraph 248 reads as follows:

> We resolve to establish an inclusive and transparent intergovernmen-tal process on sustainable development goals that is open to all stake-holders, with a view to developing global sustainable development goals to be agreed by the General Assembly. An open working group shall be constituted no later than at the opening of the sixty-seventh session of the Assembly and shall comprise thirty representatives, nominated by Member States from the five United Nations regional groups, with the aim of achieving fair, equitable and balanced geo-graphical representation.[68]

"The Future We Want" also states that the OWG would decide on its method of work, including developing modalities to ensure the full in-volvement of relevant stakeholders and expertise from civil society, the sci-entific community, and the UN system, and that it would submit a report to the 68th session of the UN General Assembly containing a proposal for SDGs for consideration and appropriate action. The agreed-upon text also states that the SDGs should be action oriented, concise and easy to com-municate, limited in number, aspirational, global in nature and universally applicable to all countries, and focused on priority areas for the achieve-ment of sustainable development.[69] These seven paragraphs, out of 283 paragraphs in "The Future We Want," became the real legacy of Rio+20.

Bringing Multilateralism Back to Life

Although delegates reached agreement on the SDGs, an issue that wasn't even originally part of the Rio+20 agenda, negotiations on sustainable de-velopment governance and the green economy were not as successful. The long, drawn-out series of preparatory negotiations in New York served only to further undermine confidence in the multilateral system and raised concerns that the process was never going to accomplish what it set out to

do. When the final PrepCom meeting in Rio failed to make sufficient progress, delegations agreed on June 17 that the host country, Brazil, should
take over and hold consultations until the start of the conference on June
20.[70] Ambassador Luiz Alberto Figueiredo Machado and Foreign Minister
Antonio Patriota opted to embark on a carefully calibrated iteration of delegations' positions, based on an intensive listening exercise.[71] The experienced Brazilian negotiators and the Rio+20 Secretariat, under the
leadership of Nikhil Seth, were able to close the remaining gaps by drafting
new language in the text, taking into account their own negotiating experience, the general thrust of the discussions, the agreements made in the
splinter groups, and the intimate knowledge of the breaking points within
the G-77.[72] The Rio+20 Secretariat worked overnight to produce a "compromise" text, weighing the different alternative texts and exercising political judgment, and then handed over the text to the Brazilian presidency of
the conference. This text, almost in its entirety, became the draft that Brazilian Foreign Minister Patriota tabled for agreement.

But things are never easy. The night before the text was to be adopted in
Rio, Secretary-General Ban's entourage, in Los Cabos, Mexico, for the G-20
Summit, made anxious calls to the Rio+20 Secretariat, expressing concern
about paragraph 248, on the SDGs. Some of Ban's senior advisers thought
that such a process was doomed and the preferred route should be similar
to the MDG process, where the goals would be drafted by a closed group of
senior advisers of the Secretary-General. Although efforts were made at
the last minute to change the text, it was too late. New proposals at that late
stage would have destroyed the hard-fought delicate compromise in "The
Future We Want."[73]

By successfully prompting—perhaps forcing—a consensus, the Brazilians preserved the quality and integrity of "The Future We Want." In doing
so they also preserved the legacy of the original Rio Earth Summit, thus
saving two summits. Had the conference negotiations been allowed to proceed in the traditional manner to the bitter end—with the media reporting
standoffs, late nights, and rumors of collapse (a real risk here)—the Brazilian hosts would have received much of the blame. By taking some of the
media attention off the negotiating text and allowing a greater focus to fall
on the more positive news generated by a festival of side events throughout

Rio, the Brazilians calculated that the outcome document would also emerge in a much better light. The host country had noted the lessons from Copenhagen, where late-night standoffs and subsequent poor decisions were followed by months of interpretation, reinterpretation, and, occasionally, breakdowns in consensus. The Brazilians had been deeply concerned about the resulting loss of confidence in the ability of the multilateral process to deal effectively with sustainable development issues. They were motivated by a desire not only to preserve the legacy of Rio but also to preserve the reputation of multilateralism itself.[74] They ensured that each regional and interest group of governments was fully represented in the consultations so the participants would not reject the outcome. This was in distinct contrast to Copenhagen, where many groups were not represented during the closed-door negotiations. Brazil's confident and high-stakes approach to the Rio+20 negotiations exemplified its status as an emerging broker and guardian of the multilateral system, thus ensuring that it repeated its 1992 achievement in bringing the conference to a successful conclusion.[75]

CONCLUSIONS AND LESSONS LEARNED

In the first decade of the twenty-first century, many were questioning the value of the United Nations in responding to the global crises in the post–Cold War era, and twentieth-century methods no longer seemed to be working. UN conferences were having difficulty coping with the growing complexity of the issues, the increase in the number of member states, the participation of hundreds of nonstate actors, and the concomitant challenges of reaching consensus. The Copenhagen Climate Conference marked a low point, where distrust between developed and developing countries and between the Danish presidency and government delegates threatened the future of the climate regime. This distrust continued as the preparatory process for the 2012 Rio+20 conference started just six months later.

Many of these lessons from this period served to shape the subsequent negotiations on the SDGs. First, strong leadership is essential. Co-chairs have to look for the common ground to guide the debate. Co-chairs must listen, identify some common positions, and be willing to accept what can be done and never let the best be the enemy of the good. If there is no agreement on the core issues, the co-chairs must be able to give the participants something else that they can agree on. They also have to assure delegations that they are working for the good of the process, not for their respective regional groups.

Second, trust is sacrosanct. Delegates must be able to put their trust in their co-chairs and/or the host country to reach an agreement. Without trust, a successful outcome is not guaranteed. After loss of trust in the Danish UNFCCC presidency and entering the Rio+20 PrepCom with a distrust of co-chairs, it looked like the Rio+20 negotiations might be doomed to failure. However, the Brazilians stepped in as the Rio+20 host country, ensured that they consulted with every regional and interest group of governments, and were able to rescue the conference from the jaws of defeat, restoring some hope for multilateralism along the way.

Third, large-scale multilateral negotiations were not working. On-screen negotiations became difficult and politically charged. Although the screen gives the illusion of transparency, it also leads the parties to defend their own proposals rather than strive for compromise, leading to gridlock. Holding numerous parallel contact (or splinter) group meetings fragmented the process, and the co-chairs essentially lost control over the negotiations. Moreover, one group didn't always know what the other group was doing. The PrepCom's working methods had to be abandoned in Rio to make progress.

Finally, sometimes it is necessary to go off script. Colombia, Guatemala, the United Arab Emirates, Pakistan, and others tipped the balance as they showed countries that something concrete could emerge as the main deliverable of Rio+20. The SDGs weren't originally on the map, and even then they were mentioned only in a couple of paragraphs in a seventy-page outcome. Yet it was already clear that the SDGs were going to be the memorable outcome of Rio+20.

3

GETTING STARTED:
Creating the Open Working Group

The SDGs seemed like yet another half-baked, crazy idea for
us to pour hours and hours into before discarding it. I was
worried that after nearly a decade of work, countries have finally figured out the MDGs, and now, we were about to change
the rules of the game on them again.

—FARRUKH KHAN[1]

It could be said that as soon as one negotiation concludes at the United
Nations, another one begins. UN diplomats spend the majority of their
time negotiating resolutions, decisions, and declarations that shape the
policies and programs of the world body and its family of organizations.

Although adopting an outcome document such as "The Future We
Want" is considered a success in itself, it represents only the first lap in a
longer race. The next set of negotiations usually consists of unpacking the
actual action items and figuring out just how to implement them. The 67th
session of the UN General Assembly had several such tasks in 2012 following Rio+20. Yet the most difficult by far was the establishment of the Open
Working Group (OWG) on Sustainable Development Goals (SDGs). This
chapter will look at what happened after Rio+20, specifically at the establishment of the OWG. We will then discuss some key elements of the

pre-negotiation phase that transpired prior to the first official meeting of the OWG.

BACK TO NEW YORK: RIO+20 FOLLOW-UP

One month after the conclusion of the Rio+20 conference, on July 27, 2012, the General Assembly met to endorse that conference's outcome document, "The Future We Want."[2] As Nassir Abdulaziz Al-Nasser, the president of the 66th session of the General Assembly, said on that day, "Member States have their work cut out for them as they discuss the definition of the sustainable development goals, the establishment of a high-level political forum, the crafting of an effective sustainable development financing strategy, the creation of a facilitation mechanism that promotes the development, transfer and dissemination of clean and environmentally sound technologies, and the adoption of modalities for the third international conference on small island developing states in 2014."[3] (See Box 3.1.)

■ **Box 3.1**

The UN General Assembly

The General Assembly (GA) is the "chief deliberative, policy-making and representative organ of the United Nations," according to the UN Charter. It comprises all 193 member states and serves as a forum for intergovernmental discussion and negotiation on all of the international issues covered by the Charter.[a]

Each session of the Assembly starts in September each year and meets through December. Thereafter, it meets from January to August, as required, to take up outstanding reports and consider current issues of critical importance to the international community in the form of high-level thematic debates organized by the president of the General Assembly in consultation with the membership.[b]

Each of the 193 Member States in the Assembly has one vote. Votes taken on designated important issues—such as recommendations on peace and security, election of Security Council members, and budgetary questions—require a two-thirds majority, but other questions are decided by a simple majority. Wherever possible, the General Assembly tries to achieve consensus on issues rather than taking a formal vote, thus strengthening support for its decisions.

The selection of the president follows an unwritten system of regional rotation. Each year one of the regional groups nominates an individual, who is then elected by the entire membership. The pattern of regional rotation since 1963 has been as follows:

- Latin American and Caribbean States

- African States

- Western European and Other States

- Asian States

- Eastern European States

The term of office is for one year, beginning in September at the opening of the session and running until the following September when the session ends. As a matter of practice (but not formal rule), the president may not be a national of any of the permanent five members of the Security Council (China, France, Russian Federation, United Kingdom, and United States).

NOTES:

[a] United Nations, *Charter of the United Nations,* 1945, https://treaties.un.org/doc/publication/ctc/uncharter.pdf.

[b] United Nations, "Functions and Powers of the General Assembly," www.un.org/en/ga/about/background.shtml.

When the General Assembly convened in September 2012, among the 170 items on the agenda[4] were a number of matters necessary to follow up on the Rio+20 conference. In addition to establishing the OWG, the General Assembly had to adopt two resolutions relating to the "institutional framework for sustainable development" theme of Rio+20: the format and organizational aspects of the High-Level Political Forum on Sustainable Development (HLPF)[5] and the strengthening and upgrading of the United Nations Environment Programme.[6] Both of these resolutions would also affect the work of the OWG and the post-2015 negotiations that followed.

The HLPF, which replaced the Commission on Sustainable Development as a more effective institutional framework for sustainable development, would later be responsible for reviewing implementation of the SDGs (see Chapter 8). The United Nations Environment Programme's (UNEP) Governing Council, which was upgraded to be a universal membership body— the United Nations Environment Assembly—with regular funding from the UN budget, was then empowered to advocate for the environmental dimensions of the SDGs and the 2030 Agenda.

And, as called for in "The Future We Want," the General Assembly agreed to convene in Samoa in 2014 the third international conference on small island developing states.[7] This conference, whose preparatory work took place in parallel with the OWG in 2013 and 2014, helped solidify the position of these nations during the OWG and later 2030 Agenda negotiations. Finally, the General Assembly adopted Resolution 67/203, which operationalized paragraphs 255–257 of "The Future We Want," on financing and technology transfer. It called for the work of the intergovernmental committee established to propose options on an effective sustainable development financing strategy to start as soon as possible.[8] Furthermore, the resolution also called for a series of workshops on the development, transfer, and dissemination of clean and environmentally sound technologies and their contribution to sustainable development with a view to proposing options for a technology facilitation, or implementation, mechanism.[9] The work of these two processes on finance and technology also contributed to the discussions on the SDGs and the 2030 Agenda (see Chapter 8).

Initial Questions About the OWG

Meanwhile, the President of the General Assembly named Ambassador Maria Luiza Ribeiro Viotti of Brazil, representing the Rio+20 host country, to aid in the establishment of the OWG on the SDGs. Ambassador Viotti began consultations on the establishment of the OWG over the summer of 2012 with the expectation that the General Assembly would be able to adopt the necessary decision or resolution and that the OWG could immediately begin its work. However, the process was not that simple.

Viotti had only the language from "The Future We Want" to guide her, and, as is often the case, the interpretation of this language varied. The sentence that caused the most trouble at this point was as follows: "An open working group shall be constituted no later than at the opening of the sixty-seventh session of the Assembly [i.e., September 2012] and shall comprise thirty representatives, nominated by Member States from the five United Nations regional groups, with the aim of achieving fair, equitable and balanced geographical representation."[10] What did this mean? Some believed that this body would comprise six countries from each of the five UN regional groups: Africa, Asia-Pacific, Eastern Europe, Latin America and the Caribbean (GRULAC), and Western European and Others (WEOG). But would these be diplomats, experts, or high-level officials? Also, which countries would be represented? And would the group have equitable geographic representation, or, given that the African and Asian regional groups were larger than the others, would they have greater representation?

Some governments envisioned the OWG to be a group of thirty experts nominated by governments who would draft the SDGs and submit them to the General Assembly for adoption. Several models for such an expert group already existed. For example, just before the Rio+20 Conference, Secretary-General Ban Ki-moon announced the creation of a twenty-seven-member high-level panel to advise on the global development framework beyond 2015, the target date for the Millennium Development Goals (MDGs), which included leaders from civil society, the private sector, and government.[11] Some governments thought that the OWG could be similar, but rather than being nominated by the Secretary-General, the experts could be nominated by member states.

Another model, one supported by Pakistan's Farrukh Khan, was the Governing Board of the Green Climate Fund (GCF). The GCF was established by the Conference of the Parties to the UN Framework Convention on Climate Change in 2010. The GCF's mandate is to respond to climate change by investing in low-emission and climate-resilient development to advance the goal of keeping the average temperature increase below 2° Celsius above preindustrial levels. The GCF helps limit or reduce greenhouse gas emissions in developing countries and helps vulnerable societies adapt to the unavoidable impacts of climate change. The twenty-four-member board governing the GCF is equally drawn from developed and developing countries—selected with the aim of an overall gender-balanced membership. To ensure fair representation, members from developing countries must span across the Asia-Pacific, Africa, and Latin America and the Caribbean, with at least one member from a least-developed country (LDC) and one from a small island developing state.[12]

There was also a question about what "open" meant. Was the OWG supposed to be an "open-ended" working group established by the General Assembly? An "open-ended" group implies that all member states can participate and meetings are generally closed to observers (representatives of UN agencies and programs, civil society, and NGOs). They can have formal and informal meetings but do not have official meeting records. Nor do they adopt resolutions or decisions. Usually, a General Assembly–established working group has one chair or two co-chairs who are appointed by the president of the General Assembly.[13] Alternatively, was this to be an "open" working group that would allow the participation of UN programs and agencies, NGOs, and others?

The negotiations almost stalled at several points on these definitional questions as well as the fact that many member states wanted to be directly involved in crafting the goals, even though the mandate was for a thirty-member group. The end of the year saw no consensus, despite weeks of consultations led by Ambassador Viotti. So on December 24, 2012, General Assembly President Vuk Jeremić informed the Assembly that negotiations had fallen short on a draft resolution to set up the OWG and that a decision on the matter would have to be postponed until a later date.[14] Heading into the Christmas break, there was a certain sense of shock, fear, and disappointment that the OWG might not be established and the negotiation of the SDGs might not happen.

Distributing the Seats

In the end, it took seven months for member states to reach agreement on how to distribute the thirty seats among the five regional groups after many arguments over what was "equitable, just and decent."[15] Following additional consultations, on January 15, 2013, General Assembly President Jeremić distributed a draft decision establishing the OWG. Member states agreed to assign seven of the seats to Asia, five to Central and Eastern Europe, five to WEOG, six to GRULAC, and seven to Africa. These numbers were in accordance with the principle of equitable geographic representation based on the number of member states from each region.[16] Each regional group was assigned the task of designating the countries that would hold the seats, but when they asked for expressions of interest, seventy countries responded.

Normally, when the number of candidates exceeds the number of vacancies, the United Nations has a selection process. Each regional group discusses its nominations, and an election is held. However, there was concern that if this protocol were followed, it might poison the atmosphere in the OWG from the outset by rejecting interested member states.[17] During informal consultations in the Asian Group, Farrukh Khan, who was representing Pakistan, chair of the Asian Group at the time (chairmanships of the regional groups rotate monthly), suggested sharing the seats, with everyone choosing the partners they felt most comfortable with.[18] This was an innovative way to accommodate all seventy interested states. The idea took hold, and the twenty-one Asia-Pacific countries vying for the region's seven seats began matchmaking. Sri Lanka approached both India and Pakistan and suggested that they share a seat. Three Pacific small island developing states (SIDS)—Nauru, Palau, and Papua New Guinea—formed another "troika," as these seat-sharing groups became known. Bhutan joined with Thailand and Vietnam. Cyprus, Singapore, and the United Arab Emirates formed another, as did China, Indonesia, and Kazakhstan, as well as Bangladesh, the Republic of Korea, and Saudi Arabia. Japan, which had initially been reluctant to share a seat, eventually ended up with Iran and Nepal, in what many thought was the most unlikely troika.[19]

The other regional groups soon followed suit. The African Group had an easier time than some of the other groups. Those countries that had been most involved in Rio+20 volunteered to serve. As a result, Benin, Congo, Ghana, Kenya, and Tanzania each had their own seat. Zambia and Zimbabwe ended up sharing, as did four North African states (Algeria, Egypt, Morocco, and Tunisia). WEOG had so many interested delegations that each seat was shared by three countries. GRULAC gave two seats to Caribbean SIDS and divided the rest. Colombia and Guatemala, which had spearheaded the SDGs during the Rio+20 process, were among those sharing a seat. The Central and Eastern Europeans, with fewer members overall, had mostly two countries sharing seats (see Box 3.2).

On January 22, 2013, the UN General Assembly adopted Decision 67/555, which established the OWG and its appendix listing the names of the seventy countries that would be sharing the thirty seats.[20] Then things moved quickly. By February 20, 2013, General Assembly President Jeremić had held consultations with the five regional groups and announced they had reached a common understanding that the first meeting of the OWG should be convened by mid-March 2013 and that additional consultations would be held on the draft agenda, the composition of the OWG leadership, and its program and modalities of work. Jeremić also announced that he had invited the permanent representative of Hungary, Ambassador Csaba Kőrösi, and the permanent representative of Kenya, Ambassador Macharia Kamau, to facilitate these consultations. He noted that Ambassador Viotti, along with one of Jeremić's own senior advisers, would also engage with the process to maintain continuity with the negotiations leading to the establishment of the OWG.[21]

Within a few weeks, Ambassadors Kőrösi and Kamau reported agreement on the agenda and the modalities of work. The agenda for the OWG was fairly open-ended because no additional guidance was available from "The Future We Want" and no one was quite sure how this process would work in practice. So the agenda was simple:

1. Election of officers.
2. Adoption of the agenda and other organizational matters.
3. Follow-up to the outcome of the United Nations Conference on Sustainable Development, relating to a proposal for sustainable development goals.
4. Other matters.
5. Adoption of the report.[22]

Modalities of Work

The modalities of work were the subject of some intense discussions, but the co-facilitators were able to bring these to a quick conclusion so

■ **Box 3.2.**

Members of the Open Working Group on Sustainable Development Goals

African Group
1. Algeria/Egypt/Morocco/Tunisia
2. Ghana
3. Benin
4. Kenya
5. Tanzania
6. Congo
7. Zambia/Zimbabwe

Asia-Pacific Group
1. Nauru/Palau/Papua New Guinea
2. Bhutan/Thailand/Viet Nam
3. India/Pakistan/Sri Lanka
4. China/Indonesia/Kazakhstan
5. Cyprus/Singapore/United Arab Emirates
6. Bangladesh/Republic of Korea/Saudi Arabia
7. Iran/Japan/Nepal

Latin American and Caribbean Group
1. Colombia/Guatemala
2. Bahamas/Barbados
3. Guyana/Haiti/Trinidad and Tobago
4. Mexico/Peru
5. Brazil/Nicaragua
6. Argentina/Bolivia/Ecuador

Western European and Others Group
1. Australia/Netherlands/United Kingdom
2. Canada/Israel/United States
3. Denmark/Ireland/Norway
4. France/Germany/Switzerland
5. Italy/Spain/Turkey

Eastern European Group
1. Hungary
2. Belarus/Serbia
3. Bulgaria/Croatia
4. Montenegro/Slovenia
5. Poland/Romania

everything would be ready for the first meeting of the OWG. Member states agreed on the following:

- In accordance with General Assembly resolution 67/203, reports on the progress of work of the OWG will be made regularly to the General Assembly, taking into account the convening of the first High-Level Political Forum on Sustainable Development, without prejudice to the format and organizational aspects of the forum, and the special event in 2013 to follow up efforts made towards achieving the MDGs.
- The OWG will submit a report to the Assembly at its sixty-eighth session, containing a proposal for the SDGs for consideration and appropriate action.
- At the beginning of its first formal meeting, the OWG shall elect two co-chairs, one from a developing country and one from a developed country.
- The group's work shall be guided by the principles of openness, transparency, inclusiveness and consensus.
- The OWG will adopt its report and recommendations by consensus, reflecting different options, if necessary.
- The following may participate as observers in the meetings of the OWG in the manner outlined in Economic and Social Council (ECOSOC) decision 1993/215:
    - Representatives of UN Specialized Agencies and related organizations; and
    - Representatives of NGOs in consultative status with ECOSOC.
- In accordance with the Rio+20 outcome document, the OWG may draw on the support of an inter-agency technical support team and expert panels, and all relevant expert advice, as needed.
- The working methods may be re-visited when deemed necessary by the open working group.[23]

Most of these modalities are fairly standard for the United Nations, including that the work of the OWG will not prejudice parallel work going on in other bodies, a deadline to submit a report to the General Assembly (by September 15, 2014, the last day of work of the sixty-eighth session of the General Assembly), and election of co-chairs. The principles of openness, transparency, inclusiveness, and consensus were added to ease member states' concerns that the work of the OWG would be shrouded in secrecy. Many member states wanted to avoid a repeat of the UN agency–dominated process that resulted in the MDGs thirteen years earlier. The "open" nature of the OWG was designed to ensure that anyone could attend the meetings, whether they were members or not. The modalities agreement invited representatives of UN agencies and NGOs into the process. This complied with the notion of an "open" working group but also guaranteed that the OWG would benefit from a wide variety of inputs and would reflect the interests and needs of not just governments but also of a range of other stakeholders. Finally, the use of an interagency technical support team and expert panels ensured the substantive integrity of the process and guaranteed that the OWG and its co-chairs could call on experts to provide information, data, and recommendations.

The proposal to allow NGOs to observe the proceedings of the OWG received a certain amount of pushback, which is often the case at the United Nations. From an institutional perspective, under Article 71 of the UN Charter only ECOSOC has the ability to make "arrangements for consultation with non-governmental organizations."[24] Although some of the UN specialized agencies, such as the UN Children's Fund (UNICEF) and the UN High Commissioner for Refugees (UNHCR), and the UN-sponsored world conferences, such as Rio+20, have introduced their own NGO accreditation procedures, NGOs have not been able to gain consultative status with the General Assembly or the Security Council.[25] The OWG was subsidiary to the General Assembly, so special provisions had to be made to enable NGO participation.

Some governments opposed any NGO participation at all, although their rationale varied. NGOs themselves argued that states that are weaker or less legitimate are the ones most concerned about NGO participation because it may undermine state sovereignty or weaken their monopoly on global decision making. Some states oppose in principle any expansion of NGO participation at the United Nations because this is an *intergovernmental* organization.[26] Some democratic states believe that NGOs have little legitimacy when compared to governments acting as the voice of their voters. Other delegates say that diplomacy is the prerogative of sovereign states and that NGOs have no legitimate role to play in global policy making.

To reach agreement, the co-facilitators needed to placate those who didn't want NGO participation by assuring them that NGOs would be allowed only to observe the proceedings. At the same time they had to assure the NGOs and the friends of NGOs that although the modalities agreement stated that NGOs could only observe the proceedings, in practice they would find a way to enable NGOs to actively contribute to the work of the OWG. The terminology wasn't anything new. But it was the OWG co-chairs' application, interpretation, and innovation that provided the flexibility to create more and more space for civil society and NGOs.

ELECTING THE CO-CHAIRS

Once the agenda and modalities were finally settled, the next step was to formally nominate the OWG co-chairs. As stated in the modalities agreement, at the beginning of its first formal meeting the OWG would elect two co-chairs, one from a developing country and one from a developed country. This system was set up to build trust. If there were a single chair from the North, many developing countries would fear that their views would not be heard and the chair would represent developed countries' interests. Similarly, if there were a single chair from the South, developed countries might distrust the process and outcome.

Although the first meeting of the OWG would formally elect the co-chairs, it was the responsibility of the relevant regional groups to put forth nominations. For the developing-country co-chair, consultations took place within the African, Asia-Pacific, and Latin America and Caribbean groups as well as in the larger Group of 77 (G-77). On the developed-country side, consultations took place within WEOG, the Eastern European Group, and the European Union, whose members span both groups.

During the discussions in the G-77, Kenya's Tobias Ogweno had assumed that Ambassador Kamau would be the co-chair from the South because he had successfully steered the modalities decision as co-facilitator.

PHOTO 3.1. At a meeting of the G-77, Kenya's Tobias Ogweno indicated that Africa was interested in taking up the position of co-chair. *Photo by IISD/Francis Dejon (enb.iisd.org)*

Kamau indicated that if the African Group endorsed him, he would be happy to co-chair. However, other members of the G-77 said that determining the working modalities was a procedural matter that was different from the substantive nature of the SDGs. In fact, some G-77 members had already met to endorse Brazil. At a meeting of the G-77, Ogweno indicated that Africa was interested in taking up the position of co-chair. Immediately, some countries asked if he had a particular country in mind. He responded, "This would be a chance for an African country and the African ambassadors will meet and decide who among them will take up the mantle." This ignited some murmurs and muted opposition. While the delegations were considering the matter, Colombia also voiced interest in co-chairing the process. Paula Caballero Gómez from the Colombian Ministry of Foreign Affairs had played an instrumental role in pushing for the SDGs during the Rio+20 process, and some went so far as to say that "the

SDGs were Colombia's baby." However, their case was not strong because Caballero was based in Bogotá and the current Colombian ambassador had been in New York for only a few months and had not really followed the process.[27]

Egypt, Argentina, India, Brazil, and Indonesia mounted strong opposition to an African co-chair. Indonesia said that although Kenya co-facilitated the drafting of the OWG's agenda and modalities and Ambassador Kamau did a terrific job, Indonesia could not agree that he should co-chair the formulation of the SDGs. At that point, Ghana responded, "What is wrong with Africa co-chairing this process? Didn't Ambassador Kamau deliver the working methods of the OWG?" Ghana's intervention was followed by a flurry of support from several African states, including Nigeria, Uganda, and Ethiopia. Brazil said that if the co-chair had to be from an African state, maybe it should be Tanzania, noting that Deputy Permanent Representative Modest Jonathan Mero "is very capable." Egypt, Cuba, and Argentina noted that they trusted Brazil to do this job.[28]

It appeared as though the majority of the G-77 countries thought that their interests would be better served if one of the so-called BASIC countries (Brazil, South Africa, India, and China) held the chairmanship. There was concern that an African country (other than South Africa) could be easily manipulated by the developed countries. Up until this point, Kenya was not really seen as a player at the United Nations. Many thought that Kenya was a Trojan horse for the Europeans or for UNEP. During the Rio+20 process, Kenya focused on UNEP and the institutional framework for sustainable development. However, now Kenya was ready to become a credible player in the international community and no longer wanted to be viewed as a single-issue delegation. But were the rest of the member states ready for Kenya?

Kenya made its case before the G-77 to deal with the concerns. First, no African country had been assigned any role in the post Rio+20 follow-up processes. Second, many African countries had not achieved all of the MDGs and needed to have a level of comfort with the SDGs. Third, Kenya would support another African co-chair, not necessarily Ambassador Kamau. Fourth, there was a need for consistency that would be better satisfied by having as a co-chair a representative from a single country, as opposed to a member of a troika. In East Africa, both Tanzania and Kenya had been nominated to the OWG as single-seat holders, not troikas (see Box 3.2). Finally, the African Group would meet and present the name of its candidate within a week. This latter step was to give the impression that the permanent representatives had already started consultations and the nomination was imminent.[29]

Following Kenya's presentation, Tanzania and Ethiopia offered support, with Ethiopia going so far as to support the nomination of Ambassador Kamau, noting that he is "one of the most knowledgeable and experienced Permanent Representatives and played a prominent role during Rio+20."[30] Fiji, which was chair of the G-77 in 2013 (the chairmanship rotates annually), then ruled that consensus was emerging that an African state would co-chair the OWG. He requested that the African Group present a name for consideration in a week. The African permanent representatives met, and Ethiopia nominated Ambassador Kamau to unanimous support.[31]

In the meantime, the developed countries had agreed that Ambassador Csaba Kőrösi of Hungary would be nominated as co-chair. The Europeans, who themselves were divided over the nature of the SDGs, needed to nominate someone who was relatively neutral. Hungary was the only developed country that had its own seat on the OWG. Some speculated that this also was a way of compensating Hungary following its loss to Azerbaijan in its bid for one of the Eastern European seats on the Security Council the year before.[32] To some degree it also made sense that the two co-facilitators for the preparations for the first session of the OWG would continue on as its co-chairs. When the first session of the OWG convened on Thursday, March 14, 2013, Ambassador Kamau and Ambassador Kőrösi were formally elected as co-chairs.

So who were the co-chairs, and what did they bring to the SDG process? Csaba Kőrösi became the permanent representative of Hungary to the United Nations in September 2010. Kőrösi was a career diplomat, having joined the Ministry of Foreign Affairs in 1983.[33] He served the government through the transition from communism to a Western-style democracy in the late 1980s and through the process of joining the European Union in 2004. Kőrösi served as the deputy chief of mission at the Hungarian

PHOTO 3.2. Ambassador Peter Thomson, permanent representative of Fiji to the United Nations, was chair of the Group of 77 in 2013. *Photo by IISD/Ángeles Estrada (enb.iisd.org)*

Embassy in Tel Aviv, chargé d'affaires at the Hungarian Embassy in the United Arab Emirates, deputy state secretary in charge of multilateral diplomacy, and as the head of the NATO-WEU (North Atlantic Treaty Organization-Western European Union) Department. From 2002 to 2006, he served as Hungary's ambassador to Greece. Prior to arriving in New York, he was the head of the first and second European departments in the Hungarian Ministry of Foreign Affairs from 2006 to 2010.[34] Kőrösi had no prior UN experience before he arrived in New York and had not focused on sustainable development issues or Rio+20. Yet his bilateral experience proved essential for the work of the OWG.

Kamau also arrived in New York in 2010 and took the position of permanent representative of Kenya to the United Nations. Unlike Kőrösi, Kamau was not a career diplomat but had years of experience within the UN system. He began his career in 1985 as a programme communication and social mobilization consultant for UNICEF's East and Southern Africa Regional Office in Nairobi.[35]

Kamau worked for UNICEF in southern Africa, New York, and the Caribbean until 1998, when he returned to Africa as the UN resident coordinator and UN Development Programme (UNDP) resident representative in Gaborone, Botswana, and then in Kigali, Rwanda, followed by a posting as the UNICEF country representative in South Africa.[36] He also served as a consultant for a number of organizations, including the Bill and Melinda Gates Foundation, the Joint UN Programme on HIV/AIDS (UNAIDS) for East and Southern Africa, the Africa Child Policy Forum, and the Africa Policy Institute. In March 2009, Kamau was appointed as Kenya's permanent representative to the United Nations Office at Nairobi, where he served concurrently as permanent representative to UNEP and to the United Nations Human Settlements Programme (UN-Habitat). This was his first diplomatic post, which was then followed by his posting in New York.[37] Once in New York, he was the focal point for the African Group at the United Nations in the lead-up to Rio+20 and was the New York liaison with the international environmental governance process under UNEP. From his experience in the UN system, Kamau brought to his position a depth and breadth of technical information, particularly about development in the context of multilateralism. He understood what was possible, and impossible, in the UN system.

The election of these two co-chairs had additional benefits beyond the experience that they brought to their position. Kenya and Hungary are both small, not-so-powerful states in the UN system. Neither country had major vested interests in the process. Neither country had other major leadership roles of committees or regional groups in the United Nations at the time. And both the governments of Kenya and Hungary gave their ambassadors independence to run the process as they saw fit. Together, all this bode well for the work of the OWG. Yet no one was totally prepared for the journey that would ensue because nothing like the OWG had ever before happened in the United Nations.

INITIAL CHALLENGES

The OWG differed from many other UN working groups from the very beginning. Most working groups established by the General Assembly develop draft resolutions and decisions that are then presented to the General

PHOTO 3.3. *Left to right:* OWG Co-chairs Ambassador Csaba Kőrösi (Hungary) and Ambassador Macharia Kamau (Kenya). *Photo by IISD/Elizabeth Press (enb.iisd.org)*

Assembly as a whole. This was the first time a working group had been tasked with producing a set of development goals. Furthermore, the scope of the issues to be considered was far broader than that of any other working group, as these groups usually deal with a single issue such as human rights for older persons or the state of the marine environment. The OWG was asked to look at the entire sustainable development agenda—an agenda that encompassed all areas of social development, economic development, and environmental protection, and expanded into areas such as peace, security, and human rights. At this point no one was even sure how to begin this monumental task. Finally, this was the first time the United Nations had ever established a body where the membership shared seats. No one was quite sure how this would work. Would each troika have to internally negotiate a single position? Would only one member speak for each troika? If others could observe, would they also be allowed to speak or submit proposals? No formal rules or procedures existed to govern the OWG's work. The co-chairs needed to discuss just how they were going to run the meetings and build the trust of the member states in this new process.

Leadership

The challenges of chairing multilateral negotiations such as the OWG have increased because of a number of features in the current era of sustainable development negotiations, making an understanding of how to success-fully chair meetings all the more important. Negotiators have to under-stand scientific evidence, and they have to grasp complex economic, environmental, and social development issues, which are not normally part of most diplomats' education.[38] At the same time, a growing number of subject experts are involved, but they do not necessarily understand all of the complexities of multilateral procedures and practice.[39] Without ef-fective leadership, negotiations can easily get bogged down in the complex-ity of the issues and the multiplicity of interests that must be reconciled. Effective leaders can guide delegates towards a formula that can embrace multiple interests and locate the small area where the interests of many parties can be satisfied or even upgraded simultaneously. Although an agreement may emerge out of the "cacophony of group interaction," it is more likely to emerge if it is articulated clearly by leaders or chairs who command respect from all parties.[40]

Chairing multilateral negotiations involves both a certain degree of imagination in inventing institutional options and skill in brokering the interests of numerous actors to line up support for such actions.[41] Effective chairs must have a number of skills, including the following:

- Patience and perseverance.
- Power to deploy threats and promises, affecting the incentives of others to accept their terms.[42]
- Leadership that demonstrates a notion of common interest, not just interest-based power politics.
- The ability to shape the perspectives of those who participate in the negotiations.
- The ability to set a good example or show the way forward on how to deal with an issue or set of issues.

- Attention to finding the means to achieve common goals and convincing others about the merits of proposed options.[43]
- The ability to work as an equal with different personalities at a very high level to deliver an outcome.[44]
- The ability to withstand pressure.
- The ability to know when to divorce themselves from the position of their own country or their regional or interest group and focus instead on achieving the best outcome possible.

Many diplomats who become chairs at the United Nations do not always demonstrate the necessary leadership skills. Many chairs are elected to these positions based on either a regional rotation or seniority, not skills or subject matter knowledge. The skills needed to chair multilateral negotiations are not usually taught in diplomatic academies. Most chairs or co-chairs are given a script by the Secretariat, which they read, and then proceed to call on countries to speak. If they are required to summarize the proceedings, the Secretariat often prepares a summary to be read aloud (see Box 3.3). But from the beginning, the OWG co-chairs realized that this process would require strong leadership to guide the membership through potentially stormy waters. In fact, without skilled co-chairs who understand the importance of timing, when to propose compromises, and when to resort to innovative working methods, it was unlikely that trust would be built or consensus found.

Before the first meeting of the OWG, the co-chairs met with their technical teams (personnel from their respective missions to the United Nations, similar to embassies) at the offices of the UN Department of Economic and Social Affairs (DESA), which was providing Secretariat services. This meeting was a bit tense at first because the Hungarians and the Kenyans had yet to find their balance and figure out how they were going to accommodate each other's working styles. In a sense, this meeting was the first round of SDG negotiations—a pre-negotiation between the two co-chairs. Often the ambassadors who are elected as co-chairs and their support teams have never worked closely together or may not have even formally met. Furthermore, the co-chairs often come from very different

■ **Box 3.3.**

What Is the United Nations Secretariat?

The Secretariat is one of the main organs of the United Nations that carries out the day-to-day work of the organization around the world, under the leadership of the Secretary-General. The Secretariat's staff is composed of permanent expert officials, constituting an international civil service. They include project directors, policy experts, administrators, technicians, clerks, translators, interpreters, and security guards.

Although the decision-making powers of the United Nations reside within its deliberative bodies (e.g., the General Assembly, Economic and Social Council, and Security Council), the Secretariat plays a key role in implementation and in setting the agenda for those bodies. The Secretariat is the main source of economic and political analysis for the General Assembly and Security Council, and operates political field missions that provide knowledge to those bodies.

The Secretariat for the Open Working Group on Sustainable Development Goals was staffed by the UN Department of Economic and Social Affairs' (DESA) Division for Sustainable Development (DSD). Based at UN Headquarters in New York, UN DESA is responsible for the sustainable development pillar of the UN Secretariat. UN DESA also collaborates closely with its partners at regional and country levels in helping countries formulate and implement national development strategies.

SOURCES: Paul Novosad and Eric Werker, "Who Runs the International System? Power and Staffing of the United Nations Secretariat," Harvard Business School Working Paper 15–018, August 30, 2014, http://ssrn.com/abstract=2498737; United Nations Careers, "Where We Are?" https://careers.un.org/lbw/home.aspx?view type=VD; United Nations, "Secretariat," www.un.org/en/sections/about-un/secretariat /index.html.

cultures and backgrounds, which can affect their personalities and their negotiating style.

National and/or ethnic cultures strongly contribute to shaping what is usually referred to as a "national negotiating style" by combining cultural influence with a country's history and political system.[45] Culture can actually serve as both an obstacle and a bridge. As an obstacle, it can always be used as an explanation or scapegoat for failure of the negotiations. But as a bridge, one party or actor can rely on certain elements of the other's culture to start building a relationship. It is not always easy and carries some risk. With regard to co-chairs of a negotiating process, learning about the other co-chair's culture instead of relying on stereotypes shows respect for that person and makes it less likely that he or she will take a defensive stance.[46] This can be done by using the other's culture to identify and build a relationship, becoming more familiar with the other's culture, or looking for a third, more common culture (for example, if both studied or worked in a common country). This can help pave the road to establishing talking points and eventually enriches the joint potential of the partnership.[47]

In an international organization such as the United Nations, the large variety of national cultures could turn it into a kind of Tower of Babel if there were no integrative dimension such as an organizational culture at work. Thus, the organizational culture of UN multilateralism creates some guidelines under which these negotiations usually occur. But in the case of the SDGs, there was no specific organizational culture or model that could be followed. The co-chairs and the OWG would be breaking new ground. So not only did the co-chairs have to learn to understand each other's backgrounds and cultures, but they also had to create a new organizational culture—and comfort—under which the SDGs would be negotiated.

Managing the Process

The co-chairs also had to determine how they were going to manage the process. How were they going to bring in the views of all member states, UN agencies, and NGOs to create a universal agenda when the OWG was limited to thirty seats filled by seventy member states? How would they keep the working group "open" yet follow the mandate for a thirty-member group provided in "The Future We Want"? Although the modalities had been agreed in principle, there was no agreement on how to honor that mandate while also ensuring that "open" meant open and that anyone who wished to speak could do so.

During the first session, some developed countries insisted that the formulation of the SDGs was a technical process and that they would be bringing in technical experts and even ministers from their capitals. Some developing countries, as articulated especially by Argentina's Josefina Bunge, wanted to ensure that if some countries brought in ministers from capitals to negotiate, it would not prejudge the participation of diplomats and technical officers in New York. Because of the sensitivity of these issues, the co-chairs assured delegates that everyone could participate in all sessions. They reassured the small states, General Assembly Second Committee officers, ambassadors, and ministers that they would all be heard. The co-chairs promised them that if they had something that would add to the process, it would be taken on board. Kamau and Kőrösi were concerned that anyone who felt left out of the proceedings or was prevented from participating could have grounds to contest the outcome when it was presented to the General Assembly. So even if this caused some friction in the beginning, the co-chairs tried to get everyone to accept working methods that recognized the members of the OWG while keeping the meetings open to anyone who wanted to participate. This would, in theory, follow the mandate of a thirty-member group while at the same time keeping it open. But no one was quite sure how it would work in practice.

Building Trust

The co-chairs also recognized that they needed to build trust in the room. Mistrust has proven to be a major obstacle to North-South cooperation in the sustainable development arena, as was seen in Copenhagen and Rio. This obstacle is largely attributable to long-standing inequalities. Inequality makes it harder for developing countries and developed countries to trust each other and establish mutually acceptable "rules of the game."[48] Such rules are important to reduce uncertainty, stabilize expectations, constrain opportunism, and increase the credibility of state commitments. The selection of co-chairs from North and South cannot necessarily solve long-standing inequality, but it can help to reduce the mistrust of the process on both sides.

Kamau noted that the first step for him, following the difficult nominating process within the G-77, was to win the confidence of his own group. There was so much skepticism and doubt about the process, and, as noted earlier, some delegations feared that Kenya was merely a Trojan horse. He knew that to succeed, he had to immediately disabuse the G-77 of that notion. To build trust and confidence, he did his homework. First, he had to understand the domestic politics of each country. What was going on in the different countries and regional and interest groups? What did they want to hear? What did they want out of this process? What were their fears? What were their agendas? He recognized that he needed to make them appreciate that he understood their concerns and was best able to champion them because he didn't have his own agenda.

For example, both co-chairs proved that they could really speak to the issues of the Bolivarian Alliance for the Peoples of Our America (ALBA) countries, including respect for Mother Earth and respect for due process in the negotiations. The concept of Mother Earth or Mother Nature is rooted in most indigenous cultures of the world. In the indigenous view, "Mother Earth" is not an inert object or the source of resources but a living entity to whom we are related. From this relationship arise the different practices in which indigenous peoples thank Mother Earth and create a relationship with birds, mountains, rivers, the wind, and everything that surrounds us. These practices are about harmony with, and respect for, nature. Therefore, the co-chairs approached Mother Earth as an indigenous-people—and even a global—concern, rather than just the ALBA political agenda.

In the case of the Africans, Kamau recognized that they needed a voice, so he assured them that they would be heard. In the case of the Arab states, there were more-complex geopolitical and economic concerns. The co-chairs realized that they had to help them get past the fear that the SDGs were part of an agenda that would upset their economies and their livelihoods—especially the fossil-fuel–dependent ones—or marginalize the region in the work of the OWG. So they tried to assure them that the SDGs were not intended to eliminate the use of fossil fuels and deprive the oil-producing states of their major source of income, but that the SDGs should be seen as an opportunity to also invest in and develop renewable energy technologies, such as solar power.

Traditionally, when there are two co-chairs, the co-chair from the North interacts more with members from Europe, the United States, Canada, Australia, New Zealand, and Japan, and the co-chair from the South interacts more with the G-77 countries. However, Kamau insisted that all countries had to trust both co-chairs, not just one. So he reached out to the developed-country delegations to ensure that he could rally them behind both co-chairs. This showed quite a bit of foresight. Not only did the co-chairs need the personal support of the members; they also had to ensure that it would be difficult for anyone to upend the process further down the road by leveraging group or regional positions.

In addition to the usual North-South mistrust and the need for the co-chairs to build trust with the membership, this was an unusual process where very little was predictable. When this is the case, anxiety often follows. As Kőrösi noted, "We may hate the [UN] procedures, but we are comfortable with them."[49] There was also lingering mistrust about the entire concept of the SDGs. It was clear that the understandings of sustainable development, the levels of expertise, and the institutional support among member states were light-years apart. Some delegations were very much about renewing the MDGs, especially those that had not been achieved. Others didn't understand what the SDGs were supposed to be, and still others didn't think that a set of goals could result from intergovernmental negotiations.

To remedy the situation, the co-chairs, in consultation with the Secretariat, decided that the OWG needed a "stocktaking" phase to create a common space, based on scientific evidence, and allow everyone to have the same terms of reference and understand the concept of sustainability and what it really means for people, planet, global prosperity, and security. Otherwise, they feared that if the OWG members didn't have a shared knowledge base when the negotiations began, it would be very difficult to achieve a substantive and transformative outcome rather than just a political one. So this became the next challenge: to define the scope of the exercise and embark on a year-long stocktaking process to build this common understanding of the issues. Given the number of days the OWG could meet and the number of issues, the co-chairs, with their teams and the Secretariat, created clusters and proposed a work program built around the main topics in "The Future We Want." They put the easier issues first and then proposed moving to the more difficult and contested issues. They felt that this would ease some of the anxiety and mistrust. Thus, the OWG agreed on a list of issues to be covered that were clustered into eight stock-taking sessions over twelve months.

CONCLUSIONS AND LESSONS LEARNED

During this pre-negotiation phase of the process, the focus was on using the language in "The Future We Want" to establish the Open Working Group, elect the co-chairs, develop the working methods, and start to establish trust in the co-chairs and the process before the negotiations of the SDGs could begin. From the outset, the co-chairs decided to manage the OWG negotiations in an iterative way. They needed to test the limits of tolerance in terms of where the innovations could be and where new arrangements could be accepted.

Several key lessons can be learned from this part of the process. First, creative problem solving is important. Usually when the United Nations decides to set up a limited-membership working group of some sort, the number of members is sacrosanct. Elections to fill the seats will result in winners and losers. Those left outside the room may challenge the outcome, as was the case during the Rio+20 PrepCom. When Pakistan's Farrukh Khan proposed sharing seats, which resulted in the agreement to have troikas of the seventy member states who wanted to be part of the OWG, the process started off by welcoming participants rather than closing the door on them. By approaching the idea of membership through creative problem solving, no one was left out or alienated from the process.

Second, chairs need to work to ensure that the membership has trust in their leadership as early as possible. Because of the difficulty in choosing co-chairs for this process, Kamau recognized that first he had to build up trust in his group (G-77) and then build trust among the developed countries, all while ensuring that he was not seen as a traitor to his own group. Both Kamau and Kőrösi knew they could not be tied down by any group's position or seen solely as an interlocutor for their own group. The principle is simple, if hard to enact: once co-chairs are "hired," they are hired for the process, not for their group.

Third, leadership includes understanding the positions, hopes, and fears of the participants. Only then can the co-chairs interpret what they can and cannot do and link the vision of what they want to do with how they are going to get there. In this case, the co-chairs realized early on that the OWG could not agree on any universal SDGs if the process was not inclusive and if the people they were working with were members of a restricted group only. So even before the first official meeting, they started the process of consulting with the different OWG members and any other delegations that wanted to meet. They went the extra mile so that they could manage the process effectively.

Finally, management of the process is important. There were many risks heading into this process, especially the risk that the negotiations would get unwieldy and resemble the Rio+20 negotiations. Many were afraid that the OWG would collapse under its own weight; in fact, some may even have been betting on it. So it was important to realize from the outset the importance of the management of people, dynamics, and process, and the ability to listen to everyone's ideas, yet still combine them over time into something coherent.

So as the OWG began its substantive work in March 2013, the co-chairs, member states, the UN Secretariat, intergovernmental organizations and agencies, and civil society were not really sure what would happen next. But there was hope that the foundations of the process and the preparation of the co-chairs, as described in this chapter, would ensure more than just a modicum of success.

4

UNCERTAIN BEGINNINGS

We are about to embark on a journey into a great unknown.
The world has rarely done anything quite so difficult as what
you are asked to accomplish.

—President of the 67th United Nations
General Assembly Vuk Jeremić[1]

The Open Working Group (OWG) met for the first time in March 2013, and, as General Assembly President Vuk Jeremić so aptly put it, the United Nations was embarking "on a journey into a great unknown."[2] This session and the seven that followed over the ensuing eleven months at UN Headquarters in New York formed the stocktaking phase, where delegates engaged in collective learning about issues on the sustainable development agenda through a series of seminars and discussions. Such collective learning is almost unheard of in UN negotiations, largely because there is rarely the luxury of time. Yet the co-chairs of the OWG, Macharia Kamau and Csaba Kőrösi, believed that this stocktaking exercise was necessary. Not only did these eight sessions build a common understanding about the issues and what was really at stake; they also built trust and understanding regarding the process for the development of a set of Sustainable Development Goals (SDGs) and dislodged delegates from their twentieth-century working methods.

This chapter provides an overview of the eight stocktaking sessions and what they contributed to the creation of the SDGs. Then we examine the impact of these sessions, the evolving coalitions, and the game changers—both within and outside the United Nations—that had an impact on the negotiations that followed.

PLAYING THE LONG GAME TO EDUCATE, DEPOLITICIZE, AND LEVEL THE PLAYING FIELD

One of the ideas behind the stocktaking sessions was to depoliticize the substance of the debate. This in itself was unique because the tradition of the United Nations is to do just the opposite: politicize technical issues. This practice can create schisms embedded in geopolitical struggles and historical injustices. During these stocktaking sessions both co-chairs constantly reminded participants that they were talking about one Earth, one climate, and one biosphere. They didn't want participants to get carried away by the tendency to fracture the process along geopolitical lines. So by the end of the stocktaking, the majority of people in the room understood that the politicization of both the debate and the substance was not going to be helpful. Sustainable development, the co-chairs stressed, is something that goes beyond a single country's borders, region, or continent. The co-chairs also wanted to start the journey by creating certain perceptions about the process. They wanted everyone to know that the co-chairs were going to be the champions for the process and the SDGs, not for any particular group or country.

The OWG demanded a different pattern of engagement, built around common interests that had to do more with the global economy, society, and environment than with parochial national interests. For much of the United Nations' seventy years, multilateral negotiations were either a narrow extension of bilateral politics meant to serve purely national interests or conducted along North-South or East-West lines. But early-twenty-first-century global sustainable development issues posed a new set of challenges that often cut across traditional negotiation patterns and groupings.

As stated earlier, many came into the OWG without a clear sense of what the group would be doing or a clear understanding of the subject matter. At first, many members prepared to negotiate in the traditional pattern along either bilateral or group lines. Breaking negotiators out of these silos required that the co-chairs (1) provide a level playing field to assure people that they could indeed negotiate differently and (2) keep the focus on the challenges of achieving sustainable development rather than on traditional politicized positions taken by negotiating groups. This recalibration of the process by the co-chairs was crucial to the ultimate success of the OWG. Luckily for the co-chairs, there was enough of a common understanding of these challenges among some member states to form a core group of negotiators that the co-chairs could rely on to move the discussions in a positive direction. Moreover, this group of states included both developed and developing countries.

Second, the co-chairs needed to assure delegates that this was a member-state–driven process. They wanted to avoid the perception that they were going to be controlled by the UN specialized agencies, funds, and programs. Some of these institutions had, over time, expanded their role in what are supposed to be negotiations handled only by member states. UN technocrats have always provided information and advice on the margins of intergovernmental negotiations, but over time they had begun to assert more influence. In some cases they would quietly champion views or ideas of certain member states, especially those that provided the most funding. Secondly, if a policy or program position under debate could affect the mandate or operations of a given organization, the technocrats would work assiduously with those countries that would protect the organization's mandate or buttress its policies.

The technocrats, as UN system employees, are omnipresent during negotiations, unlike the member state negotiators and experts who come and go at regular intervals as they are deployed and recalled by their various countries and governments. The staff of the UN agencies, funds, and programs therefore have a huge advantage in influencing negotiations, precisely because many times they form the common thread and the historical memory. Of course, this is not always the case. But in the development sphere and the OWG, there was concern that these technocrats sought to loom over the negotiations because they felt strongly, probably correctly, that the mandates and policies of their organizations would be affected and that the work of the development side of the United Nations would be influenced significantly.

The co-chairs were acutely aware of these dynamics because they played into the fears of developing countries that remembered the agency-drafted Millennium Development Goals (MDGs) and wanted to remain in control of the SDG negotiations. So even though at first the technocrats and the leadership of UN organizations expected little from the OWG's work in terms of a coherent transformative outcome, when it became obvious that the SDGs would be adopted and would be transformative, the technocrats and their executives went to great lengths to try to influence the debate. Managing the funds, programs, and organizations to ensure they were a positive rather than a threatening force was another major challenge for the co-chairs.

Third, the co-chairs wanted to assure member states that they should not fear the nongovernmental organizations (NGOs) in the room. They wanted member states to understand that they would never be cut off or prevented from taking the floor by an NGO. At the same time, the co-chairs wanted to assure NGOs that they could be in the room and they would have opportunities to speak. In spite of the growth of democracies around the world, the opening up of societies, and the expansion of the role of civil society both between and within countries, UN member states still jealously guard their privileged position at the intergovernmental negotiating table. The UN rules of engagement were built around protocols to give each member state, no matter its size, wealth, or power, an equal say in UN General Assembly negotiations. These protocols make eminently good sense, especially for small developing countries, and ensure that all countries are heard. But the protocols pose huge difficulties for civil society organizations that want to, or need to, engage in the process. Because of the growing influence and voice of civil society, especially those groups that had been engaged throughout Rio+20 and the lead-up to the OWG, the co-chairs knew that sustainable development issues are not the sole purview of state actors, so civil society needed to be accommodated.

The co-chairs may have recognized that the world had changed and the voice of civil society and NGOs needed to be heard in the OWG, but not everyone agreed. Some governments did not want to lose their privileged position as the key interlocutors and drivers of UN multilateral negotiations. There was also genuine concern among some developing countries that the developed countries, which often nurture and fund many of the most active civil society voices at the UN, would, in effect, get a second bite at the cake in the negotiations. In other words, these developing countries did not want the North to have the opportunity to use civil society organizations to drive their agenda at the expense of the South.

These conflicting dynamics needed to be managed, and the co-chairs had to work hard to create space for civil society voices to be heard without allowing the debate and the negotiations to be distorted by the overrepresentation of "Western-funded liberal entities," which some developing countries believed dominated the NGOs registered at the United Nations.

THE STOCKTAKING PROCESS

At the first meeting of the OWG, government delegates had the opportunity to express initial views on the SDGs and the challenges before them. After introductory statements by the Secretary-General and the president of the General Assembly, which demonstrated that this process was supported at the highest UN levels, Kamau and Kőrösi were formally elected as co-chairs. Nikhil Seth, director, Division for Sustainable Development (DSD), UN Department of Economic and Social Affairs (DESA), introduced the report of the Secretary-General: "Initial Input of the Secretary-General to the Open Working Group on Sustainable Development Goals" (A/67/634).[3] Seth, with his depth of experience, skills, patience, and high-mindedness, was to prove crucial to the work of the co-chairs and the OWG. From this first document through to the final text of the SDGs, the substantive inputs, organizational backstopping, and hard work of the DSD staff under Seth's leadership played an important role in the success of the OWG.

The Secretary-General's report summarized the results of a survey distributed to member states in September 2012, which included views on SDG priority areas; defining national targets for global, universally applicable goals; incorporating existing goals and targets; ensuring coherence with the post-2015 development agenda; and engaging all stakeholders.[4] Sixty-three of the 193 member states responded to the survey. Among the top priority issues identified were food security and sustainable agriculture, water and sanitation, energy, education, poverty eradication, and

PHOTO 4.1. The UN Division for Sustainable Development provided Secretariat services for the OWG, under the leadership of Director Nikhil Seth. *Photo by IISD/Francis Dejon (enb.iisd.org)*

health. Other important areas that respondents mentioned included climate change, management of natural resources, employment, gender equality, sustainable consumption and production, and cities and housing.[5] In his summary of some of the survey's findings, Seth noted that many member states believed that the priorities of the MDG agenda should continue to feature prominently in the post-2015 development agenda.[6]

During the session, the troikas—as the groups sharing the thirty seats became known, regardless of the number of countries sharing the seat—stated their initial views on both the process and substance of the SDG framework. Although most statements addressed general considerations and the OWG's work, some outlined their priorities. According to an oral summary by Kőrösi, the main areas emphasized were eradication of poverty and hunger; employment and decent jobs; sustainable consumption and production; gender equality and empowerment of women; access to and good management of the essentials of human well-being, such as food, water, health, and energy; and means of implementation (finance, trade, technology, and capacity building).[7] This session also featured the first of a series of interactive dialogues with experts that became a feature of the stocktaking sessions. In fact, by the end of OWG-8, eighty-seven experts had addressed the working group. (See Appendix I for a complete list of all of the expert presentations during the stocktaking sessions.)

Setting the Agenda

The next seven sessions addressed the key issues that were expected to form the basis of the SDGs. Not everyone initially understood the true purpose of the stocktaking exercise. The co-chairs were playing the long game, but many of the troikas were playing the short game with the old working methods—let's get a draft and start negotiating. But the co-chairs and the Secretariat recognized that the group needed to learn more about the issues before there could be any meaningful discussion about goals and targets.

The topics for each session were primarily gleaned from the headings of the Rio+20 outcome document, "The Future We Want." Seth and the Secretariat came up with the basic structure based on how many days were available, suggested how to fit the issue clusters into the eight sessions, and presented the proposal to the co-chairs. Some of the issues had to be consolidated because there were just too many.

The co-chairs and the Secretariat realized that to educate the delegates and get their buy-in, they would need to bring in experts from as many countries as possible, especially developing ones. The co-chairs consulted with many of the OWG members to ask for proposals for potential panelists from their countries, as well as for feedback on the clusters, arrangements, and agenda. They compiled the feedback they received, reevaluated the situation, and returned to the member states with a revised draft that attempted to respond to any concerns or fears.

Bringing in expert panelists from a wide range of countries was another challenge. At first, it was not easy to get panelists from anywhere, but bringing in experts from the South faced additional barriers of distance and resources. Nevertheless, the co-chairs kept selling this idea that they would bring southern thinkers and ideas to the process, and developing countries appreciated the effort.

The first few sessions generated buzz about both the OWG and the SDGs. Participants from both North and South appeared to be captivated by the panelists. When they realized that these speakers were making some really brilliant points, the OWG members began to build a common understanding around both the agenda and ideas. Delegates who were traveling back and forth to New York from their capitals talked up the OWG back home. As word spread in NGO and private sector circles about the opportunity that was created for civil society and the private sector to get involved as fully engaged partners, more and more people around the world became interested. By the fourth session of the OWG, the energy in the room was palpable. Many academics and other experts also started to recognize that this was *the* game in town, that they could influence the creation of a new sustainable development agenda, and so they wanted to be invited as panelists. Even the heads of the various UN agencies, funds, and programs, who showed little interest in the beginning, began to attend, especially when their mandate was on the agenda. Many of them also asked to be expert panelists. Although the co-chairs wanted to bring in experts from outside the United Nations—not the usual suspects—so member states could learn about the issues from new perspectives, they accommodated many UN agency experts as well (see Appendix I).

The order in which the OWG looked at the issues was also important. The co-chairs knew that to reassure many developing countries, philanthropic organizations, and the UN Development Group[8] heads, among others, they had first to address the unfinished business of the MDGs. Issues such as sustainable consumption and production and inequality were seen as "new" and contested; other issues were just plainly overly politicized, such as human rights, the rule of law, and good governance. So the co-chairs scheduled some of these newer or more-sensitive issues towards the end, especially because they had not always been seen as part of the sustainable development agenda. These newer issues, including human rights, the rule of law, and good governance, emerged from the June 2012 UN System Task Team report, *Realizing the Future We Want for All.*

The UN System Task Team was established by Secretary-General Ban Ki-moon in January 2012 to support preparations for the post-2015 development agenda (see Box 4.1). The task team report identified four core dimensions where progress would be needed in the future "to build a rights-based, equitable, secure and sustainable world for all people": inclusive social development, environmental sustainability, inclusive economic development, and peace and security.[9] The first three dimensions were the traditional pillars of sustainable development, but the fourth dimension, peace and security, was new. The task team also argued that the MDGs did not adequately address a number of issues, including "productive employment, violence against women, social protection, inequalities, social exclusion, biodiversity, persistent malnutrition and increase in noncommunicable diseases, reproductive health and complexities related to demographic dynamics, peace and security, governance, the rule of law and human rights."[10] They also noted that the MDG framework did not account for vulnerability to natural hazards and other external shocks that led to setbacks in the achievement of the MDGs.[11]

There was little doubt that some of the newer issues, especially rule of law and human rights, would cause serious anxiety among some of the members. During OWG-2 in April 2013, the co-chairs presented the draft program of work for the stocktaking sessions and allowed the troikas to

■ **Box 4.1.**

The Post-2015 Development Process

In September 2010 the General Assembly held a high-level plenary meeting to assess progress on the Millennium Development Goals (MDGs). The General Assembly reviewed MDG implementation and adopted a resolution: "Keeping the promise: united to achieve the Millennium Development Goals," which requested the Secretary-General to make recommendations for further steps to advance the UN development agenda beyond 2015, when the MDGs would expire.[a]

The UN system then embarked on consultations on the post-2015 agenda. More than 1.4 million participants from governments, civil society, the private sector, academia, and research institutions contributed to the process. Nearly ninety national consultations took place, as well as eleven thematic consultations on issues such as food security and access to water. An online platform—The World We Want

2015—connected people in a global conversation, while MY World, a survey seeking opinions on the issues that matter most, engaged people from more than 190 countries.[b]

The Secretary-General also established a UN System Task Team in September 2011 to support system-wide preparations for the post-2015 development agenda. It brought together more than sixty UN entities, agencies, and international organizations.[c] The task team presented its report, *Realizing the Future We Want for All,* in June 2012.[d] The report called for an integrated policy approach to ensure inclusive economic development, inclusive social development, peace and security, and environmental sustainability within a development agenda that responds to the aspirations of all people for a world free of want and fear.[e]

The findings from all of these consultations were presented to the Secretary-General's High-Level Panel on the Post-2015 Development Agenda for its consideration. The panel—formed in July 2012, with world leaders and representatives from civil society and the private sector—was co-chaired by President Susilo Bambang Yudhoyono of Indonesia, President Ellen Johnson Sirleaf of Liberia, and Prime Minister David Cameron of the United Kingdom. The panel's recommendations were presented to the Secretary-General and member states in May 2013.[f]

NOTES:

[a] UN General Assembly, "Keeping the Promise: United to Achieve the Millennium Development Goals," Resolution 65/1, www.un.org/en/mdg/summit2010/pdf/out come_documentN1051260.pdf.

[b] United Nations, "Beyond the Millennium Development Goals: The Post-2015 Sustainable Development Agenda," www.un.org/millenniumgoals/pdf/EN_MDG_back grounder.pdf.

[c] United Nations Department for Economic and Social Affairs, "Development Agenda Beyond 2015," www.un.org/en/development/desa/development-beyond-2015.html.

[d] United Nations Department for Economic and Social Affairs.

[e] UN System Task Team on the Post-2015 UN Development Agenda, *Realizing the Future We Want for All* (New York: United Nations, 2012), www.un.org/en /development/desa/policy/untaskteam_undf/untt_report.pdf.

[f] See High-Level Panel on the Post-2015 Development Agenda, *A New Global Partnership: Eradicate Poverty and Transform Economies Through Sustainable Development* (New York: United Nations, 2013), www.post2015hlp.org/the-report.

comment, followed by anyone else in the room. Several troikas, including Egypt/Algeria/Morocco/Tunisia, Nicaragua/Brazil, Barbados/Bahamas, Papua New Guinea/Nauru/Palau, Iran and Japan (part of the same troika but not always speaking with one voice), and Ireland/Denmark/Norway wanted to ensure that the inclusion or clustering of issues should not prejudge the eventual SDGs.

Two groups of issues generated particular discussion: (1) energy and (2) conflict, peace, and security. With regard to energy, the discussion on the agenda hinted at some of the disagreements to come on how this subject should be reflected in the SDGs. Troikas disagreed on whether it should be discussed in the context of sustained and inclusive growth and macroeconomic issues, as Egypt, Nicaragua/Brazil, Iran, Iraq, Nigeria, Libya, and Venezuela advocated, or within the cluster on transport and sustainable cities. Saudi Arabia objected to the clustering of energy with transport and climate change, saying the discussion should focus on energy access for the poor and be discussed with the session on sustained and inclusive economic growth. South Africa spoke for many countries, including Saudi Arabia, the United States, Australia, and Canada, which feared that the energy debate would be a back door to the highly technical, highly politicized UN Framework Convention on Climate Change negotiations and wanted to limit the OWG's discussion of climate change.

On conflict, peace, and security, Nicaragua/Brazil and Argentina/Bolivia/Ecuador called for it to be reworded to apply only to countries in special situations. Indonesia/China/Kazakhstan proposed its deletion. Lebanon called for the inclusion of conflict prevention, and Pakistan noted that the notion of development linked to peace and security was important. Guatemala/Colombia requested consideration of rule of law and of crime and conflict prevention.[12] The permanent five members of the UN Security Council (China, France, Russia, the United Kingdom, and the United States) were very clear and unified that the OWG should not focus on conflict, peace, and security or be used as a back door or a second track to the UN Security Council Reform process. At the same time, the United States, United Kingdom, and France wanted the discussion on rule of law to move forward. As a result of these discussions and further bilateral consultations, the co-chairs revised the program of work (see Box 4.2).

■ **Box 4.2**

OWG Stocktaking Segment: Issue Clusters

OWG-1: March 14–15, 2013

- Interactive discussion on conceptualizing the SDGs

OWG-2: April 17–19, 2013

- Conceptualizing the SDGs

- Poverty eradication

OWG-3: May 22–24, 2013

- Food security and nutrition; sustainable agriculture, desertification, land degradation, and drought

- Water and sanitation

OWG-4: June 17–19, 2013

- Employment and decent work for all, social protection, youth, education, and culture

- Health, population dynamics

OWG-5: November 25–27, 2013

- Sustained and inclusive economic growth, macroeconomic policy questions (including international trade, international financial system, and external debt sustainability), infrastructure development, and industrialization

- Energy

OWG-6: December 9–13, 2013

- Means of implementation (financing, science and technology, knowledge-sharing, and capacity building)

- Global partnership for achieving sustainable development

- Needs of countries in special situations: African countries, LDCs, LLDCs, and SIDS as well as specific challenges facing middle-income countries

- Human rights, the right to development, global governance

(Continues)

OWG-7: January 6–10, 2014

- Sustainable cities and human settlements, sustainable transport
- Sustainable consumption and production (including chemicals and waste)
- Climate change and disaster risk reduction

OWG-8: February 3–7, 2014

- Oceans and seas, forests, biodiversity
- Promoting equality, including social equity, gender equality, and women's empowerment
- Conflict prevention, post-conflict peacebuilding and the promotion of durable peace, rule of law

Establishing the Procedures

Procedurally, each of the stocktaking sessions followed a similar pattern. At 9:00 each morning, there would be an hour-long meeting with representatives of civil society. Then, when the official meeting began for the day, the OWG would first hear keynote presentations for each issue cluster, followed by an "interactive" exchange of views from the member states and observers. Then a panel of experts would speak, followed by questions and answers, as well as another interactive exchange of views. In addition, for each issue cluster the OWG Technical Support Team (TST) prepared an issue brief. The TST was co-chaired by DESA and the United Nations Development Programme (UNDP), and it included representatives from sixty programs, agencies, funds, treaty bodies, and offices throughout the UN system that contributed to different briefs. The TST prepared twenty-nine issue briefs to support the work of the OWG. (See Appendix II.) The TST also served an underappreciated function: maintaining discipline among the UN agencies, funds, and programs that were inclined to lobby delegations for their own sectoral or thematic interests. Although such lobbying is understandable, it makes the process of reaching consensus far more difficult. Thus, the TST, serving as an honest broker, channeled agency interests through the unified mechanism to the co-chairs and the negotiations.[13]

PHOTO 4.2. At OWG-7 in January 2014, Lewis Fulton, Institute of Transportation Studies, University of California, Davis, made the case that transport deserves its own SDG and set of targets. *Photo by IISD/Elizabeth Press (enb. iisd.org)*

Over time, the co-chairs established their methodology for calling on participants in a way that would respect the official members of the OWG, while allowing all interested participants the opportunity to speak during both the question-and-answer period and the interactive exchange of views. If any ministers or high-level officials came from capitals, they were allowed to speak first. Then the OWG members spoke, usually on behalf of their troikas. The next group included member states that were observing the process, followed by nonstate observers, including international organizations, UN agencies and programs, and representatives of civil society and business. The growth from thirty members in "The Future We Want" to seventy members after the UN General Assembly decision, to universal participation was an iterative process that tested the limits of tolerance in terms of what innovations could be used and where new arrangements could be accepted. This enabled most member states to develop a sense of ownership over the process and allowed the co-chairs to receive contributions from all angles. Those who were not among the seventy OWG members quickly learned that if one of their ministers attended the meeting, this person would get to speak first and have a greater impact. As a result, more and more ministers participated.

Initially, some governments, if they could afford to, sent different specialists or experts on each topic under discussion. However, this practice soon fell by the wayside. The OWG was discussing an integrated, universal set of goals, so it became evident to governments that it would be better to have a consistent team throughout the process. This was different from existing practice, where there is usually an ever-changing cast of characters in the room, leading to a loss of institutional memory and a constant reinvention of the wheel. What made this change possible was that the negotiations were all held in New York and the OWG met frequently, creating both continuity and momentum.

In addition to the thirteen scheduled meetings, the co-chairs met intersessionally with the New York–based participants and traveled extensively to meet with officials in capitals and keep them informed. The co-chairs recognized that it was important to educate these officials to bring them on board with the concept of the SDGs. In addition to these bilateral meetings, the co-chairs and many OWG participants attended a large number of intersessional activities hosted by different governments and organizations (see Box 4.3).

In addition to the expert presentations and the twenty-nine TST issue briefs, numerous organizations submitted reports on the issues under consideration, as well as the nature and format of the SDGs themselves. These reports ran the gamut from the International Council for Science's report on "Health and the Sustainable Development Goals: An Urban Systems Perspective"[14] to the 2014 Development Cooperation Forum Switzerland High-Level Symposium's report on "Development Cooperation in a Post-2015 Era: Sustainable Development for All."[15] Issue briefs and reports were also submitted by the UN Special Rapporteur on Violence Against Women: Its Causes and Consequences,[16] the Copenhagen Consensus, Save the Children, the Bill and Melinda Gates Foundation, the International Chamber

■ **BOX 4.3.**

Selected Intersessional Activities During the Stocktaking Phase

- Asia-Pacific Ministerial Dialogue on Post-2015, Bangkok, Thailand, August 26–27, 2013

- Global Compact Leaders' Summit, New York, New York, September 19–20, 2013

- Committee on World Food Security, 40th session, Rome, Italy, October 7–11, 2013

- Budapest Water Summit, Budapest, Hungary, October 8–11, 2013

- UN Development Group (UNDG) Retreat for the Latin American and Caribbean Group (GRULAC), Tarrytown, New York, October 30–31, 2013

- Means of Implementation in the Post-2015 Agenda, hosted by the Mission of Indonesia to the United Nations, New York, New York, October 31, 2013

- Africa Regional Consultative Meeting on the Sustainable Development Goals, Addis Ababa, Ethiopia, November 4–5, 2013

- Post-2015 Europe and Central Asia Regional Consultation, Istanbul, Turkey, November 6–8, 2013

- LDCs Priorities in the Post-2015 Development Agenda and the SDGs, Glen Cove, New York, November 8–9, 2013

- Arab Regional Consultative Meeting on the SDGs, Tunis, Tunisia, November 18–19, 2013

- OWG Intersessional Meeting with Major Groups and Other Stakeholders, New York, New York, November 22, 2013

- Independent Research Forum/World Resources Institute Retreats on the Post-2015 Development Agenda, Tarrytown, New York, October 2–4, 2013, February 9–10, 2014, April 6–7, 2014, and May 3, 2014 (at Columbia University)

of Commerce, the Independent Research Forum, the Sustainable Development Solutions Network, and many more. The co-chairs welcomed these reports, even though their number was often a bit overwhelming, because they demonstrated how important and alive the OWG was and that it was open to different ideas and new thinking.

CHANGING ALLIANCES

The stocktaking exercise had a number of positive effects on the negotiations that were not fully anticipated or understood at the beginning. The first of these was that traditional alliances broke down because of the use of the troikas as well as the universality and scope of the agenda. Since the early 1990s, as noted in Chapter 2, UN negotiations on sustainable development issues were often divided by blocs or coalitions along North-South lines. When negotiations devolve into bloc-to-bloc negotiations, they become rigid political and ideological battles. This instinctive clash of groups leads to polarization to the point where "if one says black the other has to say white. It is almost automatic."[17] Two formal and two informal coalitions dominated much of the sustainable development debate from 1993 to 2012: the Group of 77 and China, the European Union, the non-EU developed countries, and the countries with economies in transition.

The G-77 and China members do not always share the same interests—largely because of different stages of economic development and different degrees of vulnerability to specific threats or risks—but the coalition's strength relies on its cohesion, particularly on development issues.[18] The rotating spokesperson for the G-77 and China usually speaks on behalf of all members. More recently, on issue-specific negotiations, a number of smaller coalitions have become more active, including the least-developed countries (LDCs), the landlocked developing countries, the Arab Group, the African Group, the Latin American and Caribbean Group (GRULAC), the Bolivarian Alliance for the Peoples of Our America (ALBA), the Alliance of Small Island States (AOSIS), the Pacific Small Island Developing States, and the Caribbean Community.[19]

A second coalition is the European Union (EU), which, since the adoption of the Lisbon Treaty in 2009, has been represented primarily by a representative of the European Commission who speaks on behalf of all member states and often on behalf of all or some of the EU candidate states. A third group comprises the non-EU developed countries. Occasionally, Japan, the United States, Switzerland, Norway, Canada, Australia, and New Zealand have spoken as "JUSSCANNZ" or some variation of this group, but more often than not, they do not have joint positions. A fourth group includes the Russian Federation, some of the former Soviet republics, and non-EU Central and Eastern European countries. These countries have worked together in a loose coalition that at times has been referred to as "countries with economies in transition."[20]

The OWG's seat-sharing system democratized the process. Under the traditional coalition structure described above, one speaker represented the 134 G-77 members, one represented the twenty-eight members of the EU, and, unless speaking in other coalitions, other member states spoke on their own behalf. This structure distorts the balance of interests in the room, with the developing countries represented by only one voice but the developed countries represented by many.[21] With the seat-sharing or troika system, there were guaranteed to be at least thirty voices in the room representing seventy countries, breaking down traditional group coordination on political positions along the way. Furthermore, some of the troikas crossed traditional regional and interest groups. For example, six troikas contained both EU and non-EU countries (non-EU shown in italics): (*Montenegro*/Slovenia, *Australia*/Netherlands/United Kingdom, Denmark/Ireland/*Norway,* Italy/Spain/*Turkey,* France/Germany/*Switzerland,* and Cyprus/*Singapore*/*United Arab Emirates*). The only "pure" EU seats, interestingly enough, were held by Central and Eastern European EU members (Hungary, Bulgaria/Croatia, and Poland/Romania). Three troikas were composed of members of AOSIS: Bahamas/Barbados, Guyana/Haiti/Trinidad and Tobago, and Nauru/Palau/Papua New Guinea. Five troikas included both OECD members (Organization for Economic Cooperation and Development) and non-OECD members (OECD shown in italics): *Mexico*/Peru, Montenegro/*Slovenia, Poland*/Romania, Bangladesh/*Republic of Korea*/Saudi Arabia, and Iran/*Japan*/Nepal. Seven seats included LDCs (LDCs in italics): *Benin, Tanzania, Zambia*/Zimbabwe, Guyana/*Haiti*/Trinidad and Tobago, *Bhutan*/Thailand/Viet Nam, *Bangladesh*/Republic of Korea/Saudi Arabia, and Iran/Japan/*Nepal.*

The troikas had to first hold internal discussions that focused more on learning how their seatmates interpreted the issues rather than strategizing for negotiating advantage, which is the traditional means of managing coalitions. Then these positions were articulated publicly with everyone present, including representatives of civil society. Although each troika didn't become a de facto alliance, the seat-sharing arrangement created a more democratic, substantive conversation in the room. In fact, participants noticed that some of the most diametrically opposed and politically charged relationships mellowed over the eight stocktaking sessions. In the end, the seat-sharing structure, which forced countries that do not normally "belong" together to work together, helped the move away from traditional bloc-to-bloc negotiations.

EXPANDING HORIZONS

The discussions held in the OWG during the eleven months of stocktaking—from March 2013 to February 2014—were not the only ones that contributed to the evolution of the SDGs and targets. Numerous events both within and outside the United Nations added to delegates' understanding of the sustainable development agenda. Within the UN system, high-level events took place both at the United Nations and beyond that supported the process (see Box 4.4). There were also more than 125 side events held during the stocktaking sessions. Side events took place early in the morning, during the lunch break, or in the early evenings when the OWG was not in session. The side events were sponsored by member states, NGOs, and the UN Secretariat, funds, programs, and agencies. All of these events contributed to the process, but one event and one strategy, in particular, really expanded the horizons of member states: Joseph Stiglitz's presentation on inequalities in the United States and the co-chairs' linking of the discussions in the OWG with events outside of UN Headquarters.

Inequalities

On January 20, 2014, the Permanent Mission of Italy to the UN hosted a roundtable to discuss "The Threat of Growing Inequalities: Building More Just and Equitable Societies to Support Growth and Sustainable Development." The keynote address was given by Joseph Stiglitz, Nobel Laureate in

■ **Box 4.4.**

Selected High-Level Events to Support the OWG Negotiations

- "Sustainable Development and Climate Change: Practical Solutions in the Energy-Water Nexus," UN Headquarters, New York, May 16, 2013

- President of the General Assembly's High-Level Thematic Debate on Culture and Development, UN Headquarters, New York, June 12, 2013

- President of the General Assembly's High-Level Thematic Debate on Entrepreneurship for Development, June 26, 2013

- President of the General Assembly's Informal Thematic Debate on Inequality, July 8, 2013

- President of the General Assembly's special event to follow up efforts made towards achieving the Millennium Development Goals, September 25, 2013

- Italy's special event: The Threat of Growing Inequalities, January 20, 2014

- President of the General Assembly's Thematic Debate on Water, Sanitation and Sustainable Energy in the Post-2015 Development Agenda, February 18–19, 2014

- President of the General Assembly's High-Level Event on the Contributions of Women, the Young and Civil Society to the Post-2015 Development Agenda, March 6–7, 2014

- Joint Event of the General Assembly and the Economic and Social Council on the Role of Partnerships in the Implementation of the Post-2015 Development Agenda, April 9–10, 2014

- President of the General Assembly's Thematic Debate on Ensuring Stable and Peaceful Societies, April 24–25, 2014

- President of the General Assembly's High-Level Event on the Contributions of North-South, South-South, Triangular Cooperation, and Information and Communications Technology

(Continues)

for Development to the Implementation of the Post-2015
Development Agenda, May 21–22, 2014

- President of the General Assembly's High-Level Event on the
  Contributions of Human Rights and the Rule of Law in the
  Post-2015 Development Agenda, June 9–10, 2014

economics and author of *The Price of Inequality*. The organizers wanted to engage the scholarly and academic communities in a dialogue with the UN diplomatic corps on the impact of growing inequalities, including the political and security implications, the impact on sustainable development, the role of the United Nations and its capacity to address the threats posed by growing inequalities, and the drive towards greater justice and equity in the post-2015 development agenda.[22]

In his presentation, Stiglitz highlighted inequality in the United States, where 95 percent of all of the economic gains since 2009 had gone to only the richest 1 percent of the population. He noted that the United States had led the way in increased inequality and had less equality of opportunity than most other developed countries. He pointed out that the enormous growth in inequality is not just the result of economic forces but also of politics and policies. Even the International Monetary Fund (IMF) had pointed out that a higher level of inequality is linked to lower growth and higher instability. However, the fact that inequality is caused by policies and politics provides a glimmer of hope, he added. The United States can look to other countries that have succeeded in reducing inequalities and change its own policies. He concluded by calling for the SDGs to include a goal to reduce or eliminate inequality in its extreme forms.[23]

Some G-77 members were taken aback by Stiglitz's presentation. They couldn't believe that Americans considered inequality to be a huge problem. The G-77 countries had always seen inequality as their own agenda, and this made them realize that inequality was a global problem. Kamau and Kőrösi, who also participated in the roundtable, both noted that inequality had not been included in the MDGs and hadn't gotten the traction that it needed in the UN system. Kamau said that inequality and poverty

JOSEPH STIGLITZ

PHOTO 4.3. Joseph Stiglitz, Nobel Laureate and co-president, Initiative for Policy Dialogue, gave an eye-opening presentation on inequality. *Photo by IISD/Kiara Worth (enb.iisd.org)*

would be featured in the SDGs and that he would be surprised if this didn't translate into a goal or target. But the challenge, he added, was to make the proposition palatable to all member states.[24]

Stiglitz's presentation was not the only place where growing inequality was being discussed. As Stiglitz noted, awareness of the adverse effects of inequality had moved beyond academics and social activists, such as New York's Occupy Wall Street activists in 2011.[25] A July 2013 speech by US President Barack Obama outlined the role of inequality in creating credit bubbles (like the one that precipitated the Great Recession) and the way that inequality deprives people of opportunity, which in turn fosters an inefficient economy where the talents of many cannot be mobilized for the good of all.[26] Pope Francis, in his address in the Varginha slum of Rio de Janeiro on World Youth Day 2013, emphasized the need for greater solidarity, greater social justice, and special attention to the circumstances of youth. He declared that peace cannot be maintained in unequal societies with marginalized communities.[27] Oxfam reported in 2013 that while there had been great progress in the fight against extreme poverty, the new development goals must also tackle inequality, looking at not just the poorest but also the richest. Oxfam expressed its belief that reducing inequality is a key part of fighting poverty and securing a sustainable future for all. In a world of finite resources, Oxfam said, "we cannot end poverty unless we reduce inequality rapidly."[28] Thomas Piketty published his best-selling book, *Capital in the Twenty-First Century,* which emphasized wealth concentrations and distribution over the past 250 years, arguing that the rate of capital return in developed countries is persistently greater than the rate of economic growth and that this will cause wealth inequality to increase in the future. Piketty went so far as to propose redistribution through a progressive global tax on wealth.[29] The discussions on inequality within nations, which expanded to include inequality between nations, broadened the OWG members' horizons and affected the overall debate, especially once the negotiations began.

External Events

In addition to the side events and high-level events that convened during the stocktaking, a number of events outside the UN system had an impact on the process. Opening up UN negotiations to interact with these events was not a normal occurrence. Sometimes when UN member states sit in a conference room and negotiate a resolution, declaration, or treaty, they appear to be working in a bubble, possibly even oblivious to what is going on around the world or even just outside the doors of UN Headquarters. In fact, usually only the UN Security Council responds to events in real time. This wasn't the case for the OWG.

The co-chairs tried to remind participants of how many of the issues they were addressing in the OWG were also dominating the day's news. For example, many issues on US President Barack Obama's list of second-term priorities were also on the OWG agenda. When Obama was re-elected in November 2012, he vowed to make action on climate change one of his top priorities. Other priorities included pushing for economic policies to aid the middle class, including health care, education, and student loan debt relief, and increasing the minimum wage. He was also concerned about growing racial inequalities and worsening race relations in the country, as well as discrimination against the lesbian, gay, bisexual, and transgender communities.

Meanwhile, in New York City, Bill de Blasio was elected mayor in 2013. He ran on a platform concerned about the high level of economic inequality and continually said that New York City was a "tale of two cities," one for the rich and one for the poor. Once elected, he immediately focused on inequality and the poor, including establishing free citywide prekindergarten, imposing a rent freeze for rent-stabilized apartments, boosting the supply of affordable housing in the city, and reducing unemployment.[30] These and other events gave real-world backing to the work of the OWG in designing a new set of goals.

THE ELEPHANTS IN THE ROOM

The stocktaking exercise, combined with the reports, side events, and external events, enabled the co-chairs and the OWG members to identify specific issues that could come back to haunt them if not adequately addressed up front. The co-chairs recognized that two of these elephants in the room were the relationship between the MDGs and the SDGs, and the relationship between the post-2015 development agenda and the SDGs.

Relationship Between the SDGs and the MDGs: The Status Quo Has Its Army

It was clear from the start that certain developing countries that had not yet achieved the MDGs were concerned about the SDGs. At OWG-1, Chad, on behalf of the African Group, emphasized that most African states "remain off-track in achieving the MDGs by 2015. In this regard, the anticipated SDGs must not divert attention and resources from the implementation of the MDGs." He also noted the African Group's view that "the SDGs should be based on the MDGs, building on the outcomes of their review process as well as making a direct linkage with the post-2015 UN development agenda."[31] The EU assured the LDCs, which echoed this concern, that it agreed the SDGs should not deviate from "current efforts and attention to achieve the MDGs" and that the "EU remains committed to the MDG framework and the unfinished business of the MDG-agenda."[32]

Member states were not the only ones that wanted to ensure that the MDGs were not forgotten. As Secretary-General Ban Ki-moon said at the opening session of the OWG, "The MDGs and SDGs are mutually support-ing concepts. Greater progress towards the MDGs will fuel confidence and mobilize support for an ambitious post-2015 development agenda. And the SDGs should accelerate and continue the work begun under the banner of the MDGs."[33] The president of the General Assembly stated at the same meeting, "I strongly believe that fulfilling the MDGs should be the starting point of our endeavors. We must eradicate extreme poverty in all its forms over the next decade or so."[34] In private conversations with the co-chairs, the Secretary-General and the president of the General Assembly expressed their concern that the MDGs could be lost in the development of the SDGs and, with them, for the Secretary-General at any rate, the core business of the United Nations in development. Both the Secretary-General and the president worried that the idea of the SDGs as expressed by some delega-tions might be too ambitious and probably unrealizable through an inter-governmental process, so they advised caution.

The co-chairs recognized that the SDGs had to be built on the MDGs and ensured that all of the MDGs were addressed adequately during the stocktaking process. By bringing in speakers from both inside and outside the UN system, they wanted to demonstrate that the SDGs might even be able to resolve some of the shortcomings of the MDGs. One such speaker, Paul Polman, the chief executive officer of Unilever, echoed this point when he called on governments to recognize that they cannot do every-thing by themselves. To achieve the MDGs by 2015, he argued, "The mobi-lization and effective use of all resources, public and private, domestic and international, will be vital." In addition to championing the role of the pri-vate sector in achieving the MDGs, Polman said that the new, single set of integrated goals should reflect all dimensions of sustainability—the social, the economic, the environmental, and that of good governance; be mea-surable, time-bound, and have clear accountabilities; and finish the unfinished business of the MDGs and go beyond them.[35] Polman and the business community's contributions in private and formal meetings were as unusual as they were constructive. The private sector and the business community had found a role in the UN intergovernmental negotiation system, and they used it to very good effect.

Two Parallel Universes

Throughout most of 2013 there was still confusion and anxiety about the two parallel processes that were under way: the OWG and the post-2015 development agenda discussions (see Box 4.1). At the same time that the OWG was holding its first four meetings, General Assembly President Vuk Jeremić was organizing a special event to follow up efforts made towards achieving the MDGs, as called for by the high-level plenary meeting of the General Assembly on the MDGs in 2010.[36] On January 11, 2013, Jeremić appointed the permanent representatives of Ireland and South Africa to coordinate the preparations for the September 2013 Special Event. The two ambassadors conducted months of parallel consultations on both the agenda and the substance. In the United Nations, where conspiracy theories and deep political suspicions often prevail, some delegates saw this parallel process as an attempt to undermine the OWG and the SDGs.

Others were concerned that there was a risk of two—possibly incompatible—agendas for the post-2015 period, and this created tension during the preparations for the September 2013 Special Event. The multiple work streams that were initiated by Secretary-General Ban Ki-moon and his special adviser on Post-2015 Development Planning, Amina Mohammed, also contributed to this tension. The UN Task Team, the UN Global Compact, the High-Level Panel of Eminent Persons, and the UN Development Group delivered the input for the Secretary-General's report that provided the basis of the discussions at the Special Event. But the member states that were negotiating the proposed resolution faced the dilemma that any concrete proposal for a post-2015 agenda from their side would risk irrevocably separating the OWG and post-2015 processes. Their response was the production of a kind of "standby" resolution, the only purpose of which was to leave the door open to link the two processes.[37]

PHOTO 4.4. Amina Mohammed, the Secretary-General's special adviser on Post-2015 Development Planning, worked tirelessly to build support for the SDGs and the 2030 Agenda. *Photo by IISD/Leila Mead (enb.iisd.org)*

In the resolution adopted after the Special Event, the General Assembly noted that "we are concerned about unevenness and gaps in achievement and about the immense challenges that remain. The Millennium Development Goals are critical for meeting the basic needs of people in developing countries; as we approach the 2015 deadline, unrelenting efforts are required to accelerate progress across all the Goals."[38] With regard to the post-2015 development agenda, the resolution said that in "parallel with the intensification of efforts to accelerate the achievement of the Millennium Development Goals, we are determined to craft a strong post-2015 development agenda that will build on the foundations laid by the Goals, complete the unfinished business and respond to new challenges." The General Assembly also agreed to launch "a process of intergovernmental negotiations at the beginning of the sixty-ninth session of the General Assembly, which will lead to the adoption of the post-2015 development agenda."[39] The OWG co-chairs could not be seen to be involved in these parallel processes and negotiations, but in private and behind closed doors they pushed hard for this outcome.

The Special Event set the stage for merging these two parallel processes. The negotiations on the post-2015 agenda that were called for by the General Assembly in this resolution were not supposed to start until the beginning of the sixty-ninth session of the General Assembly, which was after the OWG's mandate expired at the end of the sixty-eighth session. Furthermore, the resolution helped to concretize some aspects of the OWG's agenda:

> Recognizing the intrinsic interlinkage between poverty eradication and the promotion of sustainable development, we underline the need for a coherent approach that integrates in a balanced manner the three dimensions of sustainable development. This coherent approach involves working towards a single framework and set of goals, universal in nature and applicable to all countries, while taking account of differing national circumstances and respecting national policies and priorities. It should also promote peace and security, democratic governance, the rule of law, gender equality and human rights for all.[40]

In other words, the General Assembly formally stressed the importance of addressing the unfinished business of the MDGs, recognized the connections between poverty eradication and the promotion of sustainable development, called for a single framework and set of goals, and, for the first time, added the promotion of peace and security, democratic governance, the rule of law, and human rights to the sustainable development agenda. So rather than creating a separate post-2015 agenda, this document paved the way for a single set of negotiations: first the goals and then the larger development agenda, which would be on sustainable development.

CONCLUSIONS AND LESSONS LEARNED

A number of lessons were learned during the stocktaking exercise that comprised the first eight sessions of the OWG from March 2013 to February 2014. First, convening the stocktaking sessions proved to be an effective icebreaker and confidence and trust builder. These sessions helped to build a common understanding of the issues and also gave delegations time to get to know one another and one another's priorities. This not only built trust between the delegates and between the delegates and the co-chairs but also strengthened the legitimacy of the process and the eventual outcome. Participants noticed that some of the most diametrically opposed and politically charged relationships mellowed over the eight sessions. The stocktaking sessions created a conversation in the room without negotiating. "The more you sit together, the more you discuss, and the more you understand the arguments," noted German delegate Stephan Contius.[41] By the time the OWG began actual negotiations in 2014, there was a high level of cohesion, a common sense of purpose, a shared understanding of the issues, and receptiveness to new ideas.

Second, the OWG members were not compelled to solidify their positions for a year, so they had the time to discuss ideas with colleagues in a more informal and nonthreatening way.[42] This also opened the door to greater participation from NGOs and civil society, for no sensitive negotiations were taking place. As a result, the OWG members developed a sense of comfort with nongovernmental observers in the room. The stocktaking process also allowed everyone to think much more critically because of the substantive and technical information received during the stocktaking. At the beginning, few had any detailed knowledge about the substance and relative importance of the issues. Towards the end there was a constant flow of ideas that opened people's eyes and built a common intellectual platform from which the negotiations could commence.

Third, the OWG's seat-sharing system proved to be quite valuable. This was a new development at the United Nations and initially led to much discomfort. Yet it inadvertently democratized the process. The seat-sharing structure or troikas, which forced countries that do not normally "belong" together to work together, aided the move away from traditional bloc-to-bloc interactions by breaking down traditional coalitions. As a result, more delegates had the opportunity to articulate their views and the OWG had much more substantive, rather than political or ideological, discussion of the issues.[43]

Fourth, there was immense value in paying attention to the action outside the room. The special events, high-level events, and side events and news of the day all played a role in educating delegates. The co-chairs and OWG members alike ensured that reports from these events and news from the outside world were brought into the proceedings. These events and the global interest in the sustainable development agenda, poverty eradication, and growing inequality around the world also gave real-world backing to the OWG's work.

Finally, it was essential for the co-chairs to allay the fears and anxieties of participants. They needed time to bring capitals up to speed and become comfortable with the idea of the SDGs. The co-chairs had to assure the Africans, the LDCs, the middle-income countries, and the EU, in particular, that the unfinished business of the MDGs would constitute the core of the new development agenda. They had to assure the UN programs, funds, and agencies, as well as NGOs and civil society, that even though this was a member-state–driven process, their participation, views, and concerns would be taken into account. And they had to ensure that the post-2015 development agenda and the OWG would not work in parallel, but together as a single, integrated sustainable development agenda.

5

THE CAST OF CHARACTERS

We have listened and talked a lot to one another over the past year. To paraphrase a popular advertisement, may I encourage you to keep talking . . . but, equally importantly, keep listening.

—Csaba Kőrösi[1]

To successfully manage multilateral negotiations, it is essential to understand the people in the room. Not only do the co-chairs need to know who everyone is, but they also need to know their positions, the issues they care about, and their concerns or fears. Do they understand the process? Are they going to be obstructionist or constructive? How much influence will they have? The eight stocktaking sessions provided an excellent opportunity for the co-chairs of the Open Working Group (OWG), Csaba Kőrösi and Macharia Kamau, to learn the answers to these and other questions as they headed into the negotiation phase.

This chapter will take a step back from the process to examine the cast of characters participating in the OWG and explain how their interests evolved during the stocktaking phase to better understand the negotiations that followed. Although government delegates were the "official" members of the OWG—as the United Nations is an intergovernmental organization—they were not the only ones in the room. So after examining the state actors, we will also look at nonstate actors, including the UN

Secretary-General, the Secretariat, UN agencies, other international organizations, civil society, and the business community.

READING THE ROOM

Multilateral negotiations are more complex than bilateral ones. This complexity reflects the great variety of interests at stake and, quite often, the high number of issues under consideration.[2] The different parties to multilateral negotiations come into the room with different interests, fears, priorities, and resources.[3] Sometimes, as was the case in the OWG, there is a great deal of fluidity in the positions. Some delegations came into the OWG with one position that evolved during the course of the stocktaking sessions. Fluid, evolving positions cause a certain amount of discomfort to chairs and other participants who are used to operating in a situation where positions are fixed. Eventually positions solidify, but until then the situation can be challenging.

It was essential for the OWG co-chairs to understand the diversity of positions and interests that can affect the creation of any package agreement such as the Sustainable Development Goals (SDGs). Once the co-chairs are able to grasp the positions and opinions in the room, they can see where there is potential for trade-offs. If the co-chairs have a clear sense of different delegations' positions, they can propose compromises or ask delegations to sit down together and reach an agreement. Recognizing that not all negotiators care equally about all of the issues on the agenda can create an opportunity to build linkages across issues and positions.[4]

Diplomats are human. Like anyone else, they have their own personalities, particularities, and emotions. They all react to anger, impatience, or gratitude. And, of course, they all have personal ambitions that may have little to do with the national interests of the country they represent.[5] Prejudices, different perceptions and interpretations of the same information, and misunderstandings caused by cultural and language differences can all come into play.[6] And such a situation is often complicated by the fact that many diplomats are functioning through the haze of jet lag.

PHOTO 5.1 To successfully manage a multilateral negotiating process, it is essential to understand the people in the room. OWG-6 met in the Trusteeship Council Chamber at UN Headquarters in New York. *Photo by IISD/ Elizabeth Press (enb.iisd.org)*

Co-chairs Kőrösi and Kamau also recognized that the members of the OWG entered into the SDG negotiations with incomplete and imperfect information and, in some cases, with tentative and vague preferences for different parts of the agenda. The stocktaking exercise, as discussed in Chapter 4, was put in place to allow the OWG members the opportunity to diagnose the problem (what should be included in the SDGs) and then discover, invent, and explore possible solutions. Yet the stocktaking meetings also gave the co-chairs the opportunity to "diagnose" the positions of the OWG members, build trust, and ascertain how expansive and encompassing the SDGs could be.[7] So by February 2014, not only had the co-chairs conducted eight meetings of the OWG; they had also held numerous intersessional consultations and had a better read of the room. Over the course of the stocktaking, several distinct types of delegations became apparent.

STATE ACTORS

UN decision-making authority is granted to its member states, so we first look at the different types of state actors that emerged during the first year of the OWG's work. Although we are categorizing countries here, there is a caveat. Not every country was progressive or conservative on every issue; not everything was black or white. Similarly, as described above, many delegations changed or adapted their positions on different issues over time. Moreover, not all groups were mutually exclusive, and some delegations straddled more than one group. Here we are using these groupings to provide our readers with an understanding of where delegations initially positioned themselves on the different issues before the actual negotiations began in March 2014.

Progressives

Some of the OWG participants were progressive when it came to the SDGs. These delegates accepted that the SDGs were supposed to be universal, aspirational, and integrated, while balancing all three dimensions of sustainable development and tackling the unfinished business of the Millennium Development Goals (MDGs). They recognized that these were not simply going to be development goals for developing countries, but, for the first time, all countries would have to achieve the goals. This went beyond the traditional UN understanding of the "development agenda." One such example was the troika of France, Germany, and Switzerland. As German Ambassador Peter Wittig noted in his speech to OWG-1,

> First: These new goals are going to be universal and valid for all countries, yet they need to be meaningful and applicable for each and every individual state. They need to reflect all three dimensions of sustainability in an appropriate manner, yet be concise and easy to communicate. . . . Second: We also need to take into account the interlinkages between different sectors, for example between water, energy and food. Third: We need convergence. We need to merge the post-MDG-process and the SDG-process. . . . The world needs one set of goals to respond to the global challenges of poverty eradication

and sustainable development. These goals are going to address all countries worldwide.[8]

The French minister of development, Pascal Canfin, also spoke at the first session. He agreed that "this sustainable development agenda is by definition universal. It involves the commitment of all. This is particularly true of our western countries, which must, without delay, begin the transition to sustainable production and consumption patterns."[9]

Colombia and Guatemala played a progressive role in the work of the OWG. Colombia's Paula Caballero Gómez and Guatemala's Jimena Leiva Roesch championed the SDGs early on and clearly understood the universal nature of the goals not just across all countries, but also the need to make gains, especially in terms of poverty eradication, within countries and across generations. As Caballero said in March 2013, the ultimate deliverables should be "an agenda of well-being beyond minimums; sustainability for long-term human progress within planetary boundaries; irreversibility of the gains achieved; MDGs are conserved; the false poverty-sustainability divide is overcome; and a universally relevant agenda sensitive to local specificities through differentiation."[10] She added that to address the eradication of poverty, sustainable development is necessary: "Degradation of natural resources and resource scarcities contribute to the root causes of poverty and undermine the well-being of present and future generations."[11] The troika of Denmark, Norway, and Ireland also took a progressive view, noting at OWG-1, "While they need to take into account different national circumstances, policies, priorities, capacities and levels of development, the SDGs should be global in nature, relevant and applicable to all countries."[12] These were not the only progressive members of the OWG, but they are indicative examples of the thinking of members of this category of countries.

Conservatives

Some of the delegates were initially more conservative in their thinking about the SDGs. They did not oppose the concept of the SDGs in principle, but they were more cautious in how they approached the work of the

OWG. Each country, or group of countries, was conservative for slightly different reasons.

For example, Brazil, India, and China were initially more concerned with managing the negotiations in the context of the "G-77 versus other countries" mind-set than with exploring new ways of moving beyond the traditional sustainable development debate. Being both emerging economies and large developing countries, they had a sharp eye on protecting or maintaining their economic, technical, and political positions. Thus, they engaged differently than other developing countries. These countries called for the new goals to adhere to the principles enshrined in the 1992 Rio Declaration on Environment and Development, particularly the principle of common but differentiated responsibilities (CBDR).[13] CBDR recognizes historical differences in the contributions of developed and developing countries to global environmental problems, and differences in their respective economic and technical capacity to tackle these problems.[14] The principle also implies that developed countries must assist developing countries with the means of implementation—financial resources, technology transfer, and capacity building—to meet these challenges. One concern of these countries was that if the SDGs were to be universal, would developed countries no longer have to assist developing countries in achieving the goals? Would emerging economies be asked to take on financing responsibilities? They were also concerned about the impact of the SDGs on their own economic growth and social development. These countries had some of the fastest-growing economies but still had low per capita income and millions of people living in poverty. They wanted to ensure they were still seen as "developing" countries. They were also skeptical of the developed countries' narrative of the need for a paradigm shift, leapfrogging from the current economic models to more sustainable ones. The historical experience in Europe, Japan, and the United States had been to grow fast, pollute, and clean up later. What would be the alternative under the SDGs?

Indian Ambassador Manjeev Singh Puri argued that the SDGs, while "universal in nature can only be meaningful if differentiation is appropriately embedded in them. It is unreasonable to craft sustainable development goals without paying due regard to the responsibility of those who rushed toward development without much regard for the needs of the global environment."[15] At OWG-1, Brazil, also on behalf of Nicaragua, with which it shared a seat, stated that the SDGs must be universal goals that recognize the "asymmetries within and between countries."[16]

China agreed with these points, especially about CBDR, but also raised other related issues. For example, at OWG-1, China said, "At the same time, the goals should respect the differences of countries in national conditions and development stage so as to ensure the right to development and policy space of all countries."[17] This added another Rio principle to the mix—the right to development. Furthermore, China resisted expanding the agenda to include such topics as peace, security, and rule of law: "[I]t is important to focus on the theme of sustainable development when selecting priority areas of the SDGs and avoid taking in areas that deviate from the main topic of development."[18]

Some of the African countries were progressive on some issues and more conservative on others. For example, Kenya, Botswana, Ghana, and South Africa were progressive with regard to the green and blue (oceans) economy and new energy paradigms that could foster development, especially because they were not oil-producing countries. However, on other agenda items, including sexual and reproductive health and rights, LGBT (lesbian, gay, bisexual, and transgender) rights, and climate change, some African countries were much more conservative.

The thirty-four least-developed countries (LDCs) in Africa and some of the Asian countries, including Timor Leste and Nepal, were initially skeptical about the SDGs because most had still not achieved the MDGs and were concerned about being left behind once again. As Ambassador Ahmad Allam-Mi, the permanent representative of Chad to the United Nations, stated on behalf of the African Group at OWG-1, "The Group also emphasizes that most of its Member States remain off track in achieving the MDGs by 2015. In this regard, the anticipated SDGs must not divert attention and resources from the implementation of the MDGs."[19]

Early on, even some of the so-called "progressive" countries, such as Germany and France, were not progressive on all issues, especially financial resources and technology transfer. Others, especially Canada and Australia, were led by more conservative governments at the time and reflected the views of their prime ministers, Stephen Harper and Tony Abbott, respectively.

Some developed countries were concerned about the SDGs being a "universal" agenda. They were not comfortable with the United Nations prescribing what they had to accomplish, and they much preferred the existing system, where they engaged in development activities in developing countries and were not held accountable by the United Nations for sustainable development at home. Historically, they were held accountable only for the means of implementation offered to developing countries, not their own unsustainable productive and consumption patterns and inequalities. The universal nature of the SDGs represented a large paradigm shift and a cause for concern. Similar to the developing countries, these developed countries wanted the SDGs to take into account the different levels of development but wanted the SDGs to focus more on the least-developed countries and fragile states, as stated by Spain, also on behalf of Italy and Turkey.[20] Others, including the United States, also on behalf of Canada and Israel, noted that while they agreed that the goals needed to be universal, "they need to be articulated in a way that can be made relevant to and responsive to different national circumstances, national priorities, and so on."[21] The Republic of Korea and the troika of Denmark, Ireland, and Norway echoed these sentiments early on in questioning the meaning of "universality."[22]

Other developed countries supported the MDGs model. In their statement of guiding principles for the post-2015 development agenda, the troika of Australia, the Netherlands, and the United Kingdom said that the priority of the SDGs should continue to be the eradication of poverty "through sustainable development":

The MDG "brand" has been successful at mobilising development efforts by the international community and developing countries. The post-2015 development framework should seek to build on the strengths of the current MDG model. . . . Any successor goals should build on the current MDGs—enhancing commitments on issues that

PHOTO 5.2. Ralien Bekkers, youth representative on sustainable development in the Netherlands, spoke on behalf of youth in the Netherlands, the United Kingdom, and Australia at OWG-4 in June 2013. *Photo by IISD/Pamela Chasek (enb.iisd.org)*

have not been fully achieved, and set more ambitious targets for those already achieved. . . . [23]

The United Kingdom, which had co-chaired the Secretary-General's High-Level Panel on Post-2015, strongly supported the panel's report, which said "it would be a mistake to simply tear up the MDGs and start from scratch."[24] Early on, these governments did not really think about how their own development affected the prospects for sustainable development in developing countries. They didn't ask this question in the beginning because they were still thinking in terms of the MDGs.

Ultraconservatives

Some countries or groupings, such as Saudi Arabia, some members of the African Group, and others such as Malta, were more narrow in their approach to the SDGs, believing that some issues should not be included on the agenda. These countries negotiated passionately on the parts of the agenda they were not happy with. Some of the most difficult issues revolved around sexual and reproductive health and rights, gender, and LGBT rights. Many wanted simply to repeat the language adopted twenty years earlier at the 1994 International Conference on Population and Development. This was just one of the instances that led Kőrösi to ask, "How can you construct a vision of the future from previously agreed language?"[25]

Saudi Arabia's Abdullah Khalid Tawlah, reflecting these concerns in a statement separate from his troika (Bangladesh and Republic of Korea), said at OWG-3 that the OWG's health focus should be on those who are sick and dying, not on sexual and reproductive rights. He cautioned that there would never be international agreement on this issue.[26] At OWG-9, Tawlah reiterated: "Sexual and reproductive issues present a sensitive cultural, moral, and religious topic and as such we should respect countries' culture and religion in this regard."[27] Nigeria concurred with this position at OWG-8, suggesting avoiding controversial issues that lack universal consensus, adding "[L]esbian, gay, bisexual and transgender rights are against [our] country's moral beliefs and cultural and religious values, and should be avoided in the Group's discussions."[28]

In the stocktaking session on health, the Holy See[29] expressed its commitment to the right to basic health care for all but called on states "to move beyond reducing the goal to sexual and reproductive health and instead have a holistic understanding of the human person and their healthcare needs."[30] As Malta added, "While the Government remains fully committed to continue to provide, and improve upon, the current services offered to the entire population of Malta, we do underline that any commitment undertaken in this process cannot in any way demand from any UN Member State the obligation to legalise abortion in any way, or to consider abortive medical practices as a method of family planning. Such medical practices remain illegal under the Laws of the Republic of Malta."[31]

There were several reasons for these countries' positions on these issues. One was domestic cultural norms. Many African societies are still primarily traditional. Seventy percent of Africans live in villages and continue long-held cultural practices. Homosexuality is taboo in most African countries and illegal in thirty-seven.[32] These countries were concerned that if LGBT rights were included in the SDGs, it could cause a problem at home. Similarly, they were concerned that a call for universal LGBT rights could become a form of conditionality for development assistance. This was not an unrealistic concern. When Ugandan President Yoweri Museveni signed a law in February 2014 imposing harsh penalties for homosexuality, Norway immediately responded by withholding $8 million in development aid, and Denmark announced that it would divert $9 million away from the government.[33] The United States followed suit, and other Western donors rechanneled aid away from the Ugandan government.[34]

Others had religious concerns. Many Muslim countries saw LGBT rights as against Islam, and some countries and the Holy See saw it as against Catholicism as well. Finally, some developing countries were concerned that if LGBT rights were included in the agenda, development assistance could be affected. Development assistance often links aid to human rights and helping vulnerable communities. If the LGBT community was considered to be a vulnerable community, this could result in the diversion of money from traditional development assistance for basic services in impoverished communities.[35]

Certain countries also tried to move the OWG away from a goal on renewable energy. Abdullah Khalid Tawlah said that Saudi Arabia's goal was to ensure access to affordable, reliable, sustainable, and modern energy for all, including clean fossil-fuel technologies. Throughout the entire process, Tawlah worked hard to ensure the SDGs would focus on access to affordable energy for the billions who do not have it and protect fossil-fuel-dependent economies such as Saudi Arabia's.[36] Saudi Arabia was among several oil-producing countries that did not want discussion on energy linked to climate change.[37]

Some countries saw the sustainable development debate in the OWG as a way to forum shop. UN member states have long shopped around for different negotiating forums to push their agenda. In the OWG, some tried to convince other delegates that it would be better to address sexual and reproductive health and rights in the Commission on the Status of Women. Others said that energy and climate change should be considered in the UN Framework Convention on Climate Change (UNFCCC). Similarly, a

PHOTO 5.3. Each delegation, even within the Group of 77, had its own priorities, which the co-chairs had to understand. Clockwise from upper left: Josefina Bunge, Argentina; Jimena Leiva Roesch, Guatemala; Abdullah Khalid Tawlah, Saudi Arabia; and Jean-Francis Régis Zinsou, Benin. *Photos by IISD (enb.iisd.org)*

number of developing countries also held firm to the argument that the SDGs must reflect the CBDR principle, fearing if they lost that battle in the OWG, they would also lose it in the UNFCCC negotiations on the Paris Agreement.

The "New York Mafia"

The UN General Assembly Second Committee experts, often referred to as the "New York mafia," were another important group of state actors. As described in Chapter 1 (see Box 1.2), the work of the General Assembly is divided into six committees, and the sustainable development agenda items are usually addressed by the Second Committee—the Economic and Financial Committee. Although some of the issues under the OWG's purview are found on the agendas of the Third Committee (Social, Humanitarian & Cultural) and, to a lesser extent, the First Committee (Disarmament and International Security), for decades sustainable development had been seen as a Second Committee issue. The New York–based delegates who serve on the Second Committee are, in a sense, the "defenders of the faith." They are the experts in how the UN system addresses these issues, the rules of procedure, and the negotiating and horse trading that leads to the adoption of resolutions. At the same time, especially among developing countries, Second Committee experts are often responsible for determining national positions on these issues.

Coordination between national governments and their New York missions (offices) is often a problem for many developing countries. In part because of the different time zones, many capitals take two to three days to respond to a question from their New York mission. In some cases a week or two could go by with no response. This is particularly common when there is a cross-sectoral agenda such as the SDGs, which requires inputs from many ministries and offices that need to develop a single coherent position. This is a difficult task, especially for LDCs. When a delegation does not receive a response from its capital, the New York–based experts have to construct their government's "official" position. They show it to their ambassador and then bring it to the regional group or the Group of 77. For better or worse, this often leads to a disconnect between New York and national capitals.[38]

This disconnect plays out in a number of ways. UN politics in New York are different from national politics. Officials in capitals often look at sustainable development in terms of how it affects their own citizens without placing these issues in a larger geopolitical context. But in New York everything is about geopolitics. For example, when peace and security were raised as a new fourth dimension of sustainable development (see Chapter 4), the reactions were different among the Second Committee experts than they were in capitals. Many capitals acknowledged that sustainable development is impossible without peace and security. However, in the context of the United Nations, the subject is viewed from a different angle. There, peace and security are under the purview of the Security Council, where the five permanent members (P5) have veto power, essentially giving

China, France, Russia, the United Kingdom, and the United States control over the agenda. So would this mean that the development agenda would become part of the Security Council and the P5 would then have the mandate to address development issues? This is not an argument that officials in capitals always understand. But the New York mafia understands that political issues are always a part of the picture.[39]

The co-chairs recognized that it was essential to get the Second Committee experts on board with the SDGs, given their potential power. To do this, the co-chairs gave them direct attention and respect. Whenever a Second Committee expert requested to speak with the co-chairs, they obliged. Many developed countries could afford to bring in experts from their capitals to the OWG meetings, but most of the developing countries relied on their Second Committee experts or ambassadors. The co-chairs knew that if they could get the support and trust of the New York mafia, it would be much easier to get officials from capitals and heads of state and government to support the outcome.

At the same time, these delegates were often some of the most challenging to deal with, especially with regard to the OWG's modus operandi. The Second Committee experts were use to the normal way of doing business, as described in Chapter 1. Spending eight sessions on stocktaking? Unheard of! Some of the G-77 OWG members constantly asked the co-chairs to start textual negotiations or convene contact groups so actual negotiations could begin. Many of them did not initially understand the importance of the stocktaking meetings, largely because there is usually no time for such a long learning process within the United Nations and, after all, they are the experts.

Issue Champions

Some groups actively promoted their own causes. For example, the small island developing states (SIDS) wanted to have an SDG on oceans. Originally, the thought was to have one goal on sustainable ecosystems. However, the SIDS argued passionately for two goals—one on terrestrial resources and one on marine resources. They argued that their main source of GDP is the ocean and that if the ocean is not sustainably managed, their livelihoods would be threatened. They also expressed concern about the impacts of climate change on the oceans, including ocean acid-ification, sea level rise, warming, deoxygenation, and soil salinization and the impacts on agriculture. The SIDS also lobbied heavily for climate change adaptation aid because of the concern that their low-lying coun-tries would be heavily affected and in some cases could disappear as a result of rising sea levels.

One group of countries formed the Group of Friends of Rule of Law. Austria, Belgium, Costa Rica, Czech Republic, Democratic Republic of the Congo, Finland, Germany, Italy, Japan, Jordan, Kyrgyzstan, Latvia, Liech-tenstein, Mongolia, Netherlands, Republic of Korea, Romania, Singapore, Slovakia, Slovenia, Sweden, and Switzerland argued passionately for the SDGs to recognize that "credible and strong institutions which operate on the basis of laws and rules set up to serve the people play a particularly important role in this context. Moreover, addressing corruption is a key element as this is one of the major obstacles to sustainable development, diverting resources away from activities that are vital for poverty eradica-tion and sustainable development."[40]

The Nordic countries championed sexual and reproductive health and rights, stating: "Advancing universal access to sexual and reproductive health and rights should be an integral part of the gender equality agenda. This includes ensuring universal access to contraception, eliminating early/forced marriages and female genital mutilation, ensur[ing] access to post-abortion care, sexual education, skilled birth attendance, post-natal care and prevention and treatment of Sexually Transmitted Diseases, in-cluding HIV/AIDS."[41]

Some issue champions that could have been negative forces in the nego-tiations actually became positive ones. For example, during the Rio+20 ne-gotiations, the Bolivarian Alliance for the Peoples of Our America (ALBA) members argued extensively against the green economy. However, in 2014 Bolivia, perhaps the most outspoken ALBA member, held the chairman-ship of the G-77. Now the Bolivians had to speak on behalf of the entire group, not just the ALBA members, which led to a moderation of posi-tions. But the Bolivians also had a vision for protection of Mother Earth, which sent a positive message and was eventually incorporated into the SDGs. Furthermore, no one insisted that the green economy be mentioned in the SDGs, which also helped. The Cubans, usually very determined negotiators, also took a more moderate position perhaps because they were in negotiations with the Obama administration about the restoration of diplomatic and trade relations.

NONSTATE ACTORS

Government delegates, while the primary decision makers, were not the only people participating in the OWG. The dynamics in the room cannot be fully understood without also looking at the role of the nonstate actors, including the UN Secretary-General; the Department of Economic and Social Affairs (DESA) Secretariat; UN agencies, funds, and programs; other international organizations; civil society; and the business sector.

The Executive Office of the Secretary-General

UN Secretary-General Ban Ki-moon made sustainable development and the implementation of the MDGs two of his priorities during his ten-year tenure (2007–2016). In 2010 the General Assembly's High-Level Plenary Meeting to assess progress on the MDGs requested the Secretary-General to make recommendations for further steps to advance the UN development agenda beyond 2015.[42] In response, in September 2011 the Secretary-General established the UN System Task Team to support system-wide preparation for the post-2015 development agenda (see Box 4.1). In June 2012 he appointed Amina J. Mohammed of Nigeria as special adviser on Post-2015 Development Planning.[43] During her tenure, from 2012 to 2015, she advised the Secretary-General and served as his link to the OWG.

Mohammed also worked with the High-Level Panel of Eminent Persons on the Post-2015 Development Agenda, which was created by the Secretary-General in July 2012 to advise him on the global development framework beyond the MDGs (see Box 4.1). This panel consulted with stakeholder groups and member states in the preparation of its report. It concluded that the post-2015 agenda needed to be driven by five "transformative shifts": leave no one behind; put sustainable development at the core; transform economies for jobs and inclusive growth; build peace and effective, open, and accountable institutions for all; and forge a new global partnership.[44]

The panel submitted its report, "A New Global Partnership: Eradicate Poverty and Transform Economies Through Sustainable Development," in May 2013. The panel listed a set of twelve indicative goals and recommended that all these goals should be universal but that almost all targets should be set at the national or even local level to account for different starting points and contexts. These goals included the following:

- End Poverty
- Empower Girls and Women and Achieve Gender Equality
- Provide Quality Education and Lifelong Learning
- Ensure Healthy Lives
- Ensure Food Security and Good Nutrition
- Achieve Universal Access to Water and Sanitation
- Secure Sustainable Energy
- Create Jobs, Sustainable Livelihoods and Equitable Growth
- Manage Natural Resource Assets Sustainably
- Ensure Good Governance and Effective Institutions
- Ensure Stable and Peaceful Societies
- Create a Global Enabling Environment and Catalyse Long-Term Finance[45]

The Secretary-General had limited involvement for most of the OWG's first year. At OWG-1, Ban told participants that he committed "the full support of the UN system to the intergovernmental process towards SDGs, drawing on the results of the post-2015 processes that we have put in place."[46] Amina Mohammed met with the OWG co-chairs and attended some of the meetings organized outside the United Nations to discuss possible SDGs. There was some discussion within the Secretary-General's office that if the OWG actually delivered a set of SDGs by the deadline, the office would be able to "fine-tune" them.[47] In fact, it was only once the European Union, the African Union, and others started hosting intersessional meetings on the SDGs and the process took on a life of its own that Mohammed and others in the Secretary-General's office—and the Secretary-General himself—took greater notice and played a more active role. During the final meetings of the OWG and throughout the year of post-2015 agenda negotiations that followed (see Chapter 8), Mohammed became an eloquent spokesperson for the SDGs, and the idea of just revamping the MDGs with a little bit of window dressing—which appeared to be the original plan for the post-2015 agenda—fell by the wayside.

The Secretariat

The DESA Secretariat was another player in the OWG. DESA's Division for Sustainable Development (DSD) was headed by Nikhil Seth during the work of the OWG. DSD had served as the Secretariat for numerous sustainable development-related processes since 1993. In his more than two decades with the United Nations, Seth had played a part in all of the major sustainable development conferences since the Earth Summit in 1992, when he was with the Indian Permanent Mission to the United Nations. In the background, Seth, because of his deep experience, played a subtle and supportive role and helped drive and explore concepts and ideas with the co-chairs and member states.

Seth and his staff had several responsibilities in the OWG. First, like most secretariats of intergovernmental organizations, they were responsible for producing documents, arranging meetings, and taking notes of the OWG deliberations. They co-chaired with the UN Development Programme (UNDP) (TST) the technical support team, that produced the issue briefs for the OWG. (See Appendix II.) As the institutional memory of sustainable development within the UN system, DSD had a crucial role to play in both the provision and synthesis of knowledge for the OWG. In fact, the final review and editing of the issues briefs and reconciling differences of opinion within the TST on substantive matters was done by DESA. Because it is a UN regular budget entity, member states usually treated DESA/DSD as a neutral observer and therefore more trustworthy than some of the UN agencies.[48]

Second, DSD was responsible for supporting the co-chairs. This task, in addition to writing background documents, often included assisting in drafting the agenda, writing scripts, preparing PowerPoint presentations for the co-chairs, and drafting the outcome documents, based on inputs received from member states and other stakeholders.

Third, DSD worked closely with the co-chairs and their teams in the drafting and redrafting of various versions of the text containing the SDGs and their associated targets. The co-chairs looked to the Secretariat to assess the feasibility of proposed targets as well as their consistency with and ambition relative to existing international agreements and commitments contained therein. In these different ways, DSD provided invaluable assistance to the co-chairs and the OWG.

Fourth, DSD staff were invited on several occasions to brief civil society on the issues and the progress of the OWG.

The Department of General Assembly and Conference Management was responsible for organizing OWG sessions. The OWG's secretary helped coordinate and run the meetings. The conference room officers and simultaneous interpreters also help to manage the room and provide interpretation in all six official UN languages (Arabic, Chinese, English, French, Russian, and Spanish).

UN Agencies and International Organizations

Another group of nonstate actors was made up of the representatives of the UN agencies, funds, and programs as well as other intergovernmental organizations, such as the World Bank, the International Monetary Fund, and the World Trade Organization. The World Bank was involved in the process from the very beginning. To a certain degree the World Bank burned its fingers on the MDGs because it had taken five years for the bank to catch up and support MDG implementation. This time, Jim Yong Kim, who was elected World Bank president in April 2012, met with the co-chairs and told them that the bank was not going to repeat this mistake. In fact, at the spring meeting of the World Bank in 2014, its Development Committee encouraged it to collaborate with the United Nations on the definition of the SDGs.[49] Kim appointed Mahmoud Mohieldin as his special envoy on the SDGs. Mohieldin played a constructive role, especially on issues of financing the SDGs and helping participants really understand the level of ambition and the trillions of dollars that achieving the goals would cost. The World Bank also held intersessional meetings at its headquarters and set up the Post-2015 Working Group, which focused largely on financing the new development agenda.

The UN agencies (see a list in Appendix II) played several roles. They contributed to the work of the technical support team that produced background documents for the OWG. In this role they provided technical knowledge to the OWG members as they embarked on the stocktaking process. The agencies also held intersessional meetings, including the regional consultative meetings on the SDGs organized by the UN regional economic commissions. Finally, agency experts gave presentations during the stocktaking process.

Throughout the stocktaking process, however, the agencies had low expectations. As Olav Kjørven, then special adviser to the UNDP administrator on the Post-2015 Development Agenda, explained, many of the agencies had

> doubts about expanding on the poverty and social sector focus of the MDGs by bringing in environmental sustainability and economic development, or doubts that the endeavor could ever succeed, that the effort was almost doomed to drown in the quick sands of yet another complex process of negotiations at the UN. Just the thought of politically negotiating the next set of global goals and targets among 193 governments seemed exhausting, perilous, even naïve. After all, the MDGs, which just about everybody now agreed had been a success as a mobilizing framework for action, had been designed by experts before being announced by the then Secretary-General, Kofi Annan.[50]

Speaking for many in the early part of the process, Kjørven believed that UN member states should entrust the Secretary-General, his experts, and the UN agencies, funds, and programs to repeat the success of the MDG process or at least develop a proposal that the membership could then consider.[51]

Most of the UN system had become comfortable with the MDGs and their respective MDG implementation programs or projects. When people realized that the MDGs were not going to be simply rolled over in a modified form for another fifteen years, they started lobbying the co-chairs and member states to ensure that there would be an SDG that spoke to their respective mandates. At all levels, agency personnel became concerned that their mandates might be lost in the transition. As it became clear that the SDGs would include elements of the MDGs and guide development policy for the next fifteen years, the UN agencies increased their engagement and provided much-needed support to the co-chairs and the OWG.

Major Groups, Civil Society, and Other Stakeholders

The final group of actors to be discussed here is made up of the Major Groups, civil society, and other stakeholders. The term "Major Groups" emerged out of Agenda 21, the program of action adopted at the Earth Summit in 1992. Agenda 21 identified nine sectors of society critical to the effective implementation of the objectives, policies, and mechanisms agreed to in Agenda 21.[52] These sectors are women, children and youth, indigenous peoples, nongovernmental organizations (NGOs), local authorities, workers and trade unions, business and industry, the scientific and technological community, and farmers. In subsequent years the representatives from these sectors organized themselves by group and often presented joint statements at UN sustainable development meetings.

As the high-level panel's slogan "Leave no one behind" became popularized by the OWG, many groups that hadn't previously been active in UN sustainable development discussions saw a way to get involved. These included local communities, older persons, persons with disabilities, migrants, LGBT groups, human rights organizations, humanitarian aid groups, and volunteer organizations.[53] The co-chairs welcomed these groups, which brought new ideas into the process. Nevertheless, there was some tension between the Major Groups that had been participating in sustainable development discussions for many years and these "new" stakeholders in the OWG. As a representative of the business community commented, there were new voices, which were good, but these voices did not always speak in a way that was carefully thought out and representative of their constituents' views.[54] Although this tension was never fully resolved, traditional Major Groups recognized the value of adding to the agenda such issues as lifelong learning (promoted by older persons) and education and employment for people with disabilities. Over time, these groups learned from their more experienced counterparts in the traditional Major Groups how to get their ideas onto the agenda and into the SDGs.

As noted in Chapter 3, it was important for the co-chairs not only to find a way to ensure that civil society had a voice but also to reassure governments that they would own the process and outcome.[55] During the first two OWG meetings, following UN sustainable development meeting protocol, the co-chairs allowed several representatives of Major Groups to speak at the end of each three-hour block, if there was time after the member states and representatives of intergovernmental organizations had spoken. During the OWG's first eight sessions, all nine Major Groups spoke on issues of relevance to them. Some civil society representatives were also panelists during the stocktaking sessions and thus were able to give longer and more-focused presentations (see Appendix I). Many member states appreciated their participation and noted that "they helped us learn."[56]

At OWG-3 the co-chairs decided to meet with Major Groups, civil society, and other stakeholders each morning from 9:00 to 10:00, before the OWG officially convened. The co-chairs encouraged member states to attend these morning meetings, but very few ever came, which was frustrating to many of the Major Groups and civil society organizations. They felt that there should have been more opportunities for direct dialogue with governments.

Nevertheless, these sessions broke new ground. Unlike in previous sustainable development negotiations, these morning meetings with the co-chairs mirrored the official negotiations. Civil society responded to the same questions asked of the member states and provided contributions to the same document. In fact, some began to believe that they were personally contributing to the final document, and that impression made a difference. In other sustainable development negotiations, the Major Groups would come to the meetings, develop a common position, and make a statement, never knowing if anyone was really listening. Yet in the early-morning sessions with the OWG co-chairs, their statements were specific, they were posted on the OWG website, and the co-chairs and participating member states listened, finding these sessions to be quite enlightening. The co-chairs believed if this was going to be a comprehensive agenda, ideas and suggestions from civil society had to be considered, even if there were some powerful countries that didn't want to see some issues (LGBT rights, for example) on the agenda.

In addition to the morning sessions, Major Groups and civil society organizations focused on lobbying delegates through side events, the distribution of reports, and during conversations in the corridors. Greenpeace, Oxfam, the Millennium Institute, the UN Sustainable Development Solutions Network (SDSN), and others proposed goals and targets. The International Peace Institute, World Resources Institute, and the Independent Research Forum hosted retreats for OWG delegations that helped to move the process forward. The UN Foundation convened discussion forums and coordinated outreach to key stakeholders, including developing-country think tanks, thought leaders, civil society, and the private sector. The UN Foundation also convened informal meetings and workshops on thematic issues to foster dialogue among member states, including engaging the US government and the Washington policy community.[57]

Other stakeholders, including the Bill and Melinda Gates Foundation, the Catholic Fund for Development, Climate Action Network, the International Chamber of Commerce, educational and academic groups, scientific organizations, and the Communitas coalition (sustainable cities) participated on issues of concern to their constituencies. We are highlighting the work of two large civil society coalitions and the business community here, but this is not to dismiss the important roles that all of the other stakeholders played in the process.

Sustainable Development Solutions Network

The Sustainable Development Solutions Network was launched in 2012 to mobilize global scientific and technological knowledge on the challenges of sustainable development, including the design and implementation of the post-2015 global sustainable development agenda. Jeffrey Sachs, the director of SDSN, was also one of the Secretary-General's advisers on the post-2015 development agenda. A highly respected American economist and then director of Columbia University's Earth Institute, Sachs met with the co-chairs numerous times and held private meetings with delegations. SDSN presented its own version of the SDGs that contained ten goals (see

Box 5.1). SDSN also produced numerous reports that assisted the OWG, including reports on climate change and sustainable development, financing the SDGs, urban sustainable development, sustainable agriculture, science, technology, and sustainable development.

■ **Box 5.1**

SDSN's Draft Sustainable Development Goals

1. End extreme poverty including hunger

2. Promote economic growth and decent jobs within planetary boundaries

3. Ensure effective learning for all children and youth for life and livelihood

4. Achieve gender equality, social inclusion and human rights for all

5. Achieve health and well-being at all ages

6. Improve agriculture systems and raise rural prosperity

7. Empower inclusive, productive and resilient cities

8. Curb human-induced climate change and ensure sustainable energy

9. Secure biodiversity and ensure good management of water, oceans, forests and natural resources

10. Transform governance and technologies for sustainable development

SOURCE: Sustainable Development Solutions Network, *An Action Agenda for Sustainable Development: Report for the UN Secretary-General,* May 5, 2014, http:// unsdsn.org/wp-content/uploads/2013/06/140505-An-Action-Agenda-for-Sustainable -Development.pdf.

Beyond 2015 Coalition

The Beyond 2015 Coalition was a global civil society campaign established in 2010 as a partnership between civil society organizations in the global North and South. The coalition eventually involved more than 1,500 organizations from 142 countries around two primary goals: the adoption of a global, overarching, cross-thematic framework to succeed the MDGs and a process of developing this framework that was participatory, inclusive, and responsive to the voices of those directly affected by poverty and injustice.[58] Beyond 2015 brought in other stakeholders that had not traditionally been part of the Major Groups system. They also contributed to "getting the practice of Major Groups more open and accountable and less dominated by Northern NGOs," which many developing countries saw as a flaw in the engagement of civil society in the United Nations.[59] This gave the campaign more credibility. The Beyond 2015 Coalition, like many of the other civil society organizations, directly engaged with governments at all levels (global, regional, and national) on concrete proposals.[60] Since December 2015, this group has been renamed "Together 2030."

Business Community

The business community was engaged with the OWG to prepare business leaders and the corporate world for the SDGs. Louise Kantrow, the permanent representative to the UN for the International Chamber of Commerce (ICC), along with other business and industry representatives from developed and developing countries, including Unilever, the International Federation of Private Water Operators (AquaFed), Safaricom, the United States Council for International Business, the International Fertilizer Industry Association, the American Chemistry Council, Dupont Sustainable Solutions, and the International Council of Mining and Metals, advocated for the important role that the business community could play in implementing the SDGs:

> The development of the SDGs should consider how to mobilize and channel resources most cost-effectively—for business, stepping up investment in and deployment of financial and technological resources, innovation and knowhow will be one of the most critical success factors for SDGs that are not unmet promises. It will be indispensable to reflect economic circumstances, opportunities and risks in designing the goals and targets as well as their necessary "support structure."[61]

PHOTO 5.4. Federica Scala (left), International Development Law Organization, and Louise Kantrow (right), International Chamber of Commerce. *Photo by IISD/Pamela Chasek (enb.iisd.org)*

The business community also wanted to make sure that the SDGs were good for business. Some issues were of particular importance for them to monitor, including calls for green procurement, trade, and intellectual property rights. They saw that promotion of renewable energy and a variety of other clean energy technologies could represent major business opportunities. But at the same time, discussions on sustainable consumption and production were of concern because this could involve a change of lifestyles, which could affect their bottom line. So the business community was not only advocating for its own role in implementing the SDGs, but it was also looking out for the economic interests of its members.

During the stocktaking and beyond, Kőrösi and Kamau encouraged civil society representatives to be bolder and more provocative and to work more closely with governments.[62] Not all of them did, but the early-morning sessions and other civil society contributions provided the co-chairs with many ideas that they could bring to the drafting process. As members of civil society saw their ideas taken on board, they felt that their proposals were legitimized; thus, their sense of ownership in the outcome increased.

CONCLUSIONS AND LESSONS LEARNED

Effective co-chairs must be able to take the temperature of the room. They must be able to identify the key actors, those most likely to cause problems, and those most likely to provide solutions. If the co-chairs are able to read the room, they can identify potential obstacles and try to "dispose of them even before they appear on the negotiating table."[63] Of course, in any UN negotiating process, the delegates often change. People arrive from capitals, new experts are transferred in, and national positions shift as a result of elections or policy changes at home. Nevertheless, if the co-chairs take the time to hold bilateral consultations with the key players and anticipate statements they will make during formal sessions, they will be better managers of the process.

The co-chairs also recognized that if they understood the delegates in the room and began to recognize each government's priority issues, they could ensure that many of these ideas would be discussed during the stocktaking sessions. This assured delegates that their concerns were important, helping to build ownership in both the process and the outcome.

But government delegates weren't the only ones in the room. So the co-chairs also had to understand how to work with and manage representatives from the UN programs, funds, and agencies, as well as the Executive Office of the UN Secretary-General and the DESA Secretariat.

Finally, the co-chairs knew that civil society would be instrumental in implementing the SDGs on the ground. So they went out of their way to incorporate the views of civil society in the process. In fact, the MDGs promoted cooperation among the public sector, private sector, and NGOs, providing a common language and bringing together disparate actors.[64] NGOs and civil society bought into the goals, worked to accomplish them, and held their governments accountable for MDG implementation, despite their frustration that the MDGs were developed "behind closed doors."[65] By incorporating ideas from civil society into the stocktaking phase, the co-chairs ensured that the work of the OWG was transparent and representative. This also ensured that civil society would be involved with the SDGs from the get-go. There was also increasing consensus that private sector businesses and industries had to be more involved in the design and implementation of the SDGs, particularly as economic growth, trade, and jobs were all high on the agenda.

As the OWG moved from stocktaking to negotiations, the fact that the co-chairs had taken the time—and this was no small feat—to meet with and understand member states, the UN system of programs, funds, and agencies, and representatives of civil society, including the business sector, was auspicious. The stocktaking meetings were complete, but the difficult work was only just beginning.

6

THE USE OF PROCESS
AND DRAMA

Ultimately the dedication and vision of two outstanding co-chairs, Ambassadors Macharia [Kamau] of Kenya and Csaba [Kőrösi] of Hungary, the discipline and commitment of 193 countries and innumerable civil society organizations, NGOs, think-tanks, private sector organizations and scientists, and a unique format that had never before been used at the UN, delivered a metric that truly has the potential to be transformational.

—Paula Caballero Gómez, former director
for Economic, Social and Environmental
Affairs, Ministry of Foreign Affairs,
Colombia[1]

For one year over eight sessions, delegates to the Open Working Group (OWG) on Sustainable Development Goals (SDGs) abided by their co-chairs' proposal to delay negotiations until they had completed a period of mutual learning and discussion. It was important for all to understand and appreciate the potential nature and scope of the SDGs and what differentiates them from other goals such as the Millennium Development Goals (MDGs). The eight "stocktaking sessions," which involved the formal discussion of more than fifty-eight issues, enhanced by presentations from eighty experts, concluded in February 2014, with the OWG's members informed about the opportunities and challenges that the SDGs had to address and the approaches that they might want to take to crafting them.

In March 2014 the ninth session of the OWG marked the turning point as delegates shifted gears from stocktaking to negotiating. The possibilities—and enormous size—of the OWG's task came into greater focus as delegates began to discuss what issues would define the goals and targets to be included in the final list of SDGs.[2] This chapter examines the final five sessions of the OWG, focusing on the strategies and tactics used by the co-chairs to bring the negotiations to a successful conclusion. However, first it is necessary to give an overview of the five negotiating sessions.

A BIRD'S-EYE VIEW OF THE SDG NEGOTIATIONS

As the co-chairs opened OWG-9 in early March 2014, they wanted to ensure that the OWG didn't immediately jump into typical UN negotiations as described in Chapters 1 and 2. They wanted to keep the OWG focused on substance and ambition rather than arguing over phrases, words, and comma placement. So the co-chairs tried to focus participants on several key questions that they should think about as they transitioned from stocktaking to negotiations:

- **What is our vision of the world we want in 2030?** How do we translate that into goals? What is needed to achieve those goals (targets)? How do we ensure they are "action oriented"? How do we address resource requirements to achieve the vision?
- **Universal yet nationally differentiated:** How do we maintain a universal set of goals and avoid proliferation of nationally specific targets and indicators that cannot be aggregated to help assess progress at the international level?
- **Few in number:** How do we deal with the broad range of topics encompassed by sustainable development? How do we prioritize?
- **Balancing the three dimensions of sustainable development:** Should we have an equal number of "environmental," "social," and "economic" goals, or do we address all three under all relevant goals?

- **Cross-cutting issues and interlinkages:** How do we address cross-cutting issues and interlinkages among goals?[3]

The co-chairs also produced a "focus areas" document, which became the basis for discussion at OWG-9.[4] (See Box 6.1.) It was called this to avoid creating the impression that it was already a first draft of the goals, which could have led either directly to negotiations or to outright rejection by member states. In introducing the document at OWG-9, the co-chairs noted that the document aimed to start the process of identifying the SDGs and accompanying targets, and was not a "zero draft" of the report that the OWG would submit to the UN General Assembly in September 2014. Macharia Kamau added that the nineteen focus areas, if they could be addressed synergistically, "can promise a more sustainable earth, societies, and economies, and ultimately a more sustainable global political framework."[5]

■ **Box 6.1.**

OWG Co-chairs' Focus Areas (February 24, 2014)

1. Poverty eradication
2. Food security and nutrition
3. Health and population dynamics
4. Education
5. Gender equality and women's empowerment
6. Water and sanitation
7. Energy
8. Economic growth
9. Industrialization
10. Infrastructure
11. Employment and decent work for all
12. Promoting equality
13. Sustainable cities and human settlements
14. Sustainable consumption and production

15. Climate

16. Marine resources, oceans and seas

17. Ecosystems and biodiversity

18. Means of implementation

19. Peaceful and non-violent societies, capable institutions

SOURCE: The complete document is available at https://sustainabledevelopment.un
.org/content/documents/3276focusareas.pdf.

The co-chairs and the Secretariat had worked together to prepare the focus areas document, based on the exchange of views during the eight stocktaking sessions and other communications from OWG members and observers. The Secretariat produced a first draft based on a best understanding of the detailed notes of the OWG discussions compiled by members of the Secretariat and the co-chairs' teams. In this regard the account of the negotiations in the *Earth Negotiations Bulletin* also provided a good cross-check, and members of the OWG and other stakeholders also submitted their written statements for reference and posting on the Division for Sustainable Development's website. The co-chairs would then review the draft. In the preparation of this document, as well as subsequent drafts of the proposed goals and targets, there was a frequent back-and-forth between the co-chairs and Secretariat until the co-chairs approved the final draft to send out to the OWG.

At the end of OWG-9, the co-chairs said they would prepare a slightly amended focus areas document, reflecting delegates' comments, to be released by March 19, 2014; a matrix document, mapping how different focus areas could come together through interlinkages;[6] a compendium document, describing existing targets that have previously been agreed upon; and a technical document, describing the differences among goals, targets, and indicators.[7]

When OWG-10 convened at the end of March 2014, the co-chairs opened the session with a recap of the process thus far. Starting each meeting with this kind of a recap to bring everyone up to speed was a good tactic in that it gave both old hands and newcomers comfort with the

PHOTO 6.1. The co-chairs had to reflect the very different positions of OWG members, including (clockwise from upper left) Hiroshi Minami, Japan; Paula Caballero Gómez, Colombia; Stephan Contius, Germany; and Taghi Ferami, Iran. *Photos by IISD/Elizabeth Press (enb.iisd.org)*

co-chairs and the process. On the first day of OWG-10, the co-chairs also had a brief discussion on methodology to ensure that everyone was on the same page. Csaba Kőrösi introduced a definitional note on goals and targets, based on the discussions at the second session of the OWG, the General Assembly outcome document from the September 2013 Special Event on the MDGs, and the call for SDGs in the Rio+20 outcome document. Kőrösi explained that a goal expresses an ambitious, specific, and actionable commitment, is concise and easy to communicate, and is aspirational. Targets identify specific measurable objectives whose attainment would contribute in a major way to achieving one or more goals. He further noted that targets should be aspirational yet attainable, nationally relevant and time bound, and adjusted as science advances and if countries raise their level of ambition.[8]

Member states and observers then commented on the revised list of nineteen focus areas, and potential targets related to each focus area, that had been prepared by the co-chairs and the Secretariat.[9] Instead of the strictly narrative version of the focus areas distributed in February, the March version listed potential topics for targets that could be included under each focus area. At the end of the week-long meeting, the co-chairs indicated that they would revise the focus areas document by April 17 to guide delegates' preparation for OWG-11.

In May 2014 the working document for OWG-11 contained a pared-down list of sixteen focus areas, a list of goals, and approximately 150 potential targets related to the focus areas.[10] (See Box 6.2.) The co-chairs took pains to assure the OWG members that this was not yet a "zero draft" but just the basis for further discussion. They asked delegates to focus on refining the targets, limiting their number, and addressing the universality of both the goals and targets. They also indicated that they would draft a "chapeau" (introduction) to focus on the principles that give direction and historical context to the SDGs.[11] The working document resembled the original focus areas documents but merged three of the previous focus areas. The focus areas on infrastructure and employment and decent work for all (formerly focus areas 10 and 11) were merged into focus area 8 (economic growth) to become "Economic growth, employment and infrastructure." The focus area on promoting equality (formerly focus area 12) was split between focus area 1, on poverty eradication (so that promoting equality *within* nations would be included), and focus area 9, on industrialization (so that promoting equality *among* nations would be included).

OWG-11 reviewed each focus area in turn. Kőrösi noted that there was general agreement that the concepts contained in the focus areas related to the "unfinished business in MDGs"—poverty eradication, food security, education, health, gender, and water—should be included as goals in the new framework. The discussion on "newer" issues on the development agenda, such as climate change, terrestrial ecosystems, oceans, sustainable consumption and production, energy, industrialization, infrastructure and economic growth and employment, human settlements, means of implementation, peaceful societies, and rule of law, revealed that there was still

■ **Box 6.2**

OWG Co-chairs' Revised Focus Areas and Draft Goals (April 17, 2014)

1. Poverty eradication, building shared prosperity and promoting equality	End poverty in all its forms everywhere
2. Sustainable agriculture, food security and nutrition	End hunger and improve nutrition for all through sustainable agriculture and improved food systems
3. Health and population dynamics	Healthy life at all ages for all
4. Education and life-long learning	Provide quality education and life-long learning for all
5. Gender equality and women's empowerment	Attain gender equality and women's empowerment everywhere
6. Water and sanitation	Water and sanitation for a sustainable world
7. Energy	Ensure access to affordable, sustainable and reliable modern energy for all
8. Economic growth, employment and infrastructure	Promote sustainable, inclusive and sustained economic growth and decent jobs for all
9. Industrialization and promoting equality among nations	Promote sustainable industrialization and equality among nations
10. Sustainable cities and human settlements	Build inclusive, safe and sustainable cities and human settlements
11. Sustainable consumption and production	Promote sustainable consumption and production patterns
12. Climate change	Take urgent and significant action to mitigate and adapt to climate change

13. Conservation and sustainable use of marine resources, oceans and seas	Take urgent and significant actions for the conservation and sustainable use of marine resources, oceans and seas
14. Ecosystems and biodiversity	Protect and restore terrestrial ecosystems and halt all biodiversity loss
15. Means of implementation/ Global partnership for sustainable development	Strengthen global partnership for sustainable development
16. Peaceful and inclusive societies, rule of law and capable institutions	Peaceful and inclusive societies, rule of law and capable institutions

SOURCE: The complete document is available at https://sustainabledevelopment.un.org/content/documents/3686WorkingDoc_0205_additionalsupporters.pdf.

no agreement on whether these focus areas should be included in the framework.

A number of delegations wanted to begin line-by-line negotiations immediately and start holding intersessional meetings. Others noted that officials from capitals would not be able to participate in intersessional meetings and supported the existing schedule. The co-chairs proposed, as a compromise, that they would hold informal consultations just prior to the start of the next session. At the close of OWG-11, the co-chairs said that the next draft of the working document would include an additional focus area—inequality—to respond to popular demand and would contain many more draft targets.[12]

During the short intersessional period, the co-chairs and the Secretariat worked on the zero draft. Although the decision on what should or should not be reflected in a stand-alone goal was ultimately based on the degree of political support shown by the OWG, the crafting of the targets was a more technically demanding matter. It was important to reflect a high level of political ambition in the goal and target language while at the same time engaging in a reality check of whether a given level of ambition was attainable in the agreed-upon fifteen-year time frame. Thus, with regard to target formulation, the Secretariat had to consult the scientific literature and experts in a given field, along with members of the UN technical support team (see Appendix II), in an effort to judge the feasibility of a proposed quantitative target, say, on maternal mortality or access to secondary education. The Secretariat would then brief the co-chairs on why a particular value was used and not another, based on available evidence.

OWG-12, which met on June 16–20, 2014, was preceded by three days of informal consultations on June 9–11. This represented the first OWG meeting where delegates worked primarily in informal sessions based on the "zero draft" of the chapeau, seventeen goals, and associated targets, distributed on June 2, 2014.[13] (See Box 6.3.) During the informal consultations, delegates considered proposed Goals 1–6, which were largely the "unfinished business" of the MDGs. OWG-12 then focused on proposed Goals 7–17.

■ **Box 6.3.**

Zero Draft of the SDGs (June 2, 2014)

On June 2, 2014, the OWG co-chairs released the "zero draft" of the proposed goals and targets. Changes from the April 17 draft (Box 6.2) are indicated in bold:

1. End poverty in all its forms everywhere
2. End hunger, **achieve food security and adequate** nutrition for all, and **promote** sustainable agriculture
3. **Attain** healthy life at all ages for all
4. Provide **equitable and inclusive** quality education and life-long learning **opportunities** for all
5. Attain gender equality, **empower** women **and girls** everywhere
6. **Secure** water and sanitation for **all for** a sustainable world
7. Ensure access to affordable, sustainable and reliable modern energy **services** for all

8. Promote **strong,** inclusive and sustained economic growth and decent **work** for all

9. Promote sustainable industrialization

10. **Reduce inequality within and among nations**

11. Build inclusive, safe and sustainable cities and human settlements

12. Promote sustainable consumption and production patterns

13. **Promote actions at all levels to address** climate change

14. **Attain** conservation and sustainable use of marine resources, oceans and seas

15. Protect and restore terrestrial ecosystems and halt all biodiversity loss

16. **Achieve peaceful and inclusive societies, rule of law, effective and capable institutions** (formerly 16)

17. Strengthen **and enhance the means of implementation and** global partnership for sustainable development (formerly 15)

SOURCE: The complete document is available at https://sustainabledevelopment.un .org/content/documents/4528zerodraft12OWG.pdf.

There was general agreement on the focus of most of the goals, but many countries proposed deleting Goal 10 (reduce inequality within and among countries), which had been removed after OWG-10 and reinserted after OWG-11, and relocating its targets to proposed Goals 1, 8, 16, and 17. Others preferred a stand-alone goal because this would send a stronger political message on reducing levels of inequality to achieve social inclusion and leave no one behind.[14]

Although a few delegations agreed with the need for fewer goals, others said that such efforts may "do us a disservice," with one suggesting that a set of twenty very clear goals with clear targets for national implementation might be preferable, and others saying that the number of goals was not as important as addressing concrete issues.[15] These back-and-forth exchanges were meant to achieve a political equilibrium. Developing countries viewed proposals to delete goals for reducing inequalities within and among countries and sustainable consumption and production as an attempt to exonerate their developed counterparts from commitments in an otherwise universal development architecture.

Many developed countries were wary of the changes in their lifestyle they would have to make under the SDGs, especially if there was a goal on sustainable consumption and production, and this posed some real challenges. Similarly, the developing world was wary of European support for a goal on climate change, fearing its enforcement could curtail their economic growth, which they saw as a necessary condition for poverty eradication. Similarly, Europe's push for the concept of "limits to growth" did not find much political traction in the developing world.

At the conclusion of the session, Kamau announced that there would be another set of informal meetings from July 9 to July 11, to be followed by the final meeting of the OWG from July 14 to July 18. He said the co-chairs would prepare a revised version of the zero draft that would have fewer targets and be a more refined, more balanced, and "tighter" document. He expressed the co-chairs' confidence that the OWG would successfully conclude its work on July 18, as scheduled.[16]

As promised, on June 30 the OWG co-chairs issued the revised zero draft. Civil society organizations and other stakeholders also released their final compilation of amendments to the goals and targets to inform the final meeting of the OWG.[17] As the co-chairs noted in their letter to delegations that accompanied the revised zero draft, "Happily the working group has lived up to its name; it has remained open to all governments and embraced the voice of civil society, including the business community, academia and United Nations Organizations, all of whom together have brought tremendous breadth and depth to our deliberations."[18]

OWG-13 conducted a complete reading of the revised zero draft of the proposed SDGs and targets. The co-chairs and the Secretariat took note of all proposals to amend the draft goals and targets, and when the reading was complete, the co-chairs issued a second draft. They followed the same process for both the second draft and a third draft. The reading of the third draft began on Friday, July 18, at 8:30 A.M. and did not conclude until Saturday afternoon, including an all-night session. This marked a critical time as outstanding issues such as the right to development, common but

differentiated responsibilities, sexual and reproductive health and reproductive rights, people living under foreign occupation, the rule of law, and
respect for human rights were squarely on the table. Delegations with
strong positions stayed throughout the night to keep abreast of any
developments.

On Saturday morning at 8:00 A.M., delegates were presented with the
final "Proposal of the Open Working Group on Sustainable Development
Goals." After consultations among the various negotiating groups and troikas, the plenary convened. At 1:20 P.M., after nearly three hours of statements—both in support of and opposed to the final document—the OWG
adopted by consensus the document containing seventeen SDGs and 169
targets.

STRATEGIES AND TACTICS

During the five OWG meetings described above, the negotiating strategies
and the tactics used by the co-chairs went a long way towards achieving a
successful outcome. The rest of this chapter focuses on these strategies and
tactics, while Chapter 7 examines the negotiations on the specific goals and
targets.

Refining the Goals and Targets:
How to Ensure Comfort

Given that the times had changed markedly since the MDGs were developed in 2000 and that Rio+20 described what the SDGs should be, a number of new questions had to be addressed by the OWG. First, given that the
MDGs were just for developing countries, how would the OWG ensure
that the SDGs would be universal in their applicability? Second, would developed countries expect emerging economies to take greater responsibility, especially with regard to the means of implementation? Third, what
transformation would the SDGs bring, and how would the three pillars of
sustainable development be balanced? This question was pertinent because
the MDGs were heavy on social development, scanty on environment, and
largely silent on the economic dimension.

Early on, the co-chairs adopted an iterative strategy, which is a process
for arriving at an outcome by repeating rounds of analysis to bring the

desired outcome closer with each repetition. The co-chairs knew that everyone first had to be comfortable with the goals, and then the targets would follow. With some convincing by the co-chairs, the OWG members agreed to leave the indicators to national statistical bodies, which would develop a set of indicators to measure progress, under the auspices of the UN Statistical Commission, following the adoption of the goals and targets.[19] There were still some who wanted the OWG to develop the indicators, as this would ensure that the General Assembly, a universal body where every country has an equal voice, would have the final say, instead of only the twenty-four member states of the UN Statistical Commission.

From the start, the co-chairs listened to everyone, putting together draft after draft. As the document took shape and someone noticed that a desired target was not in the draft, the co-chairs could either add it in, if there appeared to be consensus, or say that this item should not be considered a goal or target, but could go into the chapeau or become an indicator. For example, many developing countries called for reference to the principle of common but differentiated responsibilities (CBDR) in the text, especially in the proposed goal on climate change. At one point at OWG-12, the Group of 77 (G-77) called for CBDR to be included in every goal.[20] Developed countries, in turn, argued that CBDR should under no circumstances be included in a development agenda but should be limited to its original context of environmental degradation, if at all. The co-chairs responded by placing reference to the principle of CBDR in the chapeau, where it remained. By including CBDR in the chapeau, the co-chairs created a win-win situation. For the developing world, CBDR was preserved and would set the tone and context for the implementation and review of the SDGs. For the developed world, CBDR was not part of the actual goal set. Furthermore, not placing CBDR in the goals or in their targets maintained the universality of the goals instead of differentiating them by level of development.

Another challenge was determining the number of goals. There had been eight MDGs, and some thought that there should also be the same number of SDGs, especially those who wanted to essentially roll over the MDGs for another fifteen years. Others, including Jeffrey Sachs and the Sustainable Development Solutions Network (SDSN), argued that "To be effective, a shared framework for sustainable development must mobilize the world around a limited number of priorities and associated goals—probably not more than ten."[21] In fact, in its report to the Secretary-General, SDSN actually listed ten goals and thirty targets that its leadership council thought should be adopted by the OWG.[22] (See Box 5.1.)

The Secretary-General's High-Level Panel of Eminent Persons on the Post-2015 Development Agenda called for twelve goals and fifty-four targets in its 2013 report.[23] Nikhil Seth, director of the UN Division for Sustainable Development, commented off the record that there should be fifteen goals: fifteen goals for 2015 for fifteen years, and Kamau thought that would be a good number to aim for. The United Kingdom (as one of the co-chairs of the high-level panel), Jeffrey Sachs, the Secretary-General, and even Bill Gates put substantial pressure on the co-chairs to keep the number of goals to no more than twelve, arguing that anything more would be a recipe for implementation failure. The co-chairs kept promising them that they would keep the number down but never told them what that number would be.

The key for the co-chairs was to see where the process led them. This was a member-state–driven process, and the co-chairs believed that their consultative, iterative approach was sacrosanct. After all, it was the OWG that had the mandate to formulate the SDGs. Given the range of issues of priority to member states, the UN family of organizations, and civil society, it was not easy to limit the number of goals and targets, and in the end, the OWG members agreed on a set of seventeen goals. Although everyone was excited to have reached an agreement, there was still concern that seventeen goals were too many.

However, John McArthur, a senior fellow at the Brookings Institution, put the seventeen goals in perspective. He wrote a blog post, "Why 17 Is a Beautiful Number," explaining how he informed his mother, a retiree in Vancouver, Canada, that all 193 countries had agreed on a new set of global goals. She thought this sounded terrific. He confessed to her that there was a big problem: seventeen goals. As he wrote, "My mom's response caught me off guard, to say the least: 'Seventeen is a great number,' she enthused." When he asked her to explain, given the fact that she was the first person he had spoken to who said that, she said "It sounds like they didn't fake it.

The world is complicated. If they had come back with some Letterman-style top 10 then I probably wouldn't have believed them."[24]

The co-chairs knew if they could get the goals right, the targets would follow. But they also had trouble limiting the number of targets. The zero draft had 212 targets, with a whopping forty-six targets in proposed Goal 17 alone. This far exceeded the SDSN's proposed thirty targets and the high-level panel's fifty-four. Some wanted the number of targets under each goal to be limited to eight and thought that such a large number of targets would be impossible to manage. The co-chairs decided that they couldn't obsess over the limiting of the targets, just as they hadn't with the goals. They did their best to keep the number of targets from proliferating and welcomed suggestions to merge targets. One sticky issue was whether to have means of implementation targets in every goal or just in Goal 17. They did manage to whittle down the number of targets from 212 to 169 with an average of nine to ten targets per goal, divided between substantive targets and means of implementation targets. (See Chapter 7.)

The use of the chapeau proved to be extremely valuable during the negotiations, especially when trying to reduce the number of targets. The chapeau formed a kind of safety valve that gave delegates a certain degree of comfort when their ideas for targets needed to be deleted. Some of the proposed targets were not really targets at all but were political or aspirational language. When the endgame was in view, the co-chairs began to recognize that they would have to shift some of this political language somewhere else, and the chapeau became the place. Delegates then began to amend the chapeau to incorporate everything they had lost in the goals and targets. As the chapeau got to be quite long, like the goals and targets, the text had to be whittled down. Nonetheless, as a safety valve, the chapeau most definitely proved to be useful.

Holding the Pen

The co-chairs wanted to avoid an endless drafting process that would result in "wordsmithing" rather than focusing on the substance, so they used the strategy of a single negotiating text where they would be the ones "holding the pen," instead of a compilation document containing all amendments, as had been the norm in previous sustainable development negotiations.[25] The use of a single negotiating text is a strategy often employed in complex multiparty negotiations that can simplify the process by concentrating the attention of all sides on the same composite text.[26] In this case the single negotiating text gave drafting responsibilities to the co-chairs. Not only did this streamline the process, but it also helped delegates avoid viewing the negotiations as a "zero-sum" game, one in which any gain achieved by one side is perceived to be a loss to the other side.

As one participant noted, if the co-chairs had reverted to an inductive, on-screen exercise, as had happened with the Rio+20 compilation text (see Chapter 2), the OWG would have gotten "bogged down in endless word-smithing of a very complex document with multiple and often contradictory amendments and any technical nuances would be lost."[27] Nikhil Seth observed that Rio+20 showed that on-screen negotiations did not succeed because countries could see their positions on the screen. Each time a country saw its name removed from the screen, it represented a concession. These on-screen negotiations became very difficult, especially on politically charged issues from which delegations do not want to see their names disappear.[28] This, in effect, also reduces a chair's crucial room for maneuvering, in the privacy of his or her office, to "tweak" submitted proposals in the interest of producing a more consensual draft text. So even though a number of OWG members, especially those from developing countries, kept asking the co-chairs to move to on-screen negotiations, they stood their ground.

The only way the co-chairs could hold on to the pen was to gain the trust of the membership and be as approachable as possible to assure all parties that their input was valuable and would be incorporated into the text. They held many bilateral meetings with delegations to give them the opportunity to air their views and concerns. They also consulted with ministers and other officials in capitals between OWG sessions (see Chapter 4). These intersessional meetings played a very important role in gaining buy-in and trust.

Holding on to the pen allowed the co-chairs to keep the discussions focused and technical, and to maintain a high level of ambition. With each draft, from the original focus areas document distributed on February 24,

2014, to the March 19 revised focus areas document, to the April 17 working document, to the June 2 zero draft, and to the June 30 revised zero
draft, the co-chairs' continual avoidance of line-by-line negotiations succeeded in keeping the OWG focused on the substance. As the *Earth Negotiations Bulletin* reported, "Discussions on changes to proposed SDGs were
strikingly substantive, as delegates explained their positions and sought to
persuade others."[29] This focus on substance also enabled the co-chairs to
keep the document ambitious, with little reliance on previously agreed-
upon language.[30]

Enabling Ownership

When co-chairs hold the pen, however, it is very easy for delegations to feel
disenfranchised, especially if they do not believe that their voices and concerns are reflected in the text. When delegates engage in line-by-line negotiations, they can easily report to their capitals what they contributed to the
text, especially because in some negotiations (such as Rio+20) amendments are attributed until agreement has been reached and all amendments
have been accepted.

The co-chairs came up with a masterful way for delegations to show
their capitals that their ideas had been taken into account: "Encyclopedia
Groupinica." After the co-chairs distributed their March 19, focus areas
document, many delegations submitted amendments, proposals, and comments both during and following OWG-10. So, in advance of OWG-11, the
co-chairs asked the Secretariat to compile all the proposals submitted by
delegations, civil society, and other stakeholders into a single, organized,
and cohesive document, but not one intended to serve as the basis for negotiations. Instead, this 182-page list of proposals became "Encyclopedia
Groupinica: A Compilation of Goals and Targets Suggestions from OWG-
10 in Response to Co-Chairs' Focus Area Document Dated 19 March,
2014."[31]

When Kamau introduced this document on the first day of OWG-11, in
May 2014, he made sure that everyone knew that Encyclopedia Groupinica
contained their ideas. This served to validate all of the participants' proposals. Most experienced UN negotiators know that they will not get all their
ideas into the final text, but Encyclopedia Groupinica showed their ideas in

writing for all to see. Kamau talked up the document whenever he could because this was an essential part of the process of managing both the delegates in the room and the process. This also took some of the pressure off the co-chairs to start line-by-line negotiations. As soon as everyone knew that their voice had been heard—and they could show Encyclopedia Groupinica to their capitals to prove it—they could focus on the substance of the SDGs and avoid small skirmishes over textual proposals. Some delegates used to come to the meetings with the document and use it as a reference text. At the same time, it showed delegates in 182 pages what could have happened to the SDGs had the co-chairs not insisted on holding on to the pen. In sum, as long as delegates' ideas saw the light of day and got the attention they felt they deserved, the member states were comfortable with the process.

What Each Country Wants and Each Country Fears

Another important strategy the co-chairs used was to learn what everyone in the room wanted and, alternatively, what they feared and to use this knowledge to guide the negotiations. As noted in Chapter 5, if a chair doesn't know the room and doesn't know who the antagonists and protagonists are, the process is difficult to manage. Knowing what people want can also serve as bait. If a chair wants to get a country to shift its position, whether it is the United States, China, Brazil, or South Africa, the chair needs to understand what the country really wants out of the process and work toward the necessary trade-offs.

Some delegates saw the OWG and the SDGs as a way of making an end run on issues under negotiation in other forums, including climate change, technology transfer, and trade. Others were perceived as single-issue delegations: although they were engaged in the entire process, they put everything on the line for an issue of particular interest to their countries, including sexual and reproductive health and reproductive rights, energy, climate change, and oceans. Still others just wanted the process to be over so they could go home. This had been a nearly two-year process since Rio+20. Delegates kept asking the co-chairs when it was going to be over because their capitals wanted to know. Besides, participating in so many meetings in such a short period of time was taxing for some of the smaller countries, which really didn't have the staff for such a demanding process.

For the co-chairs to know what delegations want or fear, as formal statements do not always get at the underlying issues, they must hold numerous bilateral meetings. These meetings enabled the co-chairs to both listen to and reassure delegates, which helped them to maintain control of the room and the direction of the negotiations. The various "red lines" presented by delegates represented some deep-rooted fears often tied up with long-standing institutional, political, and economic positions, as well as the instructions from their capitals. The co-chairs needed to understand all of this to know how far they could push.

Inevitably, when the negotiations are at the eleventh hour, countries make their moves and declare their red lines on the unresolved issues. In the OWG, as the endgame approached, some countries, including the United States, China, Russia, and Brazil, became more forceful in expressing their opinions on what they did not find acceptable. When the co-chairs started getting calls from capitals, they knew that they were getting closer to their red lines. This is when Kamau and Kőrösi had to cash in on the goodwill they had built up and rely heavily on the momentum of the negotiations. They met bilaterally with different delegations and convinced them that disruptive actions could blow up in their face. Because Kamau and Kőrösi had spent months ensuring that everyone was invested in the process, they hoped that no one was prepared to see the SDGs go up in flames and that they would back down. It was their careful management of interests and fears that helped to make this possible.

Horse Trading and Creative Compromise

The co-chairs also had to use the tactic of "horse trading," another term for complex bargaining. Sometimes delegations can make trade-offs on their own, but in multilateral, multi-issue negotiating processes such as the OWG, co-chairs may need to step in and propose such trades. One such example was with Goal 16. Originally, the European Union as well as other Western states called for two separate goals: one on "peaceful and non-violent societies" and one on "rule of law and capable institutions."[32] Others did not support even a single goal on these topics, stating that they should be dealt with under the UN Human Rights Council or other, more appropriate bodies, for it was not good to conflate a development agenda with human rights, peace, and security issues. After much ado, the co-chairs were able to engineer a trade: if developing countries accepted a single goal that incorporated peace, justice, and strong institutions, the developed countries would accept goals on sustainable consumption and production, industrialization, and equality.

In some cases the co-chairs had to come up with creative compromises, such as on the issue of self-determination of peoples living under colonial and foreign occupation—in other words, the fate of the Palestinians. Throughout the United Nations, many countries, particularly in the Arab world, insert this issue into negotiations ostensibly as a means of maintaining a focus on the fate of the Palestinian people. However, the Palestinian issue can be a real lightning rod. Israel and the United States did not want reference to the Palestinian issue in the SDGs because they insisted that the SDGs were not a political agenda. Many other countries, including some Europeans, supported a reference to the Palestinians because no one was to be left behind in the SDGs. Therefore, rather than lose the SDGs over the Palestinian issue, the co-chairs were able to offer a compromise: self-determination of peoples living under occupation would be included in the chapeau rather than in SDG 16 or not mentioned at all. Although not everyone was happy, it was seen as an acceptable compromise.

Avoiding the Use of Contact Groups

Another strategy that proved crucial to the success of the OWG was the avoidance of contact groups until the very end. In many sustainable development negotiations, once a difficult issue is introduced and discussed in plenary, the chair may ask interested delegations to meet in a contact group in another room to reach agreement. In some cases, especially in climate change negotiations, multiple contact groups meet simultaneously. Kamau and Kőrösi agreed that they didn't want people leaving the room to meet in contact groups for several reasons. First, as soon as negotiations move to contact groups, the co-chairs lose control of the debate. Because co-chairs usually do not participate in the contact groups, they have no real assurance that the results of such deliberations will actually allow the process to move forward. Second, contact groups can be counterproductive and fragment the energy in the room. Finally, contact groups can create paranoia and a sense of anxiety. Countries not participating in a contact group do not always feel a sense of ownership of the outcome. So when a contact group reports back to the plenary, a disenfranchised delegate could reject the outcome, and the entire exercise could unravel.

Only on the penultimate day of OWG-13 did the co-chairs announce the formation of contact groups on four "difficult" issues: Goal 16 (peaceful and inclusive societies, rule of law, access to justice for all, and effective institutions), coordinated by Ambassador Gustavo Meza-Cuadra (Peru); Goal 6's reference to transboundary water management, coordinated by Ambassador Michael Gerber (Switzerland); Goal 7's reference to inefficient fossil-fuel subsidies, coordinated by Minister Counsellor Marianne Loe (Norway); and references to sexual and reproductive health and reproductive rights in Goals 3 and 5, coordinated by Ambassador Caleb Otto (Palau).[33]

The rationale for these four groups was that as the OWG neared the end, the co-chairs needed to be able to say that they tried everything. So if the plenary tried and failed and a contact group tried and failed, the co-chairs would have the flexibility and accumulated goodwill to put their own proposal on the table for adoption. Delegates are much more tolerant of co-chairs' proposals at the end if they believe the co-chairs have gone the extra mile to achieve consensus. This extra mile is sometimes a contact group. The co-chairs chose these four issues where agreement was elusive but gave the contact groups less than a day to reach agreement on consensus language and bring it back to the plenary. Gerber and Loe were able to bring back agreed-upon text fairly quickly. However, consensus on Goal 16 and sexual and reproductive health and rights was more elusive. So the co-chairs made sure that they had backup proposals—just in case.

THE ENDGAME

There is nothing quite like the endgame in UN negotiations. It is like chess: you don't know always what your opponent's move will be, but you must know what your countermove will be. The co-chairs knew that they would get an outcome that was flawed in some ways but fundamentally

PHOTO 6.2. Contact group coordinators (clockwise from upper left): Ambassador Caleb Otto, Palau; Ambassador Michael Gerber, Switzerland; Ambassador Gustavo Meza-Cuadra, Peru; and Minister Counsellor Marianne Loe, Norway. *Photos by IISD (enb.iisd.org)*

acceptable. But, even at the end, they had no idea how. So they prepared their countermoves. They knew where the sensitive words and paragraphs were and which delegations would put up a fight. They were confident that if they held on to the pen, continued to have consultations with delegations, and had a bit of luck, then they were going to succeed.

UN negotiators tend to use all available space and time to extract as many concessions as possible, and it is not until the time pressure posed by a hard deadline that the difficult compromises are made. No one wants to take the blame for failure. The OWG's mandate ended on Friday, July 18, 2014; however, as is sometimes the case at the United Nations, the meeting continued past that deadline and did not formally come to a close until 1:20 P.M. the next day. The thirty-six-hour endgame was marked by some elements of suspicion, exhaustion, adrenalin rushes, and tensions between delegates and between the co-chairs. At the same time, according to Kamau, there was a sense in the room that this process was going to end and was going to end well.

By this point, with the exception of Goal 16, the goals were finished, yet OWG members were still arguing over some of the targets. But even if 99 percent of the text is agreed upon, the negotiations can still collapse over disagreements on the details. The third reading of the draft SDGs and targets took place from noon on Friday until 3:45 A.M. on Saturday. Intense discussions earlier in the week resolved questions about including goals on climate change, sustainable consumption and production, and inequalities. At 3:45 A.M. the co-chairs suspended the meeting until 8:00 A.M. to meet with the Secretariat to make the final revisions and edits so that the final document could be presented to the OWG for adoption. Some delegates went to their hotels or settled in for a nap at UN Headquarters while awaiting the final draft of the SDGs. But for the Secretariat and the co-chairs, there was no rest for the weary.

The co-chairs found themselves confronted with several difficult issues. First, they had received an eleventh-hour e-mail from a representative of a powerful country asking for some major changes to the text. Although the co-chairs did not want to disappoint an ambassador who had been largely supportive throughout the process, Kamau knew that changing the text so drastically at this late hour, without discussing the proposals with the entire OWG, could do irreparable damage and upend the process completely. Kőrösi suggested accommodating this country's requests and reopening the text. Kamau strongly disagreed.

Second, there was concern that there were some changes to the text that hadn't been cleared first with the co-chairs. In this case, the thoroughness of the co-chairs came in handy. They personally reviewed the text paragraph by paragraph, and whenever they noticed an anomaly, they checked the notes that the co-chairs' teams had been taking alongside the Secretariat and reverted to the agreed-upon text. Kamau stressed that when delegates commit to such language in the room and the chair says the language has been accepted, it cannot change. If the language is changed, governments will immediately lose trust in the co-chairs and the process.

PHOTO 6.3. The co-chairs, their teams, and members of the Secretariat consulted in the UN rose garden by the East River during a short break on the final evening of the OWG on July 18, 2014. *Photo by IISD/Pamela Chasek (enb.iisd.org)*

Third, the tensions between the co-chairs were simmering. They were facing pressure from all sides on top of their own mental and physical exhaustion. In a closed meeting between the co-chairs and their teams early Saturday morning, Kamau insisted on concluding the negotiations that day. Kőrösi said there could be some flexibility with time. Kamau recognized that Kőrösi was under pressure from his capital on one side and the United States and the European Union on the other, and was concerned that he was having difficulties negotiating himself out of this bind. During this meeting the tension came to a head. After an unpleasant exchange between the co-chairs and their teams, Kamau asked both the Kenyan and Hungarian teams to leave the room. After a few words with Kőrösi, Kamau used the time-honored negotiating strategy of walking away from the table. He stood up, said he was done, and left the room.

He knew only too well that unless he took such a drastic action at this late stage, the SDGs would unravel. And they were so close to a successful conclusion.

Kamau walked out of the room and headed straight to the elevator without speaking to anyone, not even his team. A few minutes later, Kőrösi emerged and met with his team. A member of Kamau's team got into the elevator and found Kamau standing alone on the ground floor. When asked what had transpired, Kamau asked to meet with Nikhil Seth. When Seth arrived, he followed Kamau outside and convinced him to return. Seth then went back and spoke to Kőrösi and explained that the negotiations had to conclude and the co-chairs had to be on the same page so everyone understood that they were a united front.[34]

With this understanding, crisis was averted. Both co-chairs resumed reviewing the goals and targets to make sure everything was as agreed. At this stage, no member of their teams was allowed to comment on the text. It was now up to the co-chairs. If the process collapsed, it would be their fault. They moved quickly, goal by goal and target by target. When the document was approved by the co-chairs at 8:00 A.M. on Saturday morning, they gave the text to the Secretariat, who e-mailed it out to all OWG members and observers.

Shortly thereafter, another potential crisis was brewing. The G-77 and China convened and demanded to meet with Kamau. Just before he entered the room, a member of his team briefed him on the G-77's remaining concerns and the possibility of reopening some of the targets. So when Kamau walked in, he was ready. The first thing he did was thank everyone. Second, he emphatically said he had no apologies to make.[35] Third, he said the text was "take it or leave it."[36]

Some of the G-77 members then threatened to block consensus unless language on sexual health and reproductive rights was readjusted or totally expunged from the text. Kamau told those delegations that the SDGs were for everyone and that each state could choose which ones they implemented. India then read out a statement thanking Kamau for professionally steering the process and urging the G-77 to remain supportive of the co-chairs' work. There was muted acceptance. After Kamau left the G-77 meeting, some disgruntled delegates told his team that there was no consensus and that the process had collapsed. When informed of that, Kamau simply said, "Let them meet us on the floor."[37]

The co-chairs then went back to the conference room to gauge reactions to the final text and ensure that everyone was on the same page. At this time, Kamau ran into the ambassador who had submitted to the co-chairs significant proposed changes to the text at the very last minute. Kamau demurred and indicated that those changes were too extensive and too late. He indicated that the document circulated by the co-chairs was final, that it would be put on the floor for adoption, and that any delegation was free to raise concerns in front of the entire OWG. The co-chairs then quickly met with a number of delegations, indicating that some last-minute changes might be brought to the floor that could upend the process. They wanted to send the message that if delegates opened up even one word at this eleventh hour, the OWG would then have to deal with any changes that other delegations might propose. In the end, no delegation was willing to open that Pandora's box. The strategy worked.

When the co-chairs opened the closing plenary at 10:30 A.M., they were ready. Kamau said that after eighteen months, the co-chairs were pleased with the effort, especially because it is difficult to bring together 193 countries and countless NGOs to a common point on a document that would not be legally binding but nonetheless would be seen as a guiding and inspirational document. He said that like all human endeavors, the SDGs are flawed, but "we hope the result is something we can all be proud of. After 13 meetings and countless trees and lots of travel we are at the point of completion of our task. Our time is up. . . . If we had more time, we could have done a better job . . . but as far as the OWG is concerned, our work is done."[38] On behalf of the co-chairs, Kamau asked the OWG to formally adopt the proposal and send it to the UN General Assembly, and then he opened the floor for comments.

Based on his consultations between 8:00 and 10:30 that morning, Kamau knew who the naysayers were and called on them first to create a little "negative nervousness." Predictably, Nigeria wanted to amend Target 5.6 (ensure universal access to sexual and reproductive health and reproductive rights). Kamau responded that the text had been presented for adoption, not reopening, and represented "a delicate balance that could very easily unravel." Iran said it could not accept Target 5.6, suggesting that a country could not report on the implementation of a concept it does not recognize. Honduras, Chad, Egypt, and Sudan also expressed disappointment with this target. Syria expressed disappointment that reference to foreign occupation was not in the goals or targets, only in the chapeau. Venezuela expressed concern with Goal 7 (energy) and Target 12.c (fossil-fuel subsidies reform).[39]

Then the tide turned. The co-chairs had identified key countries that would be crucial to keeping the momentum alive to close the deal and adopt the SDGs, including Botswana, Tanzania, Rwanda, Ethiopia, South Africa, China, Indonesia, India, Japan, the Republic of Korea, the United States, and a number of European countries. Switzerland, also on behalf of France and Germany, took the floor and said it was not satisfied with all parts of the text but could accept it as a whole. Denmark recommended submitting the report for adoption and not reopening it. Numerous delegations followed suit, expressing where they still had problems with specific targets but stating that it was not worth reopening the text. More than thirty speakers took the floor during nearly three hours of statements on behalf of themselves, their troikas, or larger groups (G-77, European Union, etc.), supporting adoption of the SDGs. Each one was called on in a deliberate order. Finally, noting about twenty remaining requests for the floor, Kamau said the co-chairs already had a sense of the room: "As we are exhausted and will not be able to continue much longer," he requested governments to submit the proposal of the OWG to the UN General Assembly for its consideration.[40] With that, he gaveled the adoption of the proposal, giving rise to an extended standing ovation.

CONCLUSIONS AND LESSONS LEARNED

The use of strategy and tactics, as well as occasional drama, is very important for chairs of UN multilateral negotiating processes. Although not every strategy or tactic works in every situation, this chapter describes the successful ones used during the OWG negotiations.

First, an iterative strategy can be useful by repeating rounds of analysis to bring the desired outcome closer with each repetition. The co-chairs knew if they could get the goals right, the targets would follow. And to reduce the number of targets, the chapeau could be used as a safety valve. By starting with the focus area documents, the co-chairs kept delegates' attention on the substance and level of ambition, not on wordsmithing.

Second, rather than engaging in a lengthy group drafting exercise, the co-chairs used a single negotiating text where they would be the ones "holding the pen." This kept the drafting responsibilities with the co-chairs, simplified the process, and avoided a "zero-sum" game, where any gain achieved by one side is perceived to be a loss to the other side. The avoidance of a zero-sum game was also helped by the troika system, which enabled the OWG to avoid traditional North-South stalemates on many issues.

Third, because holding on to the pen can lead to a sense of disenfranchisement by delegations, the co-chairs held extensive consultations both in New York and in national capitals to listen to concerns and assure everyone that their views were important. These consultations enabled the co-chairs to learn the hopes and the fears of the different delegations. Another useful tactic, which validated all of the participants in the process and reinforced trust in the co-chairs, was the creation of Encyclopedia Groupinica.

The co-chairs also chose to limit the use of contact groups so they could maintain control of the debate and avoid fragmenting the energy in the room. When they did create four contact groups in the final hours, the purpose was more to show that they tried everything possible to reach agreement. And, in the event that consensus was elusive, as it was with rule of law in Goal 16 and sexual and reproductive health and reproductive rights in Goals 3 and 5, the co-chairs were able to successfully propose compromise text.

Finally, the use of process and drama during the endgame can lead to a desired outcome. By spreading the word that if the text was reopened by one delegation, then others would seek to further amend the text, and by managing the speakers list to allow dissenting delegates the opportunity to speak first and then start to call on supportive delegations, it was possible to create a groundswell of support for the SDGs that could not be overcome.

Managing countries and understanding their interests, wants, and needs is challenging for any chair of any UN multilateral negotiation.

However, the OWG co-chairs had momentum on their side. Once there was agreement on the conceptual framework and the nature of the SDGs, which began to emerge during the stocktaking process, OWG members realized that they could make history. By reminding delegates about the importance of the issues and the OWG's mandate, and using effective strategies and tactics, the co-chairs were able to keep the OWG's "eyes on the prize" and enable everyone to find common ground.

7

THE BIRTH
OF THE GOALS

The MDGs have helped to end poverty for some, but not for all. The SDGs must finish the job and leave no one behind. The SDGs must help us build the future we want, a future free from poverty and one that is built on human rights, equality and sustainability.

—Amina J. Mohammed, Secretary-General's special adviser on Post-2015 Development Planning and, since 2017, UN Deputy Secretary-General[1]

Determining the breadth and ambition of the Sustainable Development Goals (SDGs) was a major challenge for the Open Working Group (OWG), which had to find consensus on what the main issues were and how they affected everyone. In addition, the OWG wanted the goals and targets to be consistent and not contradict each other. It was also important for delegates not to lose sight of the big picture: how to raise living standards for all, beginning with the poorest, while keeping the global burden on food systems, biodiversity, the climate, and natural resources in check.[2] This chapter will examine the goals and targets themselves and highlight what was controversial, innovative, or groundbreaking.

GOALS 1–6:
UPDATING AND ENHANCING THE MDGS

To reassure developing countries and others who had invested in the MDGs, it was important to first address these unfinished goals. Poverty, hunger, health, education, gender equality, and clean water and sanitation became Goals 1–6. However, the OWG couldn't just roll over the MDGs, which were a limited agenda based on social development needs in developing countries. The SDGs had to be "global in nature and universally applicable to all countries."[3] In these first six goals the OWG aimed for universality in the sense of relevance to all countries' challenges, but also in the sense of ensuring all people's access to the essentials of a decent and dignified life.

GOAL 1.
End Poverty in All Its Forms Everywhere

Universality was the big story in Goal 1. The MDGs focused on reducing poverty levels in developing countries, with a particular focus on ending extreme poverty (defined in 2000 as one dollar per day per person and currently defined by the World Bank as $1.90 per day per person), but now the SDGs had to address poverty everywhere: in low-income, middle-income, and high-income countries.

Poverty wasn't only a problem in the least-developed countries (LDCs). Some of the emerging economies, including India and Brazil, spoke out about the huge pockets of poverty in their countries. The Occupy Movement (Occupy Wall Street and other protests in 951 cities in eighty-two countries[4]) and Joseph Stiglitz's presentation in January 2014 (see Chapter 4) raised awareness of poverty and inequalities in developed countries. However, the LDCs wanted to emphasize their particular challenges and insisted that they should not be left behind.

From early on, some OWG members framed the goal as not simply to end poverty but to do so irreversibly. Irreversibility had two dimensions: (1) to ensure that poverty eradication in the short term is not undermined in the medium to long term by such forces as climate change and (2) to build solid economic and social foundations for countries to be able not merely to lift but also to keep people out of poverty. Related to the previous point, delegates agreed to include a target that called for the strengthening and extension of social protection measures to keep out of poverty those who are vulnerable or who fall upon hard times and find themselves unable to earn a living income. This universal character, in combination with the scope of the targets, made a goal that may sound a lot like the first MDG but is actually very different indeed (see Box 7.1).

■ **Box 7.1.**

SDG 1. End poverty in all its forms everywhere

1.1 By 2030, eradicate extreme poverty for all people everywhere, currently measured as people living on less than $1.25 a day

1.2 By 2030, reduce at least by half the proportion of men, women and children of all ages living in poverty in all its dimensions according to national definitions

1.3 Implement nationally appropriate social protection systems and measures for all, including floors, and by 2030 achieve substantial coverage of the poor and the vulnerable

1.4 By 2030, ensure that all men and women, in particular the poor and the vulnerable, have equal rights to economic resources, as well as access to basic services, ownership and control over land and other forms of property, inheritance, natural resources, appropriate new technology and financial services, including microfinance

1.5 By 2030, build the resilience of the poor and those in vulnerable situations and reduce their exposure and vulnerability to climate-related extreme events and other economic, social and environmental shocks and disasters

1.a Ensure significant mobilization of resources from a variety of sources, including through enhanced development cooperation, in order to provide adequate and predictable means for developing

(Continues)

countries, in particular least developed countries, to implement programmes and policies to end poverty in all its dimensions

1.b Create sound policy frameworks at the national, regional and international levels, based on pro-poor and gender-sensitive development strategies, to support accelerated investment in poverty eradication actions

SOURCE: https://sustainabledevelopment.un.org/sdg1.

GOAL 2.
End Hunger, Achieve Food Security and Improved Nutrition, and Promote Sustainable Agriculture

Goal 2 evolved from MDG Target 1.c: "Halve, between 1990 and 2015, the proportion of people who suffer from hunger." Delegates agreed that this goal had to be expanded from the MDGs to address the causes of hunger. In this regard, discussions focused on improving agricultural productivity and the incomes of small-scale food producers, improving their access to land and finance, ensuring sustainable food production systems and resilient agricultural practices, and maintaining the genetic diversity of seeds, plants, and animals (see Box 7.2).

OWG participants also wanted to ensure that this goal addressed malnutrition in various dimensions, not just calorie deficiency, by sharply reducing stunting (reduced growth rate caused by malnutrition) and wasting (deficient body weight for a given height). The goal also aimed at universal food security—the ability to access safe, nutritious, and sufficient food all year round.

■ Box 7.2.

SDG 2. End hunger, achieve food security and improved nutrition, and promote sustainable agriculture

2.1 By 2030, end hunger and ensure access by all people, in particular the poor and people in vulnerable situations, including infants, to safe, nutritious and sufficient food all year round

2.2 By 2030, end all forms of malnutrition, including achieving, by 2025, the internationally agreed targets on stunting and wasting in children under 5 years of age, and address the nutritional needs of adolescent girls, pregnant and lactating women and older persons

2.3 By 2030, double the agricultural productivity and incomes of small-scale food producers, in particular women, indigenous peoples, family farmers, pastoralists and fishers, including through secure and equal access to land, other productive resources and inputs, knowledge, financial services, markets and opportunities for value addition and non-farm employment

2.4 By 2030, ensure sustainable food production systems and implement resilient agricultural practices that increase productivity and production, that help maintain ecosystems, that strengthen capacity for adaptation to climate change, extreme weather, drought, flooding and other disasters and that progressively improve land and soil quality

2.5 By 2020, maintain the genetic diversity of seeds, cultivated plants and farmed and domesticated animals and their related wild species, including through soundly managed and diversified seed and plant banks at the national, regional and international levels, and promote access to and fair and equitable sharing of benefits arising from the utilization of genetic resources and associated traditional knowledge, as internationally agreed

2.a Increase investment, including through enhanced international cooperation, in rural infrastructure, agricultural research and extension services, technology development and plant and livestock gene banks in order to enhance agricultural productive capacity in developing countries, in particular least developed countries

2.b Correct and prevent trade restrictions and distortions in world agricultural markets, including through the parallel elimination of all forms of agricultural export subsidies and all export measures with equivalent effect, in accordance with the mandate of the Doha Development Round

(*Continues*)

2.c   Adopt measures to ensure the proper functioning of food
        commodity markets and their derivatives and facilitate timely
        access to market information, including on food reserves,
        in order to help limit extreme food price volatility

SOURCE: https://sustainabledevelopment.un.org/sdg2.

GOAL 3.
Ensure Healthy Lives and Promote
Well-Being for All at All Ages

This goal evolved from MDGs 4 (reduce childhood mortality), 5 (improve maternal health), and 6 (combat HIV/AIDS, malaria and other diseases). Although acknowledging that early childhood mortality, maternal mortality, HIV/AIDS, and malaria were still important problems, OWG participants wanted to broaden the scope. Many supported adding a target on noncommunicable diseases (NCDs), which include cancer, obesity, diabetes, cardiovascular disease, and chronic respiratory diseases. In fact, according to the World Health Organization (WHO), NCDs kill forty million people each year, equivalent to 70 percent of all deaths globally.[5] Some delegates also wanted to include language promoting mental health and well-being, and addressing narcotic drug and alcohol abuse.

Target 3.7, on universal access to sexual and reproductive health care services, was particularly contentious. Although many stressed the necessity of access to sexual and reproductive services, OWG members were divided on the issue of including a target on reproductive and sexual rights (see also the discussion on Goal 5). Saudi Arabia, among others, expressed strong reservations on sexual rights and universal sexual education. Others, including many Western European countries, thought that sexual and reproductive health care services were essential. On the penultimate day of OWG-13, this target was discussed in a contact group chaired by Ambassador Caleb Otto of Palau, but delegates still could not reach agreement. So the co-chairs drafted text on universal access to sexual and reproductive health care services but did not mention rights. Despite some eleventh-hour opposition, Target 3.7 survived.

Another breakthrough was Target 3.8, on universal health coverage (UHC). Achieving UHC has been a challenge for many developing countries as well as the United States, the only major developed country without universal health care. UHC is not a new concept, but its inclusion in the SDGs is a significant acknowledgment that not only will UHC improve the health of millions of people; it will also contribute to achieving many of the other SDGs. According to the WHO, the UHC target is the linchpin of the health-related SDGs.[6] (See Box 7.3.)

■ **Box 7.3.**

SDG 3. Ensure healthy lives and promote well-being for all at all ages

3.1 By 2030, reduce the global maternal mortality ratio to less than 70 per 100,000 live births

3.2 By 2030, end preventable deaths of newborns and children under 5 years of age, with all countries aiming to reduce neonatal mortality to at least as low as 12 per 1,000 live births and under-5 mortality to at least as low as 25 per 1,000 live births

3.3 By 2030, end the epidemics of AIDS, tuberculosis, malaria and neglected tropical diseases and combat hepatitis, water-borne diseases and other communicable diseases

3.4 By 2030, reduce by one third premature mortality from non-communicable diseases through prevention and treatment and promote mental health and well-being

3.5 Strengthen the prevention and treatment of substance abuse, including narcotic drug abuse and harmful use of alcohol

3.6 By 2020, halve the number of global deaths and injuries from road traffic accidents

3.7 By 2030, ensure universal access to sexual and reproductive health-care services, including for family planning, information and education, and the integration of reproductive health into national strategies and programmes

(Continues)

3.8   Achieve universal health coverage, including financial risk protection, access to quality essential health-care services and access to safe, effective, quality and affordable essential medicines and vaccines for all

3.9   By 2030, substantially reduce the number of deaths and illnesses from hazardous chemicals and air, water and soil pollution and contamination

3.a   Strengthen the implementation of the World Health Organization Framework Convention on Tobacco Control in all countries, as appropriate

3.b   Support the research and development of vaccines and medicines for the communicable and non-communicable diseases that primarily affect developing countries, provide access to affordable essential medicines and vaccines, in accordance with the Doha Declaration on the TRIPS Agreement and Public Health, which affirms the right of developing countries to use to the full the provisions in the Agreement on Trade-Related Aspects of Intellectual Property Rights regarding flexibilities to protect public health, and, in particular, provide access to medicines for all

3.c   Substantially increase health financing and the recruitment, development, training and retention of the health workforce in developing countries, especially in least developed countries and small island developing States

3.d   Strengthen the capacity of all countries, in particular developing countries, for early warning, risk reduction and management of national and global health risks

SOURCE: https://sustainabledevelopment.un.org/sdg3.

GOAL 4.
Ensure Inclusive and Equitable Quality Education and Promote Lifelong Learning Opportunities for All

Goal 4 evolved from MDG 2, which focused on universal primary education. Great strides were made as the primary school enrollment rate in developing countries reached 91 percent in 2015, up from 83 percent in 2000.[7] However, many criticized the MDGs' focus on primary education while ignoring the importance of secondary and postsecondary education. Some critics pointed out that pushing for primary education alone resulted in more graduates who did not have the opportunity for further education. Furthermore, MDG 2 failed to ensure a *quality* education because it did not address completion rates, learning outcomes, the availability of qualified teachers, high student-teacher ratios (which were as high as 43:1 in sub-Saharan Africa), school infrastructure, and teaching materials.[8]

The OWG wanted to address these shortcomings, so delegates added targets on quality lifelong learning, including early childhood and preprimary education, free and equitable primary and secondary education, and technical, vocational, and tertiary education. The inclusion of early childhood and preprimary education was in recognition of the growing evidence that what happens developmentally in the first few years of life can have significant long-term implications. There were also calls to eliminate gender disparity in education and to ensure equal access to education and training for persons with disabilities, indigenous peoples, and children in vulnerable situations. Stakeholder groups for each of these constituencies lobbied extensively for their inclusion. The need for quality teachers, scholarships, and improved education facilities was also added (see Box 7.4).

■ **Box 7.4.**

SDG 4. Ensure inclusive and equitable quality education and promote lifelong learning opportunities for all

4.1 By 2030, ensure that all girls and boys complete free, equitable and quality primary and secondary education leading to relevant and effective learning outcomes

4.2 By 2030, ensure that all girls and boys have access to quality early childhood development, care and pre-primary education so that they are ready for primary education

(Continues)

4.3 By 2030, ensure equal access for all women and men to affordable and quality technical, vocational and tertiary education, including university

4.4 By 2030, substantially increase the number of youth and adults who have relevant skills, including technical and vocational skills, for employment, decent jobs and entrepreneurship

4.5 By 2030, eliminate gender disparities in education and ensure equal access to all levels of education and vocational training for the vulnerable, including persons with disabilities, indigenous peoples and children in vulnerable situations

4.6 By 2030, ensure that all youth and a substantial proportion of adults, both men and women, achieve literacy and numeracy

4.7 By 2030, ensure that all learners acquire the knowledge and skills needed to promote sustainable development, including, among others, through education for sustainable development and sustainable lifestyles, human rights, gender equality, promotion of a culture of peace and non-violence, global citizenship and appreciation of cultural diversity and of culture's contribution to sustainable development

4.a Build and upgrade education facilities that are child, disability and gender sensitive and provide safe, non-violent, inclusive and effective learning environments for all

4.b By 2020, substantially expand globally the number of scholarships available to developing countries, in particular least developed countries, small island developing States and African countries, for enrolment in higher education, including vocational training and information and communications technology, technical, engineering and scientific programmes, in developed countries and other developing countries

4.c By 2030, substantially increase the supply of qualified teachers, including through international cooperation for teacher training in developing countries, especially least developed countries and small island developing States

SOURCE: https://sustainabledevelopment.un.org/sdg4.

GOAL 5.
Achieve Gender Equality
and Empower All Women and Girls

Goal 5 evolved from MDG 3, which addressed gender disparity in education, male-female school enrollment ratios, women's employment, and the proportion of seats held by women in national legislatures. Although the education-related MDG targets were absorbed into SDG 4, there was recognition that ending all forms of discrimination against women and girls is not only a basic human right but also has a multiplier effect across all areas of sustainable development. The MDGs had made progress: since 1990, women held 35 percent more jobs outside of agriculture and the average proportion of women in parliaments nearly doubled,[9] but gross inequalities in access to paid employment remained in some regions, with significant gaps between men and women in earnings for comparable work. Sexual violence and exploitation, the unequal division of unpaid care and domestic work, and discrimination in public decision making remained major barriers.

There was little if any debate on the need to end all forms of discrimination against women and girls and to eliminate gender-based violence, including trafficking, sexual, and other types of exploitation. Many called for a target on eliminating all harmful practices, such as child, early, and forced marriage and female genital mutilation. Although India argued that "early" marriage may be too hard to define,[10] it was included.

Many also called for a target that would recognize the value of unpaid care and domestic work, as well as shared responsibility within the household and the family, which was seen as groundbreaking. Egypt, Iran, Indonesia, and Saudi Arabia objected, and as a compromise, the clause "as nationally appropriate" was added to the end of this target, over the objections of other delegates.

The most controversial issue was Target 5.6, on sexual and reproductive health and reproductive rights. As with Target 3.7, a number of conservative countries as well as the Holy See (the Vatican) objected to reference to reproductive and sexual rights. According to the WHO, the definition of reproductive rights may include the following: the right to legal and safe abortion, the right to birth control, the right to reproductive education, and the right to quality reproductive health care.[11] In some cultures and religions, abortion and birth control are forbidden, and the concept of reproductive rights is not recognized. In addition, some, including Nigeria, were concerned that "sexual rights" would apply to the lesbian, gay, bisexual, and transgender (LGBT) community, which they did not support.

In opposition to many participants,[12] Saudi Arabia and Qatar, among others, said there would never be agreement on a target on universal access to sexual and reproductive health and reproductive rights, so it should be deleted. Malta agreed that the term "reproductive rights" was problematic. Zimbabwe, for Southern African States, as well as China/Indonesia/Kazakhstan and Egypt, also suggested reverting to language agreed upon at the 1994 UN Conference on Population and Development (ICPD).[13] The Holy See, supported by Nigeria, said the Rio+20 outcome makes no mention of "reproductive rights," so it shouldn't be included in the SDGs.

Seeing no progress, the co-chairs assigned this target to the OWG-13 contact group chaired by Ambassador Otto, which also addressed Target 3.7, to no avail. As a result, the co-chairs proposed a formulation that included a reference to reproductive rights, but not sexual rights, and a qualifier: "in accordance with the Programme of Action of the ICPD and the Beijing Platform for Action." During the closing plenary, Nigeria, Iran, Honduras, Chad, Saudi Arabia, Egypt, and Sudan, among others, rejected Target 5.6, and some went so far as to threaten to reject the entire goal set if this target remained. Nevertheless, the goal was ultimately accepted (see Box 7.5). Some member states hoped that they could reopen discussions on this target at a later date, but relented once it became clear that the entire package of SDGs would unravel if a single target was reopened (see Chapter 8).

GOAL 6.
Ensure Availability and Sustainable Management of Water and Sanitation for All

Goal 6 emerged from MDG 7, Target 7.c, on halving the proportion of people without sustainable access to safe drinking water and basic sanitation. Many agreed that this goal epitomizes the integrated nature of the SDGs in that its cross-cutting targets address health, pollution, ecosystem

■ **Box 7.5**

SDG 5. Achieve gender equality and empower all women and girls

5.1 End all forms of discrimination against all women and girls everywhere

5.2 Eliminate all forms of violence against all women and girls in the public and private spheres, including trafficking and sexual and other types of exploitation

5.3 Eliminate all harmful practices, such as child, early and forced marriage and female genital mutilation

5.4 Recognize and value unpaid care and domestic work through the provision of public services, infrastructure and social protection policies and the promotion of shared responsibility within the household and the family as nationally appropriate

5.5 Ensure women's full and effective participation and equal opportunities for leadership at all levels of decision-making in political, economic and public life

5.6 Ensure universal access to sexual and reproductive health and reproductive rights as agreed in accordance with the Programme of Action of the International Conference on Population and Development and the Beijing Platform for Action and the outcome documents of their review conferences

5.a Undertake reforms to give women equal rights to economic resources, as well as access to ownership and control over land and other forms of property, financial services, inheritance and natural resources, in accordance with national laws

5.b Enhance the use of enabling technology, in particular information and communications technology, to promote the empowerment of women

5.c Adopt and strengthen sound policies and enforceable legislation for the promotion of gender equality and the empowerment of all women and girls at all levels

SOURCE: https://sustainabledevelopment.un.org/sdg5.

preservation and restoration, and water conservation. Many developing countries also stressed the importance of adequate facilities and infrastructure, both built and natural, for safe drinking water and sanitation systems. This aspect was eventually incorporated into SDG 9, which covers resilient infrastructure. There was some dispute on the inclusion of transboundary cooperation in Target 6.5, on integrated water resources management, largely because of geopolitical conflicts, but this was resolved in a contact group, chaired by Swiss Ambassador Michael Gerber, on the penultimate day of negotiations (see Box 7.6).

■ **Box 7.6**

SDG 6. Ensure availability and sustainable management of water and sanitation for all

6.1   By 2030, achieve universal and equitable access to safe and affordable drinking water for all

6.2   By 2030, achieve access to adequate and equitable sanitation and hygiene for all and end open defecation, paying special attention to the needs of women and girls and those in vulnerable situations

6.3   By 2030, improve water quality by reducing pollution, eliminating dumping and minimizing release of hazardous chemicals and materials, halving the proportion of untreated wastewater and substantially increasing recycling and safe reuse globally

6.4   By 2030, substantially increase water-use efficiency across all sectors and ensure sustainable withdrawals and supply of freshwater to address water scarcity and substantially reduce the number of people suffering from water scarcity

6.5   By 2030, implement integrated water resources management at all levels, including through transboundary cooperation as appropriate

6.6   By 2020, protect and restore water-related ecosystems, including mountains, forests, wetlands, rivers, aquifers and lakes

6.a   By 2030, expand international cooperation and capacity-building support to developing countries in water- and sanitation-related activities and programmes, including water harvesting, desalination, water efficiency, wastewater treatment, recycling and reuse technologies

6.b Support and strengthen the participation of local communities in improving water and sanitation management

SOURCE: https://sustainabledevelopment.un.org/sdg6.

MOVING BEYOND THE MDGS:
ENERGY, ECONOMIC GROWTH, EMPLOYMENT,
AND EQUALITY FOR THE NEW AGENDA

The next four goals represent some of the most transformational SDGs. Goal 7 begins to expand the agenda contained in the MDGs, addressing a number of root causes of poverty and inequality, as well as the linkages among the economic, social, and environmental pillars of sustainable development. With the exception of Goal 7, on energy, many developed countries did not initially support these goals, India's Amit Narang reflected, but the developing countries saw them as an important pillar of the SDGs.[14] The major challenge for the co-chairs was to achieve agreement among member states that were at different stages of—and had different views on—industrialization and economic development.

GOAL 7.
Ensure Access to Affordable, Reliable,
Sustainable, and Modern Energy for All

Energy has increasingly come to be recognized as a basic need, just like water, food, clothing, health care, and education. Nevertheless, one in five people worldwide still lacks access to modern electricity, and three billion still rely on animal waste, charcoal, coal, and wood for heating and cooking.[15] In the OWG, delegates recognized the need for an SDG on energy, which would also contribute to poverty eradication, food security, clean water, public health, education, inclusive and equitable economic growth, and tackling climate change. The big question was how the SDGs could help everyone, especially those in remote areas of the poorest countries, gain access to clean energy.

PHOTO 7.1. Amit Narang, India, consulting with Elizabeth Cousens, US ambassador to the UN Economic and Social Council, during OWG-12 in June 2014. *Photo by IISD/Pamela Chasek (enb.iisd.org)*

For many developing countries the focus was on access to energy irrespective of the technology. For example, the Saudis argued for a goal that would ensure access to affordable, reliable, sustainable, and modern energy for all, including access to clean fossil-fuel technologies.[16] The Saudis and other oil producers did not want to link energy to climate change; in contrast, the small island developing states (SIDS) argued that their survival depends on an urgent shift to renewable energy because of the dangers posed by climate change. They called for a substantial reduction of emissions from energy generation, while at the same time accelerating investment in clean and zero-emission energy technologies.[17] Many developed countries supported green technologies and green energy, but some, especially those heavily reliant on fossil fuels, were not as vocal.

There was broad support for the Secretary-General's Sustainable Energy for All initiative,[18] which already provided a substantial and widely accepted approach to the energy goal, particularly targets aimed at doubling the share of renewable energy in the global energy mix, doubling the rate of improvement of energy efficiency, and ensuring universal access to sustainable modern energy services, all by 2030.[19] This existing support paved the way for consensus on the Goal 7 targets (see Box 7.7).

The most contentious issue in this goal was energy subsidies. Some Western European and North American countries called for a target to phase out fossil-fuel subsidies that encourage wasteful consumption. However, a number of developing countries argued that some countries use energy subsidies to ensure that the poor have access to energy. They pointed out that the elimination of fossil-fuel subsidies cannot be generalized, especially if the SDGs do not leave anyone behind.[20] China and Iran argued that fossil-fuel subsidies were under discussion in other forums and should not even be included in the SDGs.[21] On the penultimate day of OWG-13, the co-chairs assigned this issue to a contact group coordinated by Norway's Marianne Loe. The contact group agreed to eliminate "inefficient" fossil-fuel subsidies, which would therefore allow continued subsidies that provide support for the poorest.[22] Although this target remained, it was eventually moved under Goal 12, on sustainable consumption and production.

■ **Box 7.7**

SDG 7. Ensure access to affordable, reliable, sustainable, and modern energy for all

7.1 By 2030, ensure universal access to affordable, reliable and modern energy services

7.2 By 2030, increase substantially the share of renewable energy in the global energy mix

7.3 By 2030, double the global rate of improvement in energy efficiency

7.a By 2030, enhance international cooperation to facilitate access to clean energy research and technology, including renewable energy, energy efficiency and advanced and cleaner fossil-fuel technology,

(Continues)

and promote investment in energy infrastructure and clean energy technology

7.b By 2030, expand infrastructure and upgrade technology for supplying modern and sustainable energy services for all in developing countries, in particular least developed countries, small island developing States, and land-locked developing countries, in accordance with their respective programmes of support

SOURCE: https://sustainabledevelopment.un.org/sdg7.

GOAL 8.
Promote Sustained, Inclusive and Sustainable Economic Growth, Full and Productive Employment and Decent Work for All

The debate on Goal 8 highlighted two very different views of economic growth. A goal on economic growth was a priority for the developing countries. Bhutan/Thailand/Viet Nam, among others, argued that it is important to underline that sustained economic growth, although not sufficient, is the necessary condition for job creation as well as generation of resources for the realization of the other goals and targets.[23] But many Europeans viewed unconstrained economic growth in potential conflict with sustainability and argued instead that economic growth must be environmentally sustainable growth. If there had to be a goal on economic growth, they believed that such a goal should highlight the positive economic benefits of greener development and decent green jobs.[24] They also urged promoting environmentally sound technologies and avoiding locking in older, environmentally unsound technologies.[25]

As negotiations continued, this goal was reframed to focus more on full and productive employment and decent work for all, which was more likely to achieve consensus. According to the International Labour Organization (ILO), decent work involves opportunities for work that is productive and delivers a fair income; security in the workplace and social protection for families; better prospects for personal development and social integration; freedom for people to express their concerns, organize, and participate in the decisions that affect their work lives; and equality of opportunity and equal treatment for women and men.[26] The focus of many previous development agendas was achieving full employment, with little attention to the type of employment, the level of pay, or the quality of the job. Developing countries argued that access to decent work must be part of the agenda; as Argentina/Bolivia/Ecuador said, the conception of work has to transcend the strictly economic and be defined as a social right.[27] Others, including Bhutan/Thailand/Viet Nam, said that any targets on employment had to include efforts to increase quality employment opportunities for women and persons with disabilities. Brazil/Nicaragua, among others, called for addressing slave and forced labor, the elimination of child labor, and improvement of conditions for migrant workers and their families.[28]

As negotiations progressed, participants began to visualize a different world—one of full and productive employment and decent work. This was another breakthrough. Not only was "decent work" in the title of goal 8, but most of the targets addressed issues of decent work and quality employment for all women and men, young people, and persons with disabilities, as well as the importance of safe and secure working environments (see Box 7.8).

■ **Box 7.8.**

SDG 8. Promote sustained, inclusive and sustainable economic growth, full and productive employment and decent work for all

8.1 Sustain per capita economic growth in accordance with national circumstances and, in particular, at least 7 percent gross domestic product growth per annum in the least developed countries

8.2 Achieve higher levels of economic productivity through diversification, technological upgrading and innovation, including through a focus on high-value added and labor-intensive sectors

8.3 Promote development-oriented policies that support productive activities, decent job creation, entrepreneurship, creativity and

(Continues)

innovation, and encourage the formalization and growth of micro-, small- and medium-sized enterprises, including through access to financial services

8.4 Improve progressively, through 2030, global resource efficiency in consumption and production and endeavor to decouple economic growth from environmental degradation, in accordance with the 10-year framework of programmes on sustainable consumption and production, with developed countries taking the lead

8.5 By 2030, achieve full and productive employment and decent work for all women and men, including for young people and persons with disabilities, and equal pay for work of equal value

8.6 By 2020, substantially reduce the proportion of youth not in employment, education or training

8.7 Take immediate and effective measures to eradicate forced labor, end modern slavery and human trafficking and secure the prohibition and elimination of the worst forms of child labor, including recruitment and use of child soldiers, and by 2025 end child labor in all its forms

8.8 Protect labor rights and promote safe and secure working environments for all workers, including migrant workers, in particular women migrants, and those in precarious employment

8.9 By 2030, devise and implement policies to promote sustainable tourism that creates jobs and promotes local culture and products

8.10 Strengthen the capacity of domestic financial institutions to encourage and expand access to banking, insurance and financial services for all

8.a Increase Aid for Trade support for developing countries, in particular least developed countries, including through the Enhanced Integrated Framework for Trade-Related Technical Assistance to Least Developed Countries

8.b By 2020, develop and operationalize a global strategy for youth employment and implement the Global Jobs Pact of the International Labour Organization

SOURCE: https://sustainabledevelopment.un.org/sdg8.

GOAL 9.
Build Resilient Infrastructure,
Promote Inclusive and Sustainable Industrialization
and Foster Innovation

Goal 9, like Goal 8, was a deal breaker for many developing countries because they knew there could not be prosperity and economic growth without infrastructure development and industrialization. However, many Europeans saw unregulated industrialization as a major cause of pollution and natural resources depletion, so initially they did not think a goal on industrialization was appropriate. Instead, they wanted to stimulate a transition towards an inclusive green economy that would aid sustainable industrialization by improving energy and resource efficiency, phasing out harmful chemicals, reducing waste and pollution, and adopting environmentally sound technologies.[29]

This debate had been going on for decades. On the one side, developing countries argued that developed countries had grown rich through industrialization, so why shouldn't they get the same benefits? On the other side, developed countries were concerned with the impact of industrialization on the environment. But they faced a dilemma. Could they really tell developing countries that they did not have a legitimate argument for wanting to industrialize? To get beyond this argument, everyone had to recognize that industrialization and infrastructure development were critical to poverty eradication, and this does not have to mean the use of dirty technologies from the nineteenth and twentieth centuries. The OWG had to reframe industrialization.

The fast pace of technological progress helped advance the OWG debate. During the course of the negotiations, many shifted their thinking from a heavy-industry, high-polluting view of the world to an ultramodern, clean-energy–driven industrialization model. The same was true for infrastructure. No one denied that infrastructure was necessary for industrialization and economic development. But infrastructure is not monolithic and not uniformly harmful to the environment. Transportation infrastructure—depending on whether it is oriented more heavily towards public or private transport—has very different environmental implications. Further, a move toward electric vehicles necessitates developing infrastructure such as charging stations. Although the manufacture and use of electric vehicles are not without pollution, such vehicles are much cleaner than their predecessors, assuming that electricity infrastructure also shifts toward low-carbon technologies. Moreover, infrastructure includes information and communication technologies, as well as "soft infrastructure" needed to deliver financial, health, and education services, all of which are relatively environmentally benign depending on their energy source.

The Central and Eastern Europeans who were facing deindustrialization recognized that they could benefit from reindustrializing with less-polluting industries, such as information and communication technologies. This also opened the door for the OWG's debate on technology transfer in Goal 17. The G-77 members were able to say that if the developed countries didn't want them to industrialize in the twentieth-century way, they would have to share the best green technologies. Two years earlier at Rio+20, few G-77 members were willing to discuss the green economy. But by 2014, many realized that this is exactly what they needed.

Developing countries weren't the only ones advocating for this goal. Louise Kantrow, on behalf of the business community, considered this goal to be of the utmost importance.[30] She called for policies to encourage innovation, research, development, deployment, and diffusion of new technologies; full access to private finance and investment in basic infrastructure, including road and rail; and electricity generation and supply, including renewable energy.[31]

The eight targets under Goal 9 (see Box 7.9) represented a sea change in the thinking about the relationship among sustainable development, industrialization, infrastructure, and innovation, including research and development, resource use efficiency, and greater adoption of clean and environmentally sound technologies and industrial processes. As the OWG kept collecting more evidence about the interplay among poverty, industrialization, the economy, and the environment, participants began to see how the various pieces of the puzzle fit together and what opportunities could be created. Before, the United Nations had always discussed these issues in silos or in oppositional terms, but now everyone began to see just how integrated the global development agenda truly was.

■ **Box 7.9.**

SDG 9. Build resilient infrastructure, promote inclusive and sustainable industrialization and foster innovation

9.1 Develop quality, reliable, sustainable and resilient infrastructure, including regional and transborder infrastructure, to support economic development and human well-being, with a focus on affordable and equitable access for all

9.2 Promote inclusive and sustainable industrialization and, by 2030, significantly raise industry's share of employment and gross domestic product, in line with national circumstances, and double its share in least developed countries

9.3 Increase the access of small-scale industrial and other enterprises, in particular in developing countries, to financial services, including affordable credit, and their integration into value chains and markets

9.4 By 2030, upgrade infrastructure and retrofit industries to make them sustainable, with increased resource-use efficiency and greater adoption of clean and environmentally sound technologies and industrial processes, with all countries taking action in accordance with their respective capabilities

9.5 Enhance scientific research, upgrade the technological capabilities of industrial sectors in all countries, in particular developing countries, including, by 2030, encouraging innovation and substantially increasing the number of research and development workers per 1 million people and public and private research and development spending

9.a Facilitate sustainable and resilient infrastructure development in developing countries through enhanced financial, technological and technical support to African countries, least developed countries, landlocked developing countries and small island developing States

9.b Support domestic technology development, research and innovation in developing countries, including by ensuring a conducive policy environment for, inter alia, industrial diversification and value addition to commodities

(Continues)

9.c Significantly increase access to information and communications technology and strive to provide universal and affordable access to the Internet in least developed countries by 2020

SOURCE: https://sustainabledevelopment.un.org/sdg9.

GOAL 10.
Reduce Inequality Within and Among Countries

As described in earlier chapters, the inclusion of a goal on reducing inequalities within and among countries was never a given. Brazil made the most impassioned pleas for this goal, particularly for reducing inequalities among countries: "If we want to be universal in our aspirations and effective in reducing inequality among human beings such asymmetry and their [*sic*] root causes need to be addressed."[32]

However, the Americans pushed back on a goal to reduce inequalities, especially among countries. In a statement, also on behalf of Canada and Israel, US Ambassador Elizabeth Cousens said the following:

> We are less convinced by a standalone goal on inequality. This could lead us to a sterile debate that economists have been having for generations and that we are unlikely to resolve here. We see much greater practical potential and concrete impact in addressing inequality through goals and targets related to poverty eradication; equal access to productive and other assets; social protection floors; gender equality; elimination of discriminatory practices, policies, and laws; and job-rich and inclusive growth. These types of measures will be a much more concrete way to hard-wire real action to reduce inequalities into our agenda.[33]

Others agreed that whether in a stand-alone goal or across multiple goals, inequality within nations had to be addressed, particularly with regard to income, gender, social inequalities, and lack of access to elements that enable upward economic mobility. After the stocktaking process and Joseph Stiglitz's presentation (described in Chapter 4), inequality within countries was recognized as a universal problem. However, developed countries—and even some developing countries—were wary about being told just how to reduce these inequalities.

The question about inequalities among nations raised different concerns. This had the potential of raising historical grievances, including the impoverishment of the global South through decades of wealth extraction where the North benefited at the expense of the South. Some saw neoliberal policies, including the deregulation of capital markets, structural adjustment policies, and agricultural subsidies and trade agreements that benefited the North, as just another way of extracting wealth and resources from the South.[34]

But there was a philosophical and conceptual breakthrough. By drafting a target—inspired by the World Bank—that focused on the relative position of the poorest 40 percent of a country's population, the co-chairs were able to slowly build consensus. Other targets addressed social, economic, and political inclusion, ensuring equal opportunity through legislation, fiscal and social protection policies, improved regulation of global financial markets, and well-managed migration policies. Target 10.6 also called for a greater voice for the developing world in global economic and financial institutions, over the objections of the United States/Canada/Israel and a few others (see Box 7.10).

The careful drafting of the targets, in addition to the repeated interventions by developing countries and strong support from civil society organizations, made Goal 10 possible. As the NGO Third World Network noted, this goal "signaled an openness to engage with complex and difficult issues that matter critically for sustainable development."[35]

■ **Box 7.10.**

SDG 10. Reduce inequality within and among countries

10.1 By 2030, progressively achieve and sustain income growth of the bottom 40 percent of the population at a rate higher than the national average

(Continues)

10.2 By 2030, empower and promote the social, economic and political inclusion of all, irrespective of age, sex, disability, race, ethnicity, origin, religion or economic or other status

10.3 Ensure equal opportunity and reduce inequalities of outcome, including by eliminating discriminatory laws, policies and practices and promoting appropriate legislation, policies and action in this regard

10.4 Adopt policies, especially fiscal, wage and social protection policies, and progressively achieve greater equality

10.5 Improve the regulation and monitoring of global financial markets and institutions and strengthen the implementation of such regulations

10.6 Ensure enhanced representation and voice for developing countries in decision-making in global international economic and financial institutions in order to deliver more effective, credible, accountable and legitimate institutions

10.7 Facilitate orderly, safe, regular and responsible migration and mobility of people, including through the implementation of planned and well-managed migration policies

10.a Implement the principle of special and differential treatment for developing countries, in particular least developed countries, in accordance with World Trade Organization agreements

10.b Encourage official development assistance and financial flows, including foreign direct investment, to States where the need is greatest, in particular least developed countries, African countries, small island developing States and landlocked developing countries, in accordance with their national plans and programmes

10.c By 2030, reduce to less than 3 percent the transaction costs of migrant remittances and eliminate remittance corridors with costs higher than 5 percent

SOURCE: https://sustainabledevelopment.un.org/sdg10.

URBANIZATION, CONSUMPTION PATTERNS, CLIMATE, AND THE ENVIRONMENT

The next five goals look at the impact that humans have on the natural environment and how this has affected both social and economic development. Goals 11 and 12 point to how people organize their lives, how they behave, and how they choose to live, consume, and produce. Goals 13, 14, and 15 examine the environmental dimension of sustainable development while incorporating social and economic concerns.

GOAL 11.
Make Cities and Human Settlements Inclusive, Safe, Resilient and Sustainable

The urban share of the world's population is expected to rise from 52 percent in 2010 to around 67 percent in 2050. Likewise, the urban share of gross domestic product (GDP) and employment will rise. If managed well, urbanization can create employment, stimulate innovation and economic growth, and become a central driver for ending extreme poverty. If urbanization is managed poorly, cities will deepen social exclusion and fail to generate enough jobs.[36] With this as the backdrop, in its call for a goal on sustainable urban development the UN Sustainable Development Solutions Network (SDSN) said, "An urban SDG is therefore important to mobilize and bring together the efforts of multiple actors and stakeholders (e.g. local authorities, national governments, businesses, knowledge institutions, and civil society) across a range of urban issues (e.g. urban jobs, housing, infrastructure, governance, disaster risk reduction, and climate change adaptation and mitigation) and mobilize the financial, institutional, and human resources to make this possible."[37]

The Major Group on Local Authorities, which brings together organizations that represent city, local, and subnational governments, agreed, noting that a stand-alone goal on sustainable urbanization would help mobilize local and subnational authorities, some of the key stakeholders in implementing the SDGs.[38] Although many supported this goal, some were a bit wary of a stand-alone goal on cities, particularly if it created an artificial distinction between urban and rural environments, livelihoods and issues.[39]

For example, India/Pakistan/Sri Lanka called for a broader approach to address all human settlements, including those in rural areas, where a large proportion of people, especially poor people, in developing countries live.[40] This issue was eventually resolved by referring to human settlements in the goal and including a target supporting positive economic, social, and environmental links among urban, peri-urban, and rural areas (see Box 7.11).

India also called for differentiation in this goal, noting that there is no one-size-fits-all approach to urban development. In developing countries, India noted, key urban challenges include providing functional cities and basic infrastructure and services, slum improvement, and job opportunities. On the other hand, India noted, key challenges facing developed-country cities include reducing use of private automobiles, energy efficiency, renovation and retrofitting of infrastructure, and increased resource efficiency.[41] The co-chairs, who wished to avoid this level of differentiation in a universal agenda, responded by ensuring that the targets address the needs of both developing and developed countries, from upgrading slums to reducing the adverse per capita environmental impacts of cities.

■ **Box 7.11.**

SDG 11. Make cities and human settlements inclusive, safe, resilient and sustainable

11.1 By 2030, ensure access for all to adequate, safe and affordable housing and basic services and upgrade slums

11.2 By 2030, provide access to safe, affordable, accessible and sustainable transport systems for all, improving road safety, notably by expanding public transport, with special attention to the needs of those in vulnerable situations, women, children, persons with disabilities and older persons

11.3 By 2030, enhance inclusive and sustainable urbanization and capacity for participatory, integrated and sustainable human settlement planning and management in all countries

11.4 Strengthen efforts to protect and safeguard the world's cultural and natural heritage

11.5 By 2030, significantly reduce the number of deaths and
the number of people affected and substantially decrease the
direct economic losses relative to global gross domestic product
caused by disasters, including water-related disasters, with a
focus on protecting the poor and people in vulnerable situations

11.6 By 2030, reduce the adverse per capita environmental impact
of cities, including by paying special attention to air quality and
municipal and other waste management

11.7 By 2030, provide universal access to safe, inclusive and accessible,
green and public spaces, in particular for women and children,
older persons and persons with disabilities

11.a Support positive economic, social and environmental links between
urban, peri-urban and rural areas by strengthening national and
regional development planning

11.b By 2020, substantially increase the number of cities and human
settlements adopting and implementing integrated policies and
plans towards inclusion, resource efficiency, mitigation and
adaptation to climate change, resilience to disasters, and develop
and implement, in line with the Sendai Framework for Disaster
Risk Reduction 2015–2030, holistic disaster risk management
at all levels

11.c Support least developed countries, including through financial
and technical assistance, in building sustainable and resilient
buildings utilizing local materials

SOURCE: https://sustainabledevelopment.un.org/sdg11.

GOAL 12.
Ensure Sustainable Consumption and Production Patterns

Goal 12 is a "messaging" goal because many recognize that production and consumption habits are at the root of the planet's sustainability problems. Many more people are expected to join the middle class over the next two decades, and although this is good for individual prosperity, it will increase demand for already constrained natural resources and place additional stresses on the environment. In fact, should the global population reach 9.6 billion by 2050, the equivalent of almost three planets would be required to provide the natural resources needed to sustain current lifestyles. Moreover, each year an estimated one-third of all food produced—equivalent to 1.3 billion tons—ends up rotting in the bins of consumers and retailers or spoiling because of poor harvesting, storage, and transportation practices.[42]

However, the discussions on sustainable consumption and production (SCP) carried baggage from twenty-five years of North-South sustainable development negotiations. Some argued that an SCP goal was not needed because sustainable consumption and production would be embedded in other goals, but not everyone was willing to accept this argument. As with gender and climate change, those who were focused on SCP were passionate about the fact that without a stand-alone goal, the concept would be lost. Moreover, a goal on sustainable consumption and production was considered central to establishing the universality of the agenda: developed countries generally have the highest per capita rates of consumption and resource use, so this goal is clearly their business. Although some developed countries continued to oppose a stand-alone goal, it was finally accepted by the developed-country holdouts in a deal with developing countries for Goal 16 (see below).

The final set of targets for Goal 12 (see Box 7.12) covers the consumer and business sectors, supply chains and procurement, waste minimization, and education and awareness raising, and may in fact underpin the other SDGs, from poverty eradication to peace and justice. However, in an increasingly consumption-influenced world, where many aspire to Western lifestyles, producing and consuming less poses a major challenge.[43]

■ **Box 7.12.**

SDG 12. Ensure sustainable consumption and production patterns

12.1 Implement the 10-year framework of programmes on sustainable consumption and production, all countries taking action, with developed countries taking the lead, taking into account the development and capabilities of developing countries

12.2 By 2030, achieve the sustainable management and efficient use of natural resources

12.3 By 2030, halve per capita global food waste at the retail and consumer levels and reduce food losses along production and supply chains, including post-harvest losses

12.4 By 2020, achieve the environmentally sound management of chemicals and all wastes throughout their life cycle, in accordance with agreed international frameworks, and significantly reduce their release to air, water and soil in order to minimize their adverse impacts on human health and the environment

12.5 By 2030, substantially reduce waste generation through prevention, reduction, recycling and reuse

12.6 Encourage companies, especially large and transnational companies, to adopt sustainable practices and to integrate sustainability information into their reporting cycle

12.7 Promote public procurement practices that are sustainable, in accordance with national policies and priorities

12.8 By 2030, ensure that people everywhere have the relevant information and awareness for sustainable development and lifestyles in harmony with nature

12.a Support developing countries to strengthen their scientific and technological capacity to move towards more sustainable patterns of consumption and production

12.b Develop and implement tools to monitor sustainable development impacts for sustainable tourism that creates jobs and promotes local culture and products

12.c Rationalize inefficient fossil-fuel subsidies that encourage wasteful consumption by removing market distortions, in accordance with national circumstances, including by restructuring taxation and phasing out those harmful subsidies, where they exist, to reflect their environmental impacts, taking fully into account the specific needs and conditions of developing countries and minimizing the possible adverse impacts on their development in a manner that protects the poor and the affected communities

SOURCE: https://sustainabledevelopment.un.org/sdg12.

GOAL 13.
Take Urgent Action to
Combat Climate Change and Its Impacts

Whether or not to have a stand-alone goal on climate change was a question that pervaded the SDG negotiations. Everyone admitted that climate change would affect the entire agenda. The problem was the overlap with the ongoing United Nations Framework Convention on Climate Change (UNFCCC) negotiations. The negotiations on a new global climate agreement, which had stalled in Copenhagen in 2009, had been reinvigorated under the leadership of UNFCCC Executive Secretary Christiana Figueres and were set to conclude in December 2015 in Paris. Many participants were worried about having a debate on climate change in the OWG that could hinder or prejudge an agreement in Paris, especially regarding a temperature target and the principle of common but differentiated responsibilities (CBDR).

Some countries were adamant that this was not the forum for negotiating climate change. Even the UNFCCC executive secretary urged the co-chairs not to include a climate goal that might compete with the UNFCCC. However, SIDS saw climate change as an issue that was so important that it deserved to be addressed across the SDGs. Even those who called for a stand-alone goal still supported its cross-cutting nature. Civil society members strongly supported both a stand-alone goal and mainstreaming climate change across all of the goals.[44]

Governments did not want to reveal their hand in the OWG when they were approaching the endgame of the climate change negotiations, especially if they wanted to extract last-minute concessions from their negotiating partners. Developing countries were not yet willing to concede on CBDR in Paris, still insisting that industrialized countries had to take the lead in reduction of greenhouse gas emissions. However, they also had to come to terms with the fact that the SDGs were universal and applicable to all countries, which which could be seen as at odds with the CBDR principle. But if they relented on CBDR in the SDGs, what would be the implications under the UNFCCC? A few countries said that if the SDGs were to have a climate change goal, then it should also contain a temperature target. Yet the debate between holding the increase in the global average temperature to either 2°C or the more ambitious 1.5°C was resolved only at the eleventh hour in Paris. It seemed unlikely that the SIDS would have been willing to concede to a 2°C target in the SDGs when they were trying to have a stronger reference to 1.5°C in Paris.[45]

In the meantime, the co-chairs met bilaterally with delegations and lobbied them on the inclusion of the climate goal, working hard to convince countries such as South Africa, the United States, and China that this was in their best interest. At one point even the SIDS were persuaded by some developed countries to delete the climate goal because they would get a better deal out of the UNFCCC negotiations. The co-chairs were shocked. Kamau met with the SIDS behind closed doors and asked them to stand by this goal, and they were eventually persuaded.

Outside forces also helped. Jeffrey Sachs wrote a series of editorials and also personally helped to mobilize the White House, the vatican, and others. France, the host of the Paris Conference, and other European countries

PHOTO 7.2. Jeffrey Sachs, Sustainable Development Solutions Network and Columbia University, wrote a series of editorials and also personally helped to mobilize the White House and others. *Photo by IISD/Francis Dejon (enb.iisd.org)*

advocated for a climate goal. Many tugged at delegates' consciences, including Kőrösi, who said that he couldn't go home and face his young
daughter if they completed the SDGs without a goal on climate change, the
biggest threat to her future.[46] The absence of a climate goal in a set of sustainable development goals risked undermining their credibility in the
eyes of the wider world.

Goal 13 finally survived, even if lacking in crucial details such as a temperature target (see Box 7.13). As a compromise, the OWG included a footnote to the goal acknowledging that the UNFCCC is the primary
international, intergovernmental forum for negotiating the global response
to climate change. Did the inclusion of a climate change goal in the SDGs
influence the Paris outcome? Probably not in terms of its substance, but
possibly by creating a positive momentum towards a reasonably ambitious
deal in Paris.[47]

■ **Box 7.13.**

SDG 13. Take urgent action to combat climate change and its impacts*

13.1 Strengthen resilience and adaptive capacity to climate-related
hazards and natural disasters in all countries

13.2 Integrate climate change measures into national policies, strategies
and planning

13.3 Improve education, awareness-raising and human and institutional
capacity on climate change mitigation, adaptation, impact
reduction and early warning

13.a Implement the commitment undertaken by developed-country
parties to the United Nations Framework Convention on Climate
Change to a goal of mobilizing jointly $100 billion annually by
2020 from all sources to address the needs of developing countries
in the context of meaningful mitigation actions and transparency on
implementation and fully operationalize the Green Climate Fund
through its capitalization as soon as possible

13.b Promote mechanisms for raising capacity for effective climate
change-related planning and management in least developed

countries and small island developing States, including focusing on women, youth and local and marginalized communities

SOURCE: *Acknowledging that the United Nations Framework Convention on Climate Change is the primary international, intergovernmental forum for negotiating the global response to climate change. https://sustainabledevelopment.un.org/sdg13.

GOAL 14.
Conserve and Sustainably Use the Oceans, Seas and Marine Resources for Sustainable Development

Although oceans and marine resources were discussed during the stock-taking phase, there might not have been a dedicated ocean goal if it were not for the efforts of the Pacific SIDS. Tommy Remengesau, Jr., president of the Republic of Palau, came to OWG-8 in February 2014. Calling SIDS "large ocean states," he made an impassioned plea for a goal on oceans and seas. He said that such a goal should meet three main targets: a healthy and well-managed marine environment, healthy fish stocks, and assistance to LDCs, African countries, and SIDS so they could realize the benefits of their sustainably developed marine resources.[48] This speech from the only head of state to attend the OWG gave momentum to this goal.

A few delegations called for merging the proposed goals on oceans and terrestrial ecosystems, but the vast majority, in the words of New Zealand, "opposed any effort to undermine the dedicated and integrated approach the co-chairs have taken to oceans and seas."[49] The United States "loved the idea of an oceans goal" but was wary that a specific goal for oceans could open the floodgates for other ecosystem goals regarding mountains and forests, which would lead to goal proliferation.[50] However, by OWG-12 there was strong support for two separate goals, one on oceans and seas and one on terrestrial ecosystems.

On the targets (see Box 7.14), delegates wanted to ensure they did not impinge on other negotiations on fisheries subsidies under the World Trade Organization (WTO), on marine biodiversity in areas beyond national jurisdiction under the UN General Assembly, and under the UN Convention on the Law of the Sea (UNCLOS). In fact, the most contentious issue during the negotiations related to UNCLOS. Adopted in 1982, it defines the rights and responsibilities of nations with respect to their use of the world's oceans, establishing guidelines for businesses, the environment, and the management of marine natural resources. To date, UNCLOS has been ratified by 168 countries. UN member states that are not parties to UNCLOS did not think it was appropriate to reference the full implementation of UNCLOS in Target 14.c. For example, Venezuela referred to this target as a "very, very thick red line" and wanted to delete the reference to UNCLOS or specify that this target is only "for states parties to UNCLOS." Others underscored that the specific reference to UNCLOS was essential in this target.[51] When the co-chairs redrafted Target 14.c to add in Venezuela's proposed qualifier, others argued that the target was now too weak. A number of states, including Mexico, Argentina/Bolivia/Ecuador, and Venezuela, still expressed reservations on this target during the closing plenary but did not block consensus.[52]

■ **Box 7.14**

SDG 14. Conserve and sustainably use the oceans, seas and marine resources for sustainable development

14.1   By 2025, prevent and significantly reduce marine pollution of all kinds, in particular from land-based activities, including marine debris and nutrient pollution

14.2   By 2020, sustainably manage and protect marine and coastal ecosystems to avoid significant adverse impacts, including by strengthening their resilience, and take action for their restoration in order to achieve healthy and productive oceans

14.3   Minimize and address the impacts of ocean acidification, including through enhanced scientific cooperation at all levels

14.4   By 2020, effectively regulate harvesting and end overfishing, illegal, unreported and unregulated fishing and destructive fishing practices and implement science-based management plans, in order to restore fish stocks in the shortest time feasible, at least to levels that can produce maximum sustainable yield as determined by their biological characteristics

14.5   By 2020, conserve at least 10 percent of coastal and marine areas, consistent with national and international law and based on the best available scientific information

14.6   By 2020, prohibit certain forms of fisheries subsidies which contribute to overcapacity and overfishing, eliminate subsidies that contribute to illegal, unreported and unregulated fishing and refrain from introducing new such subsidies, recognizing that appropriate and effective special and differential treatment for developing and least developed countries should be an integral part of the World Trade Organization fisheries subsidies negotiation

14.7   By 2030, increase the economic benefits to small island developing States and least developed countries from the sustainable use of marine resources, including through sustainable management of fisheries, aquaculture and tourism

14.a   Increase scientific knowledge, develop research capacity and transfer marine technology, taking into account the Intergovernmental Oceanographic Commission Criteria and Guidelines on the Transfer of Marine Technology, in order to improve ocean health and to enhance the contribution of marine biodiversity to the development of developing countries, in particular small island developing States and least developed countries

14.b   Provide access for small-scale artisanal fishers to marine resources and markets

14.c   Enhance the conservation and sustainable use of oceans and their resources by implementing international law as reflected in UNCLOS, which provides the legal framework for the conservation and sustainable use of oceans and their resources, as recalled in paragraph 158 of The Future We Want

SOURCE: https://sustainabledevelopment.un.org/sdg14.

GOAL 15.
Protect, Restore and Promote Sustainable Use of Terrestrial Ecosystems, Sustainably Manage Forests, Combat Desertification, and Halt and Reverse Land Degradation and Halt Biodiversity Loss

With different constituencies supporting targets on conservation and restoration of ecosystems, biodiversity conservation, sustainable forest management, combating desertification, avoiding habitat loss, cracking down on poaching and trafficking of protected species of flora and fauna, preventing the introduction of invasive alien species, and protecting natural and cultural heritage, mountains, and wetlands, the challenge with this goal was to come up with a limited set of targets where each member state and civil society organization could see its issues of concern. Yet many wanted to include all of these issues not only in the targets but also in the title of the goal. Despite the co-chairs' best intentions, they were never able to get agreement on the concise goal title that they wanted.

Another complicating factor was ensuring that the targets were consistent with existing international treaties, including the Convention on Biological Diversity (CBD), the UN Convention to Combat Desertification (UNCCD), the Convention on International Trade in Endangered Species of Wild Fauna and Flora (CITES), and the Ramsar Convention on Wetlands. Two of these proved to be particularly challenging.

The first was the Aichi Biodiversity Targets, which had been adopted by the CBD in 2010, to be achieved by 2020. The twenty Aichi targets range from reducing direct pressure on biodiversity and mainstreaming nature across different sectors to promoting sustainable use and providing benefits to all from biodiversity and ecosystem services.[53] Although most OWG members and stakeholders supported SDG targets that were consistent with the Aichi targets, others argued that many of the targets were already covered by the CBD, so there was no need to repeat them in Goal 15. The second challenge was the dates: the deadline for the Aichi targets was 2020, but the deadline for the SDGs was 2030. The CBD Secretariat and some delegations were resistant to having Aichi-like targets for 2030 because that would undermine the actual Aichi 2020 deadline. A compromise resulted in nine targets related to the Aichi targets (6.6, 14.2, 14.4, 14.5, 15.1, 15.2, 15.5, 15.8, and 15.9—see Boxes 7.6, 7.14, and 7.15) containing a 2020 deadline.[54]

A second challenge was Target 15.3's reference to achieving a land degradation neutral world (LDNW). At OWG-3 in May 2013, then UNCCD Executive Secretary Luc Gnacadja proposed an SDG target aiming to achieve a LDNW by 2030. He argued that productive land is central to the poverty, food, water, energy, and environmental health nexus at the heart of sustainable development.[55] Thus, land degradation neutrality, "a state whereby the amount and quality of land resources necessary to support ecosystem functions and services and enhance food security remain stable or increase within specified temporal and spatial scales and ecosystems,"[56] would add value to the SDGs.

During the negotiations, many supported the LDNW language; however, a constituency of Latin American countries and the United States objected. Brazil/Nicaragua argued that LDNW could not be translated into targets and indicators and that despite its inclusion in paragraph 206 of the Rio+20 outcome, its feasibility was not technically confirmed.[57]

Others were concerned that an LDNW target could allow some countries to "trade" land with other countries, thus allowing them to continue to degrade their own land. Proponents stressed that the phrase is "not a license to degrade."[58] The United States continued to object to this target during the closing plenary: "We continue to have major concerns that this concept could undermine decades of conservation and development efforts and lead to increased land degradation. True neutrality can only be achieved at the scale of national, subnational, and local landscapes."[59] Even though they still objected, the United States, Brazil, and a few others did not block consensus.

THE ENABLING ENVIRONMENT

The final two goals create the enabling environment for the achievement of the SDGs and were among the most difficult to negotiate. As discussed in Chapter 4, human rights, peace and security, and rule of law were "new" to the sustainable development agenda. But acceptance of Goal 16 sent a powerful signal that these issues are fundamentally important for achieving sustainable development. The means of implementation (MOI) targets in Goal 17 represent one of the overarching debates of the process: how will the goals and targets be implemented, what technological and financial resources will be needed, and who will pay?

■ **Box 7.15**

SDG 15. Protect, restore and promote sustainable use of terrestrial ecosystems, sustainably manage forests, combat desertification, and halt and reverse land degradation and halt biodiversity loss

15.1 By 2020, ensure the conservation, restoration and sustainable use of terrestrial and inland freshwater ecosystems and their services, in particular forests, wetlands, mountains and drylands, in line with obligations under international agreements

15.2 By 2020, promote the implementation of sustainable management of all types of forests, halt deforestation, restore degraded forests and substantially increase afforestation and reforestation globally

15.3 By 2030, combat desertification, restore degraded land and soil, including land affected by desertification, drought and floods, and strive to achieve a land degradation-neutral world

15.4 By 2030, ensure the conservation of mountain ecosystems, including their biodiversity, in order to enhance their capacity to provide benefits that are essential for sustainable development

15.5 Take urgent and significant action to reduce the degradation of natural habitats, halt the loss of biodiversity and, by 2020, protect and prevent the extinction of threatened species

15.6 Promote fair and equitable sharing of the benefits arising from the utilization of genetic resources and promote appropriate access to such resources, as internationally agreed

15.7   Take urgent action to end poaching and trafficking of protected species of flora and fauna and address both demand and supply of illegal wildlife products

15.8   By 2020, introduce measures to prevent the introduction and significantly reduce the impact of invasive alien species on land and water ecosystems and control or eradicate the priority species

15.9   By 2020, integrate ecosystem and biodiversity values into national and local planning, development processes, poverty reduction strategies and accounts

15.a   Mobilize and significantly increase financial resources from all sources to conserve and sustainably use biodiversity and ecosystems

15.b   Mobilize significant resources from all sources and at all levels to finance sustainable forest management and provide adequate incentives to developing countries to advance such management, including for conservation and reforestation

15.c   Enhance global support for efforts to combat poaching and trafficking of protected species, including by increasing the capacity of local communities to pursue sustainable livelihood opportunities

SOURCE: https://sustainabledevelopment.un.org/sdg15.

GOAL 16.
Promote Peaceful and Inclusive Societies for Sustainable Development, Provide Access to Justice for All and Build Effective, Accountable and Inclusive Institutions at All Levels

The idea for a goal addressing peace and security and good governance emerged from the UN System Task Team Report on the Post-2015 Development Agenda (see Chapter 4), when the report proposed a fourth pillar of sustainable development: "Peace and security, including freedom from political persecution, discrimination and all forms of violence, are critical for development and a major component of it."[60] However, not everyone was convinced that these issues should be part of the SDGs. As India's Amit Narang stated at OWG-10,

> The relationship between peace and development is self-evident. However, we feel that in this group we would do well to focus on the developmental links of peace rather than the other way round. We should focus on how development leads to peace and not how peace can link to development. . . . There can be no durable peace without economic growth and development and this group can and will make a lasting contribution to the creation of peace, if we are able to create conditions for rapid sustained and inclusive economic growth and put the world on a more sustainable pathway. For this reason, we are not fully convinced with the need to have a separate goal on peace and security.[61]

Many developing countries and emerging economies agreed. In the words of Nicaragua/Brazil, these issues were "a distraction that runs the risk of deviating us from the core social, economic and environmental challenges we have been mandated to address."[62] Also, there were other important institutions and forums that could discuss these issues.[63] On the other hand, many developed countries supported two separate goals, one on stable and peaceful societies and one on good governance, rule of law, and effective institutions.

During OWG-8, Austrian Ambassador Martin Sajdik, on behalf of the twenty-two members of the Group of Friends of the Rule of Law, bridging North and South, East and West, noted that rule of law and development are strongly interrelated and mutually reinforcing, and stressed that the rule of law must be considered by the OWG.[64] Timor-Leste Ambassador Sofia Borges described her country's experience with war and recognized that resilience and peace are central to eradicating poverty and achieving sustainable and inclusive development, adding "Only through this inclusion can the post-2015 development framework be transformative and leave no one behind."[65] Timor Leste and several African countries that had recently emerged from violent conflicts used their moral authority to push for this goal. Their activism prevented a G-77 consensus to drop the goal and contributed to its eventual adoption.

By OWG-13, there was still no consensus. The emerging economies (China, Brazil, and India) argued vociferously that there is no intergovernmentally agreed-upon definition of "rule of law" and that they did not want to be subject to a "Western" definition in their own sovereign states. Given the impasse, the co-chairs established a contact group coordinated by Peruvian Ambassador Gustavo Meza-Cuadra on the penultimate day of OWG-13. Reporting back to the OWG co-chairs the following evening, Meza-Cuadra said that although they could not reach consensus, they did have a common understanding that a goal would be feasible and asked the co-chairs to move this forward.[66]

When plenary discussions resumed, China complained that the OWG had spent more time on this goal than on the rest of the other goals together. Brazil, supported by Cuba and Saudi Arabia, said a goal without consensus is a nonexistent goal. India was willing to negotiate but didn't think the objective of the OWG's negotiations was to achieve peace. Egypt, supported by Saudi Arabia, Syria, and Palestine, argued that people under foreign occupation had to be included. When the co-chairs suspended discussion at 12:45 A.M., it still wasn't clear that Goal 16 could be adopted.[67] The co-chairs were worried that those who did not want this goal would be willing to "throw out the baby with the bathwater" and reject the SDGs.

Through the use of bilateral and small group discussions, the co-chairs were able to do some horse trading and leveraged acceptance of Goal 16 in exchange for the goals on inequality, industrialization, and sustainable consumption and production. By dealing with this goal last, the co-chairs were able to engineer the trade-off. Once there was tacit agreement to have a single goal that did not mention rule of law in the title, the group was also able to agree on the language on peaceful and inclusive societies (see Box 7.16). This successful outcome stemmed from countries' being able to express their own views with their own voices, rather than only hearing the voices of larger regional or interest groups, such as the G-77 or the European Union, as well as from a willingness on all sides to compromise.[68]

■ **Box 7.16**

SDG 16. Promote peaceful and inclusive societies for sustainable development, provide access to justice for all and build effective, accountable and inclusive institutions at all levels

16.1 Significantly reduce all forms of violence and related death rates everywhere

16.2 End abuse, exploitation, trafficking and all forms of violence against and torture of children

16.3 Promote the rule of law at the national and international levels and ensure equal access to justice for all

16.4 By 2030, significantly reduce illicit financial and arms flows, strengthen the recovery and return of stolen assets and combat all forms of organized crime

16.5 Substantially reduce corruption and bribery in all their forms

16.6 Develop effective, accountable and transparent institutions at all levels

16.7 Ensure responsive, inclusive, participatory and representative decision-making at all levels

16.8 Broaden and strengthen the participation of developing countries in the institutions of global governance

16.9 By 2030, provide legal identity for all, including birth registration

16.10 Ensure public access to information and protect fundamental freedoms, in accordance with national legislation and international agreements

16.a Strengthen relevant national institutions, including through international cooperation, for building capacity at all levels, in particular in developing countries, to prevent violence and combat terrorism and crime

16.b Promote and enforce non-discriminatory laws and policies for sustainable development

SOURCE: https://sustainabledevelopment.un.org/sdg16.

GOAL 17.
Strengthen the Means of Implementation and Revitalize the Global Partnership for Sustainable Development

Everyone knew there could not be a credible goal set that did not include the means of implementation. But an underlying issue was how MOI would appear in a universal agenda where, historically, developed countries supported developing countries through bilateral and multilateral assistance. How would financing be addressed in a universal agenda and in a world where the per capita GDP of some "developing" countries exceeded that of some European countries that were among the traditional providers of development assistance?

As the discussions on Goal 17 and on the MOI targets that appeared in the other goals (the targets denoted by letters—e.g., 3.a—are MOI targets) progressed, the understanding of CBDR also evolved. Unlike the twentieth-century versions of CBDR, as enshrined in Agenda 21 and the UNFCCC, the OWG recognized that the SDGs are a universal agenda and everyone has to work together, acknowledging that countries and people are starting from different places with different capabilities. The chances of achieving the SDGs and targets depend on how much each country had succeeded in development in the past, the co-chairs argued, recognizing that the LDCs clearly had the greatest journey to achieve the goals. The LDCs needed assurance that they would have the MOI to support their efforts.

Some developed countries argued that the OWG should not consider MOI because the financial elements fell under the mandate of the Intergovernmental Committee of Experts on Sustainable Development Financing, which was established by Rio+20, the 2015 Third International Conference on Financing for Development (FfD), the follow-up process to the 2011 Busan Conference on Aid Effectiveness, and the UNFCCC (in the case of climate finance) and WTO negotiations (in the case of trade).[69] Peru advocated against waiting for the conclusion of other processes, suggesting that the OWG represented governments' opportunity to create synergies across processes. Moreover, as India commented, "We cannot freeze the substance of the SDGs now and address MOI later."[70] At first, the co-chairs were not sure how to handle the MOI targets given these divisions. Then they found that they could use the 2015 FfD conference in Addis Ababa to their advantage. The co-chairs told delegates that they could adopt the MOI targets, and then the FfD conference could flesh them out. Delegates accepted this, but how far the FfD conference actually succeeded in finalizing the MOI targets is open to debate (see Chapter 8). Nevertheless, the MOI targets remained essentially unchanged.

The revised zero draft distributed before OWG-13 tried to take all of this into account. The nineteen proposed targets under SDG 17 were organized along thematic lines: trade, finance, technology, capacity building, policy and institutional coherence, multi-stakeholder partnerships, and data, monitoring, and accountability. At the end of the first reading, the co-chairs agreed with those who said that the OWG had to make sure that MOI speak to all countries, and that all countries would have to make contributions singularly and together to achieve sustainable development. However, Kamau reiterated, "It is my deep belief that the development agenda recognizes first and foremost that those who have the first call on resources are the least developed countries." Unless there is greater effort at closing this intellectual gap, it will be difficult to bring this ship home in a manner that will make us all happy, he concluded.[71]

The co-chairs presented two more revised drafts of Goal 17 before the final reading, which didn't even begin until 12:45 A.M. on Saturday, July 19. When the SDGs were finally adopted twelve hours later, Goal 17 reflected both old and new realities. The goal recognizes the need to mobilize existing and additional resources: technology development, financial resources, and capacity building. LDCs are given special consideration, and developed countries are called on to fulfill their existing ODA commitments. Yet the goal also recognizes that ODA is not enough. Resources need to be mobilized from domestic and international sources, as well as from the public and private sectors. Investment, trade, macroeconomic stability, and policy coherence are all part of the picture. Furthermore, multi-stakeholder partnerships, including public, public-private, and civil society partnerships, are crucial to leverage the linkages among the goals to accelerate progress in their achievement (see Box 7.17).

PHOTO 7.3. OWG delegates consulting during the final hours of the final session of the OWG in July 2014. *Photo by IISD/Pamela Chasek (enb.iisd.org)*

■ **Box 7.17**

SDG 17. Strengthen the means of implementation and revitalize the global partnership for sustainable development

Finance

17.1   Strengthen domestic resource mobilization, including through international support to developing countries, to improve domestic capacity for tax and other revenue collection

17.2   Developed countries to implement fully their official development assistance commitments, including the commitment by many developed countries to achieve the target of 0.7 percent of ODA/GNI [gross national income] to developing countries and 0.15 to 0.20 percent of ODA/GNI to least developed countries; ODA providers are encouraged to consider setting a target to provide at least 0.20 percent of ODA/GNI to least developed countries

17.3   Mobilize additional financial resources for developing countries from multiple sources

(Continues)

208

17.4 Assist developing countries in attaining long-term debt sustainability through coordinated policies aimed at fostering debt financing, debt relief and debt restructuring, as appropriate, and address the external debt of highly indebted poor countries to reduce debt distress

17.5 Adopt and implement investment promotion regimes for least developed countries

Technology

17.6 Enhance North-South, South-South and triangular regional and international cooperation on and access to science, technology and innovation and enhance knowledge sharing on mutually agreed terms, including through improved coordination among existing mechanisms, in particular at the United Nations level, and through a global technology facilitation mechanism

17.7 Promote the development, transfer, dissemination and diffusion of environmentally sound technologies to developing countries on favorable terms, including on concessional and preferential terms, as mutually agreed

17.8 Fully operationalize the technology bank and science, technology and innovation capacity-building mechanism for least developed countries by 2017 and enhance the use of enabling technology, in particular information and communications technology

Capacity-building

17.9 Enhance international support for implementing effective and targeted capacity-building in developing countries to support national plans to implement all the sustainable development goals, including through North-South, South-South and triangular cooperation

Trade

17.10 Promote a universal, rules-based, open, non-discriminatory and equitable multilateral trading system under the World Trade Organization, including through the conclusion of negotiations under its Doha Development Agenda

17.11 Significantly increase the exports of developing countries, in particular with a view to doubling the least developed countries' share of global exports by 2020

17.12   Realize timely implementation of duty-free and quota-free market access on a lasting basis for all least developed countries, consistent with World Trade Organization decisions, including by ensuring that preferential rules of origin applicable to imports from least developed countries are transparent and simple, and contribute to facilitating market access

Systemic issues

Policy and institutional coherence

17.13   Enhance global macroeconomic stability, including through policy coordination and policy coherence

17.14   Enhance policy coherence for sustainable development

17.15   Respect each country's policy space and leadership to establish and implement policies for poverty eradication and sustainable development

Multi-stakeholder partnerships

17.16   Enhance the global partnership for sustainable development, complemented by multi-stakeholder partnerships that mobilize and share knowledge, expertise, technology and financial resources, to support the achievement of the sustainable development goals in all countries, in particular developing countries

17.17   Encourage and promote effective public, public-private and civil society partnerships, building on the experience and resourcing strategies of partnerships

Data, monitoring and accountability

17.18   By 2020, enhance capacity-building support to developing countries, including for least developed countries and small island developing States, to increase significantly the availability of high-quality, timely and reliable data disaggregated by income, gender, age, race, ethnicity, migratory status, disability, geographic location and other characteristics relevant in national contexts

17.19   By 2030, build on existing initiatives to develop measurements of progress on sustainable development that complement gross domestic product, and support statistical capacity-building in developing countries

SOURCE: https://sustainabledevelopment.un.org/sdg17.

CONCLUSIONS AND LESSONS LEARNED

From the Rio+20 conference in June 2012 until the closing of the OWG in July 2014, the development of the SDGs was a long journey. The negotiation of seventeen goals and 169 targets required trust, compromise, and a new development paradigm for the future. The seventeen SDGs go well beyond the MDGs in their scope and ambition. The SDGs commit every country to take action to address the root causes of poverty, to increase economic growth and prosperity, and to meet people's health, education, and social needs, all while protecting the environment. With the careful guidance of the co-chairs, the OWG was able to reach agreement on a number of important issues where the SDGs broke new ground: universal health coverage, inequalities, economic growth, decent jobs, industrialization, infrastructure, energy, climate change, protecting the ocean, sustainable consumption and production, and peace and justice. In some areas, such as sexual and reproductive health and rights, rule of law, and means of implementation, the co-chairs had to dig deep to draw on their knowledge of where they could get countries to accept bargains and compromise. In others, such as noncommunicable diseases, lifelong education, education and employment for the disabled, and the needs of older persons, women, and girls, agreement was comparatively easy.

Notably, the SDGs are universal and apply to all countries. They have changed the traditional development agenda, where the focus was only on developing countries, and developed countries were responsible for providing the necessary finance, technology, and capacity building. The SDGs are applicable to all countries regardless of their level of development, while recognizing the varying starting points of countries and their different challenges to achieve the goals.

Now the United Nations had to develop the rest of the agenda to be built around the SDGs and adopted at the September 2015 Sustainable Development Summit. This next phase, which began six months later, was a new round of negotiations, which resulted in the 2030 Agenda for Sustainable Development.

8

PULLING IT ALL TOGETHER:
The SDGs and the
Post-2015 Development Agenda

We have a truly historic opportunity on the occasion of the
70th anniversary of the United Nations to agree on an inspiring agenda that can energize the international community,
governments everywhere and the citizens of the world.

—SAM K. KUTESA, PRESIDENT OF THE 69TH SESSION
OF THE GENERAL ASSEMBLY[1]

When the Open Working Group (OWG) on Sustainable Development
Goals (SDGs) concluded on July 19, 2014, everyone took a deep breath,
perhaps even a sigh of relief. It had been an exhausting sixteen-month process including thirteen official meetings, several all-night sessions, and
seemingly endless consultations. And while there was now a set of SDGs
and targets, the work was not yet complete. The ambitious SDGs still
needed an effective "delivery system." The post-2015 development agenda
(later renamed the 2030 Agenda for Sustainable Development) had to provide the vision for a sustainable, equitable, and prosperous world and the
operational context, including how to mobilize political will, adequate financial resources, technology, and institutional and technical capacity, and

211

create a follow-up and review mechanism to track progress with implementation.

The path to the post-2015 development agenda was not always clear. In fact, it wasn't until after the SDGs were formulated that it became clear these goals and targets would become the basis of the new development agenda. Once this hurdle was cleared, the next round of negotiations could begin, to elaborate the 2030 Agenda for Sustainable Development. But this time, there was no OWG and there were no troikas. For these negotiations, member states returned to their traditional working methods . . . with a twist. The success of the OWG, including how the co-chairs conducted its proceedings, created a sense of goodwill, flexibility, and confidence as negotiations resumed in January 2015.

This chapter examines the negotiation of the post-2015 development agenda, which took place over eight sessions in 2015. We look at the similarities and differences between the OWG and the post-2015 negotiations, the politics surrounding the process, the balancing act of elaborating an agenda in one room while parallel negotiations for the Third International Conference on Financing for Development were taking place in the same building, and the challenges in achieving a final outcome.

BEGINNING ANEW

On September 10, 2014, the UN General Assembly, in Resolution 68/309, welcomed the report of the OWG and, notably, decided that the SDGs "shall be the main basis for integrating sustainable development goals into the post-2015 development agenda, while recognizing that other inputs will also be considered. . . ."[2] This resolution was important in that, after several years of confusion about the relationship between the SDGs and the post-2015 development agenda, the two were now officially merged. The Group of 77 and China (G-77 and China) were the driving force behind this resolution. In his statement on behalf of the G-77 and China to the General Assembly, Bolivian Ambassador Sacha Sergio Llorentty Solíz said that his group firmly believed that the OWG's outcome needed to be fully preserved and should not be reopened or renegotiated: "We are happy, therefore, that the resolution that we have adopted today clearly recognizes that this proposal will be the basis for integrating the SDGs into the post-2015 development agenda."³

Not all of the delegates were completely on board, even though they did not formally oppose the resolution. The United States, Japan, and some Europeans were hoping that the Secretary-General's synthesis report on the post-2015 development agenda, which was due to be released in December 2014, would provide a vehicle through which they could address what they saw as the unfinished business of the OWG, including renegotiating some of the SDGs and targets. However, once the post-2015 negotiations began, they quickly found that this was not to be the case.

A week later, the 69th session of the UN General Assembly opened under the presidency of Sam K. Kutesa, the minister of foreign affairs of Uganda. Kutesa knew that delivery of the post-2015 development agenda would be the biggest responsibility of his presidency and that he had to ensure its success. Furthermore, the seventieth anniversary of the United Nations was in 2015, and the post-2015 development agenda would be the perfect deliverable for this momentous occasion. So when it came for him to choose the co-facilitators for the post-2015 negotiations, he had to be strategic.

In the meantime, Ambassador Csaba Kőrösi had finished his term in New York and returned to Hungary to take up the role of special adviser to the president. Ambassador Macharia Kamau also thought he would be leaving New York as his term was concluding. However, Kutesa was convinced by his colleagues and peers who had witnessed the work of the OWG that it would be foolhardy not to have Kamau continue as co-facilitator for the post-2015 negotiations. This would ensure continuity with the OWG, and there was already comfort with his chairing style and working methods, including his perceived evenhandedness. So Kutesa had the president of Uganda, Yoweri Museveni, speak to his good friend Uhuru Kenyatta, the president of Kenya, and ask to have Kamau extend his term as Kenya's permanent representative to the United Nations. Then Kutesa asked Kamau to moderate the post-2015 negotiations. Kamau had been intellectually and emotionally drained after the SDG negotiations. He couldn't imagine himself back in the game and taking on such an

PHOTO 8.1. Sam K. Kutesa, the minister of foreign affairs of Uganda, served as president of the 69th session of the UN General Assembly. *Photo by IISD/ Francis Dejon (enb.iisd.org)*

onerous task. But after a three-week holiday, he began to feel mentally re-charged and believed that he could see the process through.

Because Kőrösi had left, Kutesa had to select a co-facilitator from the North. After a series of consultations, David Donoghue's name emerged as a front-runner. Donoghue arrived in New York in September 2013 to assume the position of permanent representative of Ireland to the United Nations. His distinguished career in the Irish Department of Foreign Affairs, which began in 1975, included three terms in the Anglo-Irish Division, dealing with Northern Ireland and Anglo-Irish relations. He was involved in the negotiation of both the Anglo-Irish Agreement and the Good Friday Agreement. He had also served in the Irish embassies to the Holy See, Germany, the United Kingdom, the Russian Federation, and Austria and had previous experience at the United Nations, the European Union (EU), and IrishAid.[4] Donoghue had participated continuously in the second year of the OWG negotiations, even after he broke his leg. He had a balanced idea of how North-South relations should be, understood development, and, based on Kutesa's consultations, was the right person for the job. On October 17, 2014, Kutesa appointed Kamau and Donoghue as co-facilitators "to lead open, inclusive, and transparent consultations on the post-2015 development agenda."[5]

While Kamau was the force of continuity, Donoghue needed a period of transition. The legacy of the OWG was subject to interpretation, and many were itching to open up parts of the SDGs with which they were not completely happy. Initially it seemed that Donoghue was receptive to the idea of "flexibility" on the OWG text. It was only through the experience of the post-2015 negotiations that the perils of indiscriminate opening up of the OWG agreement were better appreciated. Donoghue's understanding of the consequences of reopening the basic goal/target structure, his diplomatic skills, and his gifted drafting skills were a great relief to Kamau and the Secretariat.[6]

The first task for the co-facilitators, as was the case with the OWG, was to get their teams together so they could get to know one another. Donoghue went out of his way to make this a smooth transition. The Kenyan and Irish teams listened to each other and showed mutual respect. The two co-facilitators then began consulting with member states. But unlike the OWG, they did not have to consult with troikas. Instead, the consultative process was more in line with "usual" UN negotiations: meeting with the G-77 and China, the EU, the non-EU developed countries, and the Central and Eastern Europeans. They also held several open informal preparatory sessions.

Kutesa was a strong General Assembly president, supporting the co-facilitators throughout the months that followed. He also trusted Donoghue and Kamau to deliver the post-2015 agenda and did not interfere in the process. As a result, member states knew that they had to deal with the co-facilitators and could not do an end run around them through the president's office.

By December 2014, the dates and the agenda for the Intergovernmental Negotiations on the Post-2015 Development Agenda (IGN) had been established, and Kamau and Donoghue submitted a draft decision through

PHOTO 8.2. David Donoghue, the permanent representative of Ireland to the United Nations, was named co-facilitator for the Intergovernmental Negotiations on the Post-2015 Development Agenda. *Photo by IISD (enb.iisd.org)*

President Kutesa for approval by the UN General Assembly. On January 16, 2015, the General Assembly adopted draft decision A/69/L.46:

- the proposal of the OWG on SDGs will be the main basis for integrating the SDGs into the post-2015 development agenda, while other inputs will also be taken into consideration;
- "every effort shall be made" to ensure effective coordination between the IGN and the preparatory process for the third International Conference on Financing for Development, and other relevant UN intergovernmental processes;
- the outcome document for adoption at the September 2015 Sustainable Development Summit "may include" as main components: a declaration, the SDGs and targets, means of implementation and global partnership for sustainable development, and follow-up and review; and

- the initial draft of the outcome document shall be prepared by the co-facilitators "on the basis of views provided by Member States," as well as "taking into account substantive discussions in the process of intergovernmental negotiations," and issued by May 2015.[7]

The decision also set a schedule of eight meetings (see Box 8.1), beginning in January 2015 and concluding six months later.

■ **Box 8.1.**

Schedule of the Intergovernmental Negotiations on the Post-2015 Development Agenda

- January 19–21, 2015   Stocktaking

- February 17–20, 2015   Declaration

- March 23–27, 2015   Sustainable Development Goals and Targets

- April 20–24, 2015   Means of Implementation and Global Partnership for Sustainable Development

- May 18–22, 2015   Follow-Up and Review

- June 22–25, 2015   Intergovernmental Negotiations on the Outcome Document

- July 20–24, 2015   Intergovernmental Negotiations on the Outcome Document

- July 27–31, 2015   Intergovernmental Negotiations on the Outcome Document

CHANGING DYNAMICS

Once the IGN began, the co-facilitators decided to mirror the OWG's approach as much as they could. However, the post-2015 negotiations differed from the OWG in several key ways. First, unlike the SDG negotiations, there was already agreement on the new agenda with the SDGs as the core, so the co-facilitators didn't have to start from scratch. Second, they had to manage the more traditional structure of the post-2015 negotiations and their increasingly political nature. And third, they had to keep their eye on ongoing negotiations in other forums that could make or break the post-2015 agenda. But with the success of the OWG behind them, the co-facilitators were able to build on that experience, hold on to the pen, and keep the process open to nonstate stakeholders.

Jumping on the SDG Bandwagon

Whereas the SDG negotiations started with no initial consensus on how the goals and targets should be structured, their number, and their content, the post-2015 negotiations began quite differently. By January 2015, there was a global consensus on the SDGs and recognition that the United Nations' credibility relied on a strong sustainable development agenda going forward. Furthermore, the Secretary-General, whose term was ending in 2016, knew that his legacy was at stake and was committed to the successful adoption of the new sustainable development agenda as well as a successful climate change agreement in Paris.

By this time, the Secretary-General, his team, and the UN programs, funds, and agencies had jumped on the SDG bandwagon. Secretary-General Ban Ki-moon and his team were particularly pleased with Goal 16, which dealt with peace, justice, and accountable institutions, especially because they never thought such a goal was possible. Most of the UN programs, agencies, and funds, which had been variously laissez faire and combative during the OWG, now accepted that these goals would form the centerpiece of the next development agenda.[8] Kamau was confident that, amid such fervent support, the co-facilitators wouldn't be second-guessed.

The member states also were supportive of the co-facilitators. Kamau brought continuity to the process that gave comfort to the delegates who had just participated in the OWG. Furthermore, the chair of the G-77 and China for 2015 was the South African permanent representative to the United Nations, Ambassador Kingsley Mamabolo. Often negotiations get into trouble when the chair of the G-77 has a different agenda than the co-chairs or co-facilitators. But in this case, one of the co-facilitators, the chair of the G-77, and the president of the General Assembly were all Africans. This created a sense of cooperation at the highest levels.

Yet the co-facilitators knew by the end of the January 2015 stocktaking session that, although there was support for the process, the devil was in the details; formidable hurdles still faced the adoption of the post-2015 agenda. The first of these was to avoid reopening the SDGs.

In December 2014 the Secretary-General released his "synthesis report" on the post-2015 sustainable development agenda as an input to the IGN (see Box 8.2). This report was supposed to support the negotiations by reviewing lessons from the Millennium Development Goals (MDGs). The synthesis report also presented dignity, people, prosperity, the planet, justice, and partnerships as an integrated set of "essential elements" aimed at providing conceptual guidance during discussions of the agenda.[9]

■ **Box 8.2.**

The Secretary-General's Synthesis Report on the Post-2015 Sustainable Development Agenda[a]

The Secretary-General's synthesis report on the Post-2015 Sustainable Development Agenda, titled "The road to dignity by 2030: Ending poverty, transforming all lives and protecting the planet" (document A/69/700), was released on December 4, 2014. It was built on the experience of the development community over the previous twenty years and the outcomes of the 1992 UN Conference on Environment and Development (Earth Summit), the 2000 Millennium Summit, the 2005 World Summit, the 2010 Summit on the Millennium Development goals, and the 2012 UN Conference on Sustainable Development (Rio+20).

The report also benefited from the unprecedented consultations and outreach efforts of organized civil society groups, as well as from the global conversation led by the UN Development Group on "A Million

NOTE:
[a] See the full report at www.un.org/ga/search/view_doc.asp?symbol=A/69/700&Lang=E.

(Continues)

Voices: The World We Want," "Delivering the Post-2015 Agenda: Opportunities at the National and Local Levels," and the "MY World" survey. Millions of people, including children and youth, took part in these processes through national, thematic, and online consultations and surveys.

In addition to the SDGS and targets from the OWG, the report also benefited from the contributions of the following:

- The High-Level Panel of Eminent Persons on the Post-2015 Development Agenda
- Academics and scientists convened through the Sustainable Development Solutions Network
- The report of the UN Global Compact, which reflected the contributions of the business community
- Reports of the UN regional commissions, which highlighted the importance of regional efforts
- The report of the UN system task team on the post-2015 development agenda and the work of the technical support team
- The contributions of the UN System Chief Executives Board for Coordination (CEB)
- The Secretary-General's High-level Panel on Global Sustainability
- The report of the Intergovernmental Committee of Experts on Sustainable Development Financing
- The summary of the discussions and recommendations on possible arrangements for a facilitation mechanism to promote the development, transfer, and dissemination of clean and environmentally sound technologies

Paragraphs 136–139 of the Secretary-General's synthesis report addressed the SDG targets, noting that while the proposed 169 targets "go a long way in defining the substance of what we need to achieve," some of them are less ambitious than existing targets, some may be better as indicators, and some would be better elsewhere. The report called for a "technical review" of the SDGs to ensure that each goal is framed in language that is "specific, measurable, achievable and consistent with existing United Nations standards and agreements, while preserving the important political balance that they represent."[10] This created an opening for those who were still not satisfied with all the SDGs and targets.

At the January 2015 stocktaking session, Tony Pipa, the US lead negotiator for the post-2015 process, said that the OWG "experience built a strong foundation of shared vocabulary, understanding of mutual interests and concerns, and of course a report that serves as an important departure point today for our discussions about goals and targets."[11] Ambassador Michael Grant of Canada also hinted at a need to reopen the SDGs: "We have a total of 169 targets—and we are not convinced all these targets fit the criteria of being quantifiable and measurable, or consistent with the latest evidence and technical thinking."[12] The United Kingdom and Japan both said that while the OWG report served as the main basis, the post-2015 negotiations should recognize and draw on other inputs, including the reports of the high-level panel, the Intergovernmental Committee of Experts on Sustainable Development Financing, and the UN Secretary-General's synthesis report.[13]

South African Ambassador Mamabolo, on behalf of the G-77 and China, disagreed. The G-77 and China argued that any "technical review" used to redraft the SDGs and targets would only threaten the OWG's delicate political compromise.[14] Although some G-77 members had entered formal reservations about aspects of the SDGs and targets when the OWG's proposal was adopted, they recognized that the outcome represented a careful and hard-fought compromise. No one had gotten everything they wanted; everyone had had to swallow hard and accept the parts they were not comfortable with. The G-77 and China feared that something presented as a "technical" improvement of a target could in fact amount to a substantive change, which could create a slippery slope towards effective renegotiation of the targets.[15] So after several governments (notably the United Kingdom) indicated a desire to see a reduction in the number of the goals, the G-77 and China resisted. Even if there was agreement to reduce the number of goals, based on the OWG experience they knew there would never be agreement on which goals should be dropped or merged.

Carrying the OWG Torch

Another dynamic that quickly became apparent was the increasingly political nature of the proceedings. Because the IGN would have to address means of implementation and follow-up and review, everyone expected North-South political debates to dominate the sessions. The OWG had been a fairly technical process, especially for the United Nations. Although political positions and geopolitical realities were never far from participants' minds, the OWG co-chairs worked tirelessly to keep the discussions focused on the substance rather than the politics for as long as they could. The question at the beginning of the IGN was whether the focus member states showed in the OWG would carry over to this political process. Would the IGN return to the "usual" UN negotiations? Not every IGN delegate had participated in the work of the OWG. Many OWG members had moved on to other posts or other portfolios as part of a normal four- to five-year rotation. For those who continued on from the OWG, there was a certain camaraderie born of the intense nature of the SDG negotiations. In addition, these delegates, as well as the civil society organizations and other stakeholders, valued the working methods of the OWG, had become accustomed to Kamau as their chair, and appreciated the open nature of the group, where people could speak independently of the regional or interest groups to which they belonged. However, the new delegates did not have this shared history and did not have the same level of ownership of the SDGs or the process.

For example, there was some reluctance to accept the schedule for the eight sessions, with many developing countries calling for a zero draft to be available earlier than the sixth meeting in June. These calls echoed those during the OWG, when many of the same countries wanted to start line-by-line negotiations on a screen in front of the room for all to see. Both Kamau and Donoghue stood firm and introduced the zero draft in June as scheduled, did not allow on-screen negotiations, and held on to the pen until the end.

Although the G-77, China, and the EU presented statements and intervened regularly at each session according to historical UN practice, some of the OWG practices seeped in. The regional groups did not dominate the negotiations to the extent that the co-chairs and some member states had

PHOTO 8.3. Joseph Enyegue Oye, Sightsavers Cameroon, as part of the Royal Commonwealth Society for the Blind, and Veronica Robledo, WWF Colombia, participating in one of the stakeholder dialogues. *Photo by IISD/ Pamela Chasek (enb.iisd.org)*

anticipated, and this allowed for a more fluid discourse. Even some of the OWG troikas continued to work together, albeit informally. It was tacitly accepted that individual member states could convey their own views, and the co-facilitators actively encouraged this because it gave them more room to maneuver as they tried to find compromise and consensus.[16]

The OWG experience also paved the way for engaging civil society and other nongovernmental stakeholders. Building on the success of the OWG, Kamau and Donoghue established a three-hour structured session with civil society organizations and other stakeholders at each IGN session. These dialogues included participants from both civil society and member states seated alongside each other without official nameplates. What was particularly interesting was the lack of opposition from member states. Usually, some member states want to limit nongovernmental participation, noting the *intergovernmental* nature of the United Nations. In fact, in most cases during final negotiations, civil society organizations and other non-governmental stakeholders are asked to leave the room, especially when sensitive compromises have to be made. During the IGN, however, no such efforts were made, much to the co-facilitators' surprise. This enabled civil society representatives to bring a wider public perspective to the process and contribute substantial expertise relating to the entire agenda.[17]

Keeping an Eye on the Road

The IGN also had to keep an eye on several parallel processes in the UN system that would have a direct impact on its work. The first was the climate change negotiations under the UN Framework Convention on Climate Change (UNFCCC). As noted during the SDG negotiations, the Paris Agreement was scheduled to be adopted in December 2015, just a few months after the September 2015 Sustainable Development Summit that would adopt the 2030 Agenda. So, as was the case in the OWG, the co-facilitators had to balance the needs of countries that wanted strong language on climate change with those that were concerned about prejudging or prejudicing the outcome of the climate negotiations.

The second was the work of the UN Statistical Commission, which was the designated intergovernmental focal point on the development of the SDG indicators, which would be used to monitor progress, inform policy, and ensure accountability. Many, especially developing countries, wanted the indicators developed by the Statistical Commission to be global indicators and let individual countries develop their own national indicators referring, as appropriate, to the global ones. Their argument, as summarized by Ambassador Mamabolo, was that "Governments should implement the post-2015 development agenda according to their national circumstances, capability and development stages, on a voluntary basis and it is for this reason that the Group insists on the need for respect of the national policy space of Member States."[18]

There was also some apprehension that the indicator framework could be a back door to changing the SDGs and targets. Although the indicators would not be developed and approved until after the IGN concluded, the co-facilitators invited Stefan Schweinfest, the director of the UN Statistics Division, which served as the Secretariat for the Statistical Commission, to periodically brief the IGN. This built a sense of comfort not only with the future global indicators but also with the sanctity of the goals and targets.

The third process, and perhaps the most difficult, was the Third International Conference on Financing for Development (FfD), which was taking place in July 2015, just before the final meeting of the IGN. Two prior FfD conferences had been held, in Monterrey, Mexico, in 2002 and in Doha, Qatar, in 2008.[19] This third conference was convened to assess the progress made in the implementation of the Monterrey Consensus and the Doha Declaration, address new and emerging issues, and reinvigorate and strengthen the financing for development follow-up process. In addition, many hoped that the outcome document, the Addis Ababa Action Agenda (AAAA), would launch a renewed and strengthened global partnership for financing people-centered sustainable development that could provide the means of implementation (MOI) for the 2030 Agenda.

The co-facilitators of the FfD process, Ambassador Geir Pedersen of Norway and Ambassador George Talbot of Guyana, were appointed in October 2014 at the same time as the co-facilitators for the IGN. They were charged with leading the negotiations on the AAAA, with their meetings alternating with those of the IGN. This made the IGN discussions challenging, particularly on MOI. To help coordinate the two processes, which involved many of the same delegates, Donoghue, Kamau, Pedersen, and Talbot held several joint briefing sessions. This improved coordination but didn't make the negotiations any easier.

THE POLITICS OF A DECLARATION

The first part of the 2030 Agenda to be discussed was the political declaration, which would set the tone for the new agenda. UN summits, which are attended by heads of state and government, almost always adopt political declarations. The drafting of the political declaration faced a question of purpose: was it supposed to communicate the 2030 Agenda to "ordinary" people, or was it to serve as an introduction to the agenda, like the chapeau in the report of the OWG? Delegates soon agreed that the declaration should be "concise," which the co-facilitators hoped would be about six to eight pages. They also agreed that the declaration should communicate the 2030 Agenda to the widest possible audience, in that it should be easily readable and be written in inspiring and motivating terms. Although this sounded good in theory, in practice delegates and regional groups wanted more.[20] The G-77 and China wanted the declaration to draw from agreed-upon outcomes from previous summits and processes, including the Millennium Declaration, the World Summit Outcome, the Johannesburg Plan of Implementation, "The Future We Want," and the chapeau of the OWG's report.[21] Others wanted it to include references to a range of principles and commitments. For example, the EU noted that universality, human rights, democratic governance, gender equality, climate action, and respect for international law must be emphasized in the declaration.[22]

For the second session of the IGN, the co-facilitators produced a discussion document[23] for the declaration as well as an elements paper,[24] which guided discussions. They proposed that the declaration could be framed around the six elements introduced in the Secretary-General's synthesis report: dignity, people, prosperity, planet, justice, and partnership. In response, some saw the declaration as the last chance to make a large and unwieldy agenda concise and understandable, and they called for creative new approaches to its formulation. For example, Sierra Leone called for the declaration to be "the billboard of the SDGs."[25] The delegate from the Netherlands hoped that his thirteen-year-old daughter would be able to relate to simple language in the declaration and suggested that a group of young people be involved in "proofing" it for their generation.[26]

However, not everyone agreed with this interpretation of the declaration's intent. The Maldives, on behalf of the Alliance of Small Island States, for one, cautioned that the use of the word "simple" might detract from the complex, multidimensional issues contained in the agenda.[27] India said the declaration shouldn't be simplified to the extent that it is understandable to a thirteen-year-old, for ease of reading should not come at the cost of substance.[28] Brazil suggested that the six elements proposed in the Secretary-General's synthesis report might be a useful idea, but not all of them adequately conveyed the priority and essence of this agenda. So Brazil proposed "four P's" to capture the integration of the three dimensions of sustainable development and one for MOI: people, prosperity, planet, and partnerships.[29] However, many delegates from both North and South thought that a fifth "P"—peace—needed to be added to highlight the relationship between peace and sustainable development. Although Canada, Israel, the United States, the Republic of Korea, Finland, and Spain, among others, expressed support for the five "P's" as a tool to communicate the agenda,[30] Brazil continued to oppose "peace" because it was "not a Rio+20 overarching concept, nor an inherent pillar of sustainable development."[31] But the five "P's" survived.

There were also lengthy discussions on the content of the declaration. Some wanted to reiterate or restate all or some of the goals, but others wanted to rectify problems that they had with the goals or otherwise address contentious issues, including common but differentiated responsibilities (CBDR), colonial and foreign occupation, sexual and reproductive health and rights, climate change, and migration.[32] The co-facilitators tried various approaches in successive drafts of the outcome document.

By July, delegations were able to agree to a short, one-page preamble that captured the essentials of the 2030 Agenda under five simple headings reflecting the five "P's": people, planet, prosperity, peace, and partnerships. The declaration set out the overarching vision, described more fully what the agenda was about, summarized its key provisions (in a way that would guard against allegations of "cherry-picking" specific goals), and ended with a stirring "call to action to change our world."[33] One major concern was to ensure that a meticulous balance was maintained among the three dimensions of sustainable development, the holistic nature of the agenda, and the need to transcend traditional "silo" approaches. A paragraph on the positive contribution of migrants to sustainable development was inserted, responding to a request from many delegations as the world was experiencing the greatest forced-migration crisis since World War II, despite the reservations of some developed countries.

There were inevitably many trade-offs within the declaration, with paragraphs of particular interest to one or another group balanced by paragraphs to satisfy others. Some elements could be agreed on only at the last moment, including CBDR, reference to the climate change negotiations, reference to the Addis outcome, and reference to people living under occupation. The final preamble and declaration, although difficult to negotiate, met the criteria that the IGN and the co-facilitators had identified at the outset and were well received.[34]

PHOTO 8.4. Delegates had to make many trade-offs during the negotiations on the 2030 Agenda. Clockwise from top left: Lu Mei, China; David Hallam, United Kingdom; Guilherme de Aguiar Patriota, Brazil; and Henry de Cazotte, France. *Photos by IISD (enb.iisd.org)*

"TWEAKING" THE TARGETS

During the rush to complete the SDGs at the end of the OWG, because of lack of time and consensus, some of the targets had missing numerical values, and instead the text included references to "[x] percent" in nine targets.[35] The co-facilitators knew that they couldn't forward text with missing values for formal adoption at the September 2015 summit, but they also didn't want to risk reopening all of the targets. The G-77 and China remained adamant that the SDGs and targets should not be renegotiated. However, at a December 2014 meeting with interested delegates prior to the official start of the IGN, the co-facilitators proposed requesting the relevant members of the UN System Task Team on the post-2015 development agenda[36] to review each target to make sure that it was clear, specific, measurable, and consistent with all relevant international standards and agreements.[37]

During the March 2015 IGN meeting, which focused on the goals and targets, the co-facilitators circulated a document containing nineteen targets that had been identified as requiring some technical "tweaking."[38] For each of the nineteen targets, the document showed a proposed revision and a justification for that revision. These revisions were welcomed by the developed countries, but the G-77 and China stood firm. South African Ambassador Mamabolo, on behalf of the G-77 and China, said that his group opposed technical proofing of the goals and targets and any repackaging or clustering of the SDGs.[39]

The standoff with the G-77 continued, but the co-facilitators did not back down, and they included these technical revisions of the nineteen targets in the June zero draft and subsequent revisions. Over time, even if their opposition in principle remained, some G-77 members were willing to discuss the substance of the proposals. It was not until the final week of negotiations that the G-77 expressed willingness to engage constructively on proposals to replace the missing numerical values, despite the group's consistent position that the goals and targets should not change. South Africa specified that the G-77's engagement on the technical revisions did not indicate any intention or will to engage on any other goals and targets beyond the technical revisions proposed by the co-facilitators.[40] However, members of the G-77 and China, along with others, did propose some additional "tweaks" and rejected others. In the end, seventeen targets were tweaked . . . and accepted.[41]

MEANS OF IMPLEMENTATION AND
THE GLOBAL PARTNERSHIP: ALMOST A DISASTER

The means of implementation for the 2030 Agenda was very sensitive, and the co-facilitators had to find a way to work with the parallel FfD process while taking into account the outcomes from other UN processes (see Box 8.3). When the co-facilitators set the IGN's schedule, they postponed consideration of MOI until after the FfD negotiations had begun in mid-April 2015. It proved to be an awkward situation. There was continuous tension over the relationship between the IGN and FfD tracks and, in the final stages of the IGN, over the manner in which the Addis Ababa outcome would be reflected in the 2030 Agenda.[42] Kamau and Donoghue coordinated with the FfD co-facilitators, Pedersen and Talbot, to ensure that the two processes would not meet at the same time and that Pederson and Talbot could also participate in IGN meetings. They all knew that the FfD conference had to succeed for the IGN to succeed.

■ **Box 8.3.**

UN System Inputs into the Post-2015 Development Agenda Negotiations on Means of Implementation

Intergovernmental Committee of Experts on Sustainable Development Financing

The Rio+20 outcome document called for the establishment of a thirty-member intergovernmental expert committee on financing. Established on June 21, 2013, the experts were nominated by regional groups with equitable geographical representation. In August 2014 the committee adopted its report, which provides a menu of ways to mobilize resources for sustainable development.[a]

Technology

Rio+20 contained a section on technology, including a request to relevant UN agencies to identify options for a facilitation mechanism that promotes the development, transfer, and dissemination of clean and environmentally sound technologies. The president of the General Assembly convened four workshops on the subject of the development, transfer, and dissemination of clean and environmentally sound technologies in developing countries. Building on the workshops, the General Assembly held a series of four one-day structured dialogues to consider possible arrangements for a facilitation mechanism. The dialogues resulted in a summary of the discussions and recommendations, including the possible modalities and organization of such a mechanism.[b]

Third UN Conference on Financing for Development

The Third International Conference on Financing for Development (FfD) was mandated by the General Assembly to focus on assessing progress in the implementation of the Monterrey Consensus and the Doha Declaration, from the two previous FfD conferences; addressing new and emerging issues; and reinvigorating and strengthening the financing for development follow-up process.[c] The conference, which took place in July 2015, adopted the Addis Ababa Action Agenda.

NOTES:

[a] See United Nations, "Report of the Intergovernmental Committee of Experts on Sustainable Development Financing," A/69/314, August 15, 2014, www.un.org /ga/search/view_doc.asp?symbol=A/69/315&Lang=E.

[b] See United Nations General Assembly, "Summary Report on the General Assembly Structured Dialogues on: Possible Arrangements for a Facilitation Mechanism to Promote the Development, Transfer and Dissemination of Clean and Environmentally Sound Technologies," August 13, 2014, https://sustainable development.un.org/content/documents/4673techreport.pdf.

[c] See United Nations, "Addis Ababa Action Agenda," 2015, www.un.org/esa/ffd /wp-content/uploads/2015/08/AAAA_Outcome.pdf.

The negotiations leading up to Addis Ababa were difficult and needed more time than the originally scheduled three drafting sessions (January, April, and June 2015). Additional sessions were convened in May and June that ate into the IGN's time, for many of the same delegates were participating in both negotiations. The final session did not come to a close until July 7, 2015, less than a week before the conference opened in Ethiopia on July 13. With member states still unable to reach consensus on the draft outcome document, the co-facilitators proposed continuing negotiations in Addis. This put a lot of pressure on the IGN because its MOI negotiations could not be completed until there was agreement in Addis.

There were deep divisions between developed and developing countries about the relative weight to be given to MOI. Although the G-77 position was not monolithic and key players had significant differences, the overarching G-77 view was that sufficient MOI and a credible global partnership were critical to the success of the 2030 Agenda. They argued that these topics should be discussed both in the IGN and the FfD.[43] South Africa, on behalf of the G-77 and China, argued that FfD was a separate process and its scope went beyond merely financing the SDGs. Furthermore, the MOI for the 2030 Agenda needed to go beyond just the FfD outcome document.[44]

Developed countries put more weight on the FfD negotiations. The zero draft of the AAAA had come out of the work of the Intergovernmental Committee of Experts on Sustainable Development Financing (see Box 8.3), where the developed countries had more influence, especially on issues like the weight to be assigned to domestic resource mobilization relative to foreign aid (official development assistance). In addition, the FfD negotiations involved the World Bank and the International Monetary Fund (IMF) as equal partners with the United Nations, which gave the FfD process more gravitas in the eyes of the developed countries. Failure to integrate the Addis outcome into the 2030 Agenda, the EU said, would significantly detract from the credibility, consistency, and impact of the Agenda.[45] The developed countries also made it clear that they would be unwilling to reopen issues in the IGN that had been settled in Addis.

Attempts at Coordination

The April 2015 session of the IGN was convened as a joint meeting between the IGN and the FfD and was co-chaired by the facilitators of both processes. Research done by the World Bank and the IMF, whose representatives briefed delegates during the session, informed everyone that funding must increase from "billions to trillions" in order to achieve the SDGs.[46] On more than a few occasions, participants reminded one another of the weight and reality of the issues before them and the importance of matching their ambitious agreement on "what" to do (the SDGs) with resources for "how" to do it.

In opening the April session, Kamau offered delegates a "reality check" by reading newspaper headlines about tragedies that resulted from inequalities and violence, including the drowning of nine hundred migrants in the Mediterranean, Saudi-led airstrikes in Yemen, an Al-Shabab bomb explosion on a bus carrying UN employees in northern Somalia, the Islamic State battle for Ramadi, and the death of Freddie Gray, a twenty-seven-year-old African American man, after an arrest by Baltimore police. He reminded delegates that they were dealing with "very real challenges and issues" as they attempted to end poverty, reduce inequality, and protect the planet.[47] Later in the session, to remind delegates of the high stakes involved in finding the means to support this ambitious agenda, one civil society representative silenced the room as she presented a personal account of female genital cutting and appealed for funds to educate others about the practice. Her courage and story were applauded by delegates, although it was far from clear whether the outcome would be filled with an equivalent level of courage.[48]

A day long discussion devoted to the proposal for a technology facilitation mechanism (TFM) made significant progress on this issue, which had been hotly contested between North and South. The two co-chairs of the United Nations General Assembly structured dialogues on possible arrangements for a TFM, Brazilian Ambassador Guilherme de Aguiar Patriota and Swiss Ambassador Paul Seger, briefed delegates on the recommendations of the dialogues, which ended in July 2014. After a robust discussion on this topic, the IGN and FfD co-facilitators met to discuss the way forward.

At the May IGN meeting, the co-facilitators jointly presented a "Food for Thought Paper on a Possible Technology Facilitation Mechanism."[49] This paper built on existing proposals included in the FfD revised draft outcome document of May 6, 2015, discussions during the joint FFD/post-2015 negotiations in April, and discussions during the FfD intersessional meeting on May 15. The content also reflected the work being undertaken by an informal interagency working group on a technology facilitation mechanism and benefited from ideas advanced by France. This paper suggested that the mechanism include an online knowledge hub and information-sharing platform; an annual (or biennial) forum on science, technology, and innovation (STI) for the SDGs; a UN system interagency working group on STI for the SDGs; and a coordinated STI capacity-building program. Because this "food for thought" paper was issued by both sets of facilitators, it compelled developed countries to take the technology facilitation mechanism seriously. After further consultations, they agreed that the substance of the mechanism would be negotiated under the FfD but that the agreement would also be included in the 2030 Agenda and the mechanism would be launched with its adoption.[50]

Kamau and Donoghue went to Addis in July, for they knew it was crucially important to push for a successful outcome. It was a nerve-racking process where deals were cut in the old-school way: behind closed doors. Expectations were high that there would be more money for official development assistance (ODA), but the promises that were made were bound to disappoint many. The onus was put on developing countries to finance their own development through domestic resource mobilization, with the private sector called on to contribute significant resources. This challenged the traditional ODA-dominated paradigm of international development cooperation. Other contentious issues, such as an international tax body to deal with tax evasion and avoidance and to regulate tax cooperation, technology transfer, the illicit drug trade, and debt, were difficult to resolve. Without the political will of the host country, the Addis Ababa Action Agenda might not have been adopted.

Final Negotiations

Three days after the FfD conference concluded in Addis Ababa, exhausted delegates returned to New York, where the IGN resumed for its final two weeks. Kamau opened the session on July 20, 2015, and said that the FfD outcome adopted in Addis Ababa should not be reopened, but governments must decide how to handle it in the 2030 Agenda: annex the AAAA in its entirety, refer to it, include its introduction, or address issues not included in it.[51]

The G-77 was not totally happy with the outcome in Addis, and nerves were frayed. A number of issues of priority to its members were, in their opinion, not adequately accommodated in the text, including explicit reaffirmation of the principle of CBDR; the need for developed countries to meet existing commitments and to upscale ODA; the diverse and specific development needs of middle-income countries; the need to fully upgrade the UN Tax Committee into an intergovernmental body; explicit reference to countries and people living under foreign occupation; lifting and terminating coercive measures, including unilateral economic sanctions; and explicit recognition that climate financing is new and additional to, and cannot be counted as, ODA.[52]

At the July IGN session many developing countries proposed "welcoming" and not "fully endorsing" the AAAA and opposed integrating or attaching it as an annex. Developed countries requested the "full endorsement" of the AAAA, and many proposed annexing it as an integral part of the 2030 Agenda.[53] There was also some confusion with the placement of SDG 17 (means of implementation) itself—should it be separated from the goals and used as the MOI section, should it be repeated in its entirety in the MOI section, or should it remain with the other SDGs?

One of the challenges was to get the G-77 members to think beyond historical ODA obligations of the North that had not been met. Although the views of the G-77 had to be respected, the co-chairs wanted them to recognize that the 2030 Agenda represented a huge opportunity to expand development finance. Kamau worried that the G-77 would end up fighting over hundreds of millions of dollars in ODA and put at risk the opportunity to mobilize trillions of dollars from a variety of sources, including private investors and businesses, South-South cooperation, and triangular cooperation (where donor countries and international organizations aid South-South cooperation), that could have a real impact on people's lives. This debate was difficult to close because delegates had to move beyond a seventy-year-old negotiating pattern around ODA. But Kamau and Donoghue persisted, and the result was a major expansion of the development cooperation equation in the UN system.

The FfD had reached agreement on the technology facilitation mechanism, largely on the same lines as the "food for thought" paper distributed in May. The mechanism was to be composed of a UN interagency task team on STI for the SDGs; a collaborative multi-stakeholder forum on STI for the SDGs supported by a ten-member multi-stakeholder expert group; and an online platform to map, and serve as a gateway for, information on existing STI initiatives, mechanisms, and programs, within and beyond the United Nations. The multi-stakeholder forum on STI for the SDGs would be convened once a year for two days to discuss STI cooperation around thematic areas for SDG implementation, congregating all relevant stakeholders to contribute in their areas of expertise.[54] Despite the excitement in Addis about agreement on the technology facilitation mechanism, delegates disagreed on how to refer to it in the 2030 Agenda. Some wanted the language to be essentially cut and pasted from the AAAA, but others wanted it only to be referenced.

After much back-and-forth over those final two weeks, the eleven paragraphs in the MOI section of the 2030 Agenda agreed that the AAAA was an integral part of the 2030 Agenda and included a footnote noting that the AAAA had been adopted by the UN General Assembly. The co-facilitators didn't annex the AAAA and didn't include the goal-by-goal MOI targets and SDG 17, but they did copy paragraph 123 of the AAAA on the technology facilitation mechanism in its entirety.

FOLLOW-UP AND REVIEW:
ANOTHER ELEPHANT IN THE ROOM

Another significant challenge for the IGN was to find a common understanding on the arrangements that would be needed to follow up and review implementation of the SDGs and targets for the next fifteen years. Although it was recognized that most of the implementation efforts would be at the national level, effective follow-up and review arrangements would also be needed at the regional and global levels. Once again, there was a clash between North and South. Some of the developed countries that were still not comfortable with the universality of the 2030 Agenda did not like the idea that they would have to report to the United Nations on their implementation. However, the EU did call for an integrated "monitoring, accountability and review" process operating at local, national, regional, and international levels.[55]

Developing countries did not want to be judged by developed countries as they had been under the MDG paradigm. The G-77 and China strongly resisted any mechanism that would place them under unreasonable pressure, bearing in mind that many of their members were at levels of development well behind the North, the limited institutional capacities of many of their governments and, in particular, their lack of data collection capacity.[56] They emphasized that any international follow-up and review arrangements should be voluntary, government-led, and under the United Nations' High-Level Political Forum on Sustainable Development (HLPF), which was established following Rio+20. Furthermore, they argued that each government should determine how it would implement the SDGs at the national level, based on national circumstances and level of development.[57]

In successive drafts of the 2030 Agenda, the co-facilitators tried to find a model for the follow-up and review arrangements that would balance these various concerns. In one draft the pendulum was considered to have swung too far towards a rigorously structured approach. Accordingly, in the next version it swung back towards a more voluntary approach and the need to take account of individual national circumstances. Gradually a text emerged that balanced these positions.[58]

The final text stated that the follow-up and review process is voluntary and country-led; will track progress on all goals and targets; will be open, inclusive, participatory, transparent, and supportive of contributions from all relevant stakeholders; will use existing platforms and processes; and will be conducted on the basis of the indicators under development by the UN Statistical Commission. The 2030 Agenda distinguishes among national, regional, and global follow-up and review, and agrees that the HLPF will play a central role in overseeing a network of follow-up and review processes at the global level.[59] The final text did not go into detail about the precise functioning of the arrangements at the three levels. Instead, it was understood that these details would be fleshed out both in capitals and by the HLPF.[60]

THE FINAL PUSH

The endgame of the IGN played out over a tense forty-eight-hour period from 7:30 P.M. on Friday, July 31, 2015, already ninety minutes past the official end of the process, until the 2030 Agenda for Sustainable Development was formally accepted by the IGN at 6:30 P.M. on Sunday, August 2. The co-facilitators distributed a revised draft text at 7:30 P.M. on Friday. After breaking for five hours for regional and interest groups to consult, the IGN resumed at 12:30 A.M. Although there was broad consensus on about 99 percent of the text, four hours of statements revealed that there were still problems to be overcome on some of the same issues that had plagued the OWG: climate change, migrants and migratory status, human rights (including people living under occupation), MOI, and countries in special circumstances.[61] On this last item, Benin, speaking on behalf of the least-developed countries (LDCs), caused an eleventh-hour near-crisis. The final draft of the 2030 Agenda had introduced a substantial discussion of the concerns of middle-income countries, including reference to poverty eradication in those countries. This change had been put in as a response to a World Bank report that the largest numbers of poor people are actually in middle-income countries, not LDCs. So if the goal of the 2030 Agenda was to eradicate poverty, its actions couldn't be limited to LDCs. Benin also argued that the draft did not give LDCs the attention they deserve and proposed numerous amendments throughout the text that would add reference to the special situation of LDCs.[62] In response, the landlocked developing countries and the small island developing states also called for additional references to the special situations of their own groups.

At 4:45 A.M. the co-facilitators suspended the meeting for additional consultations on these issues. These consultations lasted thirty-six hours as informal discussions continued all day Saturday, and the reconvening of plenary was postponed several times, from noon to 4:00 P.M., 5:00 P.M., and 7:00 P.M. The co-facilitators then advised everyone that the plenary would not resume until Sunday morning as consultations continued. Delegations began convening for the announced plenary at 11:00 A.M. on Sunday, but the informal talks continued in the corridors and behind closed doors. At 2:00 P.M., the plenary convened, and a revised version of the outcome document was circulated. Kamau flagged changes from the previous version and said that all of these changes had been agreed upon by the major groupings of member states, with the exception of one paragraph on peace and security, which was still under discussion. He suspended the meeting once again. When the IGN finally convened at 4:40 P.M. on Sunday afternoon, Kamau and Donoghue introduced the document, titled "Transforming Our World: The 2030 Agenda for Sustainable Development," adding that it had been negotiated "to the comma." After nearly two hours of comments, in which the tension between the LDCs and the small island developing states and landlocked developing countries was prominently on

PHOTO 5.5. Delegates applaud the adoption of the 2030 Agenda for Sustainable Development on August 2, 2015. *Photo by IISD/Pamela Chasek (enb.iisd.org)*

display, at 6:25 P.M. on Sunday, August 2, 2015, the co-facilitators declared the document officially adopted.[63]

CONCLUSIONS AND LESSONS LEARNED

The moment of gaveling through the 2030 Agenda for Sustainable Development was the culmination of two extraordinary negotiation processes that defied conventional UN experience. First, the agreement reached was without precedent in UN history. The two negotiating processes, the OWG and the IGN, created the most comprehensive sustainable development agenda ever negotiated by UN member states. Second, the IGN successfully concluded six weeks ahead of the UN Sustainable Development Summit in late September, when the 2030 Agenda was to be adopted by the world's leaders. This was almost unheard of at the United Nations. In fact, when the co-facilitators had announced that July 31, 2015, would be the deadline and insisted that this was feasible, nobody believed them. Everyone thought the IGN would be working into late August or early September. Third, the co-facilitators managed to keep the IGN a member-state–driven process while carefully managing the mediation role of the Secretary-General's office, calling upon Amina Mohammed, the Secretary-General's special adviser on Post-2015 Development Planning, for strategic interventions. And fourth, the process remained open and transparent, allowing civil society to have an unparalleled level of access to, participation in, and influence on the negotiations throughout the process.[64]

With the negotiations complete, and as member states and the world geared up for the September 2015 Sustainable Development Summit, it was now time to share the 2030 Sustainable Development Agenda and the SDGs and targets with the world.

9

TRANSFORMING OUR WORLD

The world needs a change. It cannot change itself. It is me, it is
you, it is all of us who have to bring that change.

—Malala Yousafzai,
Nobel Peace Prize Laureate[1]

With a thunderous standing ovation, on September 25, 2015, the 193
member states at the United Nations unanimously adopted "Transforming
Our World: The 2030 Agenda for Sustainable Development," with the seventeen Sustainable Development Goals (SDGs) at its core. Speaking at the
opening ceremony of the three-day UN Sustainable Development Summit,
UN Secretary-General Ban Ki-moon said, "Seventy years ago, the United
Nations rose from the ashes of war. Governments agreed on a visionary
Charter dedicated to 'We the Peoples.' The Agenda you are adopting today
advances the goals of the Charter. It embodies the aspirations of people
everywhere for lives of peace, security and dignity on a healthy planet. Let
us today pledge to light the path to this transformative vision."[2]

The summit was the culmination of a unique three-year intergovernmental process, supported by civil society, the private sector, academia,
and specialists from the United Nations system and international financial
institutions. Individuals had the opportunity to voice their needs and priorities through surveys and consultations in more than one hundred countries. The 2030 Agenda for Sustainable Development is truly an agenda of
the people, for the people, by the people.

This chapter reviews the launch of the goals both within and outside the United Nations and the initial efforts by multiple stakeholders to implement the goals.

LAUNCHING THE GOALS

The 2030 Agenda for Sustainable Development was launched in a multipronged series of events surrounding the Sustainable Development Summit. Within the United Nations, world leaders and other high-level officials welcomed the goals and committed to their implementation. Outside UN Headquarters a multimedia public awareness campaign introduced the goals to people around the world. The negotiations were complete, and the agenda was adopted, but the only way it would be effectively implemented was if the news of the SDGs was spread at all levels—from presidents and prime ministers to children in remote villages and everyone in between.

Inside the Sustainable Development Summit

Inside the United Nations, more than 9,000 people and 136 heads of state and government, including US President Barack Obama, Chinese President Xi Jinping, Prince Albert II of Monaco, and Pope Francis, attended the Sustainable Development Summit. The United Nations had at least two purposes in convening the summit—to adopt its sustainable development agenda for the next fifteen years and to demonstrate that all countries are committed to its implementation. Although member states had agreed on the 2030 Agenda on August 2, 2015, their presidents and prime ministers needed to look one another in the eye—figuratively, literally, collectively, and publicly—to affirm their commitment.[3]

One by one, world leaders and other officials welcomed the 2030 Agenda. As Liberian President Ellen Johnson Sirleaf said, "[W]e made history today by adopting the 2030 Development Agenda to replace the Millennium Development Goals. In so doing, we have assumed a challenge and responsibility to deliver to the future generation, in the next 15 years, a world free of poverty and hunger and a more secure planet for everyone. This must be our legacy."[4] This was largely a celebration of the decision to move collectively in a new direction, but participants were also fully cognizant that they would be judged on the implementation of the agenda and not only by their words.[5] Many expressed sentiments similar to those of Sheikh Hasina, prime minister of Bangladesh: "To deliver on the SDGs, robust global cooperation is critical. In realizing the Agenda, we have to recognize the diverse national realities, capacities and levels of development. . . . We will have to address all forms of inequalities across the Agenda. In this 'collective journey,' the international community must deliver on the means of implementation for each Goal and across the Agenda."[6]

Others noted the important transition from the Millennium Development Goals (MDGs) to the SDGs. Laments about unachieved MDG targets were voiced alongside reports on successes in increasing levels of education, raising citizens out of poverty, and empowering women and girls.[7] Many echoed Jamaican Foreign Minister Arnold J. Nicholson's sentiments that Agenda 2030 was a "worthy successor" to the MDGs: "For while the MDGs provided a useful tool for focusing development efforts, this Agenda will help ensure that these efforts are sustainable. It is no coincidence that it is an Agenda for people, planet, prosperity, peace and partnerships. These are the ingredients that will make for a world free of extreme poverty, where prosperity can be achieved and sustained."[8]

But, as Swiss President Simonetta Sommaruga concluded, "We all know the 2030 Agenda for Sustainable Development is not a magic wand which will simply wish away all the problems of this world. However, I firmly believe that the agenda is an extremely promising approach to resolving many of the world's problems, and that with it we can set a great deal in motion and make big changes."[9]

World leaders also took part in six interactive dialogues during the summit:

- Ending poverty and hunger;
- Tackling inequalities, empowering women and girls, and leaving no one behind;
- Fostering sustainable economic growth, transformation, and promoting sustainable consumption and production;
- Delivering on a revitalized Global Partnership;

- Building effective, accountable, and inclusive institutions to achieve sustainable development; and
- Protecting our planet and combating climate change.

These dialogues emphasized the need to forge innovative partnerships among governments, businesses, and civil society.[10] This marked a major paradigm shift from previous development agendas that focused primarily on North-South cooperation and the use of official development assistance (ODA).

During the summit, two figures received repeated requests to appear in other participants' photos and "selfies": Malala Yousafzai and Mark Zuckerberg. Well below the average age of the world leaders, they drew a level of attention and celebrity to both the agenda and the summit. As an activist for girls' education and chief executive of Facebook, respectively, their messages resonated with participants because they were not just talking about lofty ideas; despite their age, they have a real, global impact on the issues about which they are passionate. The endorsement of the 2030 Agenda by these two cultural icons was seen as a hopeful sign for its future.[11]

Introducing the Goals to the World

As part of the global launch, filmmaker Richard Curtis helped the United Nations design a campaign that would be "fun, bright, entertaining, and interesting" to attract attention, especially that of young people. This groundbreaking collaboration of public figures, companies, and civil society groups, with support from the Bill and Melinda Gates Foundation and numerous other private sector donors and social movements, including Global Citizen,[12] united to tell "seven billion people in seven days that 'it's time to change the world.'"[13] Curtis, the filmmaker behind major international hits such as *Four Weddings and a Funeral, Notting Hill,* and *Mr. Bean,* created "Project Everyone," a short, dynamic, and snappy explanation of the SDGs. His goal was to make these new goals more famous and more well-known than the MDGs and to ensure that everyone on the planet knew about the SDGs so that they would stand the greatest chance of being achieved.[14]

Curtis worked with a Swedish-based communication company, The New Division, to create colorful icons of the SDGs to engage the public.[15]

Not only did these icons become omnipresent in the months and years following the summit; they also popularized the goals and could even fit on a business card, something that Jeffrey Sachs had favored all along. Curtis wanted to call the SDGs "The Global Goals," which he thought would be less UN-like and more enticing to the public. However, there were some at the United Nations who strongly believed that "sustainable development" must be included. Curtis relented and called them "The Global Goals" and, in smaller letters, "for sustainable development."

Project Everyone also created "The World's Largest Lesson," an initiative delivered in partnership with the United Nations Children's Fund (UNICEF) to raise young people's awareness of the SDGs and encourage them to be actively involved. Schools were asked to teach students a lesson about the goals and encourage them to share their experience on social media. In the first year, the SDGs were taught in more than 160 countries in thirty languages, with millions of children taking part.[16]

Curtis also created the world's first global cinema ad, voiced by Liam Neeson and Michelle Rodriguez, which premiered across thirty-four countries through the Global Cinema Advertising Association.[17] On the eve of the summit, thousands attended the Global Citizens Festival, headlined by Beyoncé and Coldplay, in New York's Central Park, and a highlights show was broadcast in 150 countries. Global icons including Stephen Hawking, Daniel Craig, Jennifer Lawrence, and Meryl Streep contributed to the crowd-sourced short film "We the People" to raise awareness about the SDGs.[18] The SDGs in Action smartphone app was developed, and mobile phone operators texted almost one billion people about the SDGs and spread the word to 5.2 billion customers. The Global Goals campaign took over twenty of the biggest online sites, 1.3 million people shared #globalgoals on social media, more than 250 million people engaged via Radio Everyone in seventy-five countries with six hundred radio partners, 140,000 "Posterscope" (digital advertising) sites across the world spread news of the goals, and football (soccer) players and other athletes, including Usain Bolt, posted "Dizzy Goals" challenge videos on YouTube to raise awareness of the SDGs, leading to more than 250 million views.[19]

During the summit itself, Project Everyone video mapped the UN building with a projection highlighting the icons for the seventeen goals,

PHOTO 9.1. The United Nations projected the icons for the seventeen Sustainable Development Goals on its headquarters building during the Sustainable Development Summit in September 2015. *Photo by IISD/Pamela Chasek (enb.iisd.org)*

and flags representing each of the goals were sent to iconic locations to represent the highest, farthest, and lowest points around the globe. All in all, it was an unprecedented global launch for a UN development agenda.

OWNERSHIP IN IMPLEMENTATION

The 2030 Agenda was adopted against the backdrop of immense global challenges, including high levels of poverty and hunger, rising inequality, the refugee and migration crisis, a rapidly warming world, and growing violence and insecurity. It is perhaps no exaggeration to consider this generation the last to have a "chance of saving the planet," as the 2030 Agenda states, requiring people around the world to address, fundamentally and structurally, many of these pressing challenges and ensure that no one is left behind.[20]

When the SDG era officially began on January 1, 2016, it already appeared that people not only in Delhi and Dakar but also in Berlin and Ottawa were up to the challenge of the United Nations' ambitious, first-ever universal sustainable development agenda. Governments had to figure out just what they needed to do to honor their new commitments. The United Nations and its funds, programs, and agencies, along with other international organizations, including the World Bank, had to refocus their priorities in line with the 2030 Agenda. The nongovernmental organization (NGO) community, philanthropies, the business community, and the scientific community began to consider how their work could align with the SDGs. Within countries, regional and local governments began reevaluating their sustainable development priorities.[21]

The examples below are by no means comprehensive but are presented to provide evidence of early implementation only, with the recognition that much remains to be done.

National Governments

In the first year of the SDG era, governments got off to a respectable start. The 2030 Agenda had given the High-Level Political Forum on Sustainable Development (HLPF) responsibility for regular review of implementation. As part of its follow-up and review mechanisms, paragraph 79 of the 2030 Agenda encourages member states to "conduct regular and inclusive reviews of progress at the national and sub-national levels, which are country-led and country-driven."[22] These voluntary national reviews (VNRs) are expected to serve as a basis for the regular reviews by the HLPF and enable the sharing of experiences, including successes, challenges, and lessons learned, with a view to accelerating the implementation of the 2030 Agenda. The VNRs also seek to strengthen government policies and mobilize multi-stakeholder support and partnerships for the implementation of the SDGs.[23]

At its July 2016 meeting, less than a year after the adoption of the 2030 Agenda, twenty-two member states volunteered for the first round of VNRs. This was a surprisingly large number for the first year, and what was even more noteworthy was that countries at all levels of development voluntarily took part: four least-developed countries, one small island developing state, four lower-middle-income countries, five middle-income countries, and eight high-income countries.[24] Their presentations revealed that these countries had begun to put institutional mechanisms in place to coordinate implementation, had already or were considering integrating the SDGs into national development plans and international cooperation strategies, and had started to adjust their national data collection and analysis processes to monitor progress towards the SDGs.[25] Even developed countries identified gaps in their performance against the SDGs. For example, Finland discovered that it still had work to do to address the gender pay gap and its economy's energy intensity. Germany flagged the need to reduce municipal waste and freshwater withdrawals.[26] This beginning sounded good, but many were still somewhat skeptical: after all, it was only six months into the SDG era. Several countries readily admitted that SDG implementation for them really entailed pursuing existing national priorities. Although this admission could be seen as an indication that the SDGs had traction at the national level, it does lead to the question of whether the SDGs could be really "transformational" without additional action that reflected a significant shift from business as usual.[27] Nevertheless, VNR momentum grew, and in July 2017, forty-three countries volunteered to present their reviews to the HLPF.[28] What is already clear is that implementing the 2030 Agenda is complicated, cutting across many, if not all, areas of government policy and that within specific SDGs can be found targets pertaining to economic, social, and environmental dimensions of sustainable development. Thus, most governments have found it helpful if not essential to enhance institutional and policy coordination to make sure that policies in one area do not undercut those in another.[29] Moreover, because many of the actions needed to achieve the SDGs require investment, finance ministries and parliaments, which legislate budgets, must also be engaged in SDG implementation. For example, in Norway the parliament receives reports on SDG implementation and approves the budget proposals submitted by different ministries and consolidated by the ministry of finance.[30]

In comparison, MDG implementation got off to a particularly slow start. As Jeffrey Sachs pointed out in 2006, six years after the launch of the MDGs, "There was a long, slow start after 2000 to actual implementation and indeed it remains slow in many ways, promises remain far ahead of reality on the ground."[31] In comparison, as the 2016 HLPF review demonstrated, less than a year after adoption of the 2030 Agenda, SDG implementation was already off and running.

NGOs and Philanthropies

During the negotiation of the SDGs, NGOs and philanthropies were of two minds. Environmental NGOs supported a more robust set of environment-oriented goals and targets, but the traditional development-focused NGOs and philanthropies were lobbying for a continuation of the MDGs. The Bill and Melinda Gates Foundation was the strongest proponent of an MDG+ approach. Bill Gates argued that the MDGs had helped achieve tremendous progress on child mortality and health but that more work needed to be done, and broadening the agenda would cause greater competition for scarce attention and resources.[32] Ultimately, the Gates Foundation and other philanthropies came to embrace the SDGs and be committed to their achievement. It perhaps helps that Gates had come to appreciate that climate change poses a real threat to the development progress of the past few decades and can have an adverse impact on food security, health, and incomes of the poor.[33]

Other philanthropies and NGOs around the world have been incorporating the SDGs into their work. For example, the SDG Philanthropy

Platform is a collaboration led by the Foundation Center, the United Nations Development Programme, and Rockefeller Philanthropy Advisors and supported by the Conrad N. Hilton Foundation, Ford Foundation, MasterCard Foundation, Brach Family Foundation, and other key organizations to enable partnerships on global development as the world transitions to the SDGs.[34] A group of Brazilian-based foundations and associations including Banco do Brasil Foundation, Sabin Institute, Roberto Marinho Foundation, Itaú-Unibanco Foundation, C&A Foundation, GIFE, and the Institute for the Development of Social Investment (IDIS) are launching the SDG Philanthropy Platform in Brazil.[35]

National NGOs are already producing reports to hold their governments accountable and to raise awareness on the SDGs. These reports provide a critical analysis of the state of progress of the SDGs, as was the case with the Swiss NGO coalition Alliance Sud.[36] Some NGOs, including a German coalition, are even presenting "shadow reports"—independent of the official VNR—at the HLPF to attract the attention of the international community. The SDGs have also become a valuable advocacy tool for a large number of charitable and human rights NGOs that haven't always been part of the sustainable development agenda. The SDGs are also leading to greater collaboration among development, environmental, and social NGOs, and this collaboration has been breaking down traditional silos at both the national and international levels. SDG Watch Europe is one of the first of these types of alliances to be created.[37] African Monitor, an independent pan-African body that monitors development commitments, delivery, and the impact on grassroots communities, has developed a program to accelerate the implementation of the SDGs in Africa and promote multi-stakeholder engagement on the SDGs at the national and regional levels, with a focus on the needs of vulnerable groups.[38] In other countries, such alliances are beginning to emerge.[39]

Business Community

The business community has not always been receptive to goals, programs, and projects emanating from the United Nations. However, this time the business community participated in the post-2015 and SDG processes from the beginning. Two representatives from the business sector were on the Secretary-General's High-Level Panel of Eminent Persons on the Post-2015 Agenda: Paul Polman, CEO of Unilever, and Betty Maina, CEO of the Kenya Association of Manufacturers. During the negotiations the business community contributed proposals for the SDGs and the 2030 Agenda.

Since the adoption of the SDGs, a number of progressive companies—some, such as Unilever, among the world's largest—see a tremendous business opportunity in embracing the SDGs. Scott Mather, chief investment officer of Pimco, is getting his company involved in the SDGs and expects to see an explosion of SDG bond issuance, which he hopes to tap into.[40] Frans van Houten, head of Royal Philips, sees the SDGs as a way to expand the Dutch company's brand around the world.[41] "We all see commercial opportunities," says Bob Collymore, head of Safaricom.[42] Safaricom, a leading telecommunications company in Kenya, has developed a framework for integrating the SDGs into its corporate strategy.[43] A 2016 survey by GlobeScan found evidence that the SDGs may be affecting corporate sustainability agendas more than anticipated in that nearly one in five companies are already implementing the goals.[44] The International Copper Association has done an audit of its initiatives, which shows alignment with all seventeen SDGs.[45] The International Chamber of Commerce, the world's largest business organization, with a network of more than 6.5 million members in more than 130 countries, has laid out plans for new collaborative efforts to advance the SDGs.[46]

In January 2016, at the annual World Economic Forum in Davos, Switzerland, the chief executive officers of Unilever, Alibaba, Mars, Safaricom, and a number of other large companies launched the Commission on Business and Sustainable Development. The commission brings together leaders from business, finance, civil society, labor, and international organizations with the twin aims of mapping the economic benefits that could be available to business if the SDGs are achieved and describing how business can contribute to delivering the goals. The commission's first report, *Better Business, Better World,* identifies the sixty biggest market opportunities related to delivering the SDGs, adding up to some $12 trillion by 2030, across four broad areas: food and agriculture, cities, energy and materials, and health and well-being. A sample of the top opportunities in each area includes reducing food waste, providing affordable housing and

PHOTO 2.2. The American pharmaceutical company Pfizer highlights its commitment to the SDGs outside its headquarters building in New York City. *Photo by Pamela Chasek.*

energy-efficient buildings, expanding renewable energy, risk pooling, and remote patient monitoring.[47] In March 2017 the UN India Business Forum, which includes prominent Indian and international businesses, including Tata, Godrej, YES Bank, Aditya Birla Group, Jain Irrigation, Unilever, and Shell, was created to build a tangible long-term partnership of ideas and solutions for sustainable development.[48]

In April 2017, UN General Assembly President Peter Thomson convened a high-level SDG financing lab to discuss the need to increase private investment to support the SDGs. Executives from various financial firms, including JP Morgan Chase, Citibank, UBS, MasterCard, and Aviva Investors, joined member states in discussing ways to align financial markets with the 2030 Agenda. Participants agreed that private investment in development could be scaled up dramatically by reducing risk and educating companies about the bottom-line benefits of sustainability. Matt

Arnold, Chase's global head of sustainable finance, suggested that, if persuaded of the business case, the financial sector could play a leading role in support of the SDGs. A handful of SDG-committed financial institutions could drive change across the industry. Steve Waygood, Aviva's chief responsible investment officer, proposed that corporations be benchmarked for their performance in advancing the SDGs, with publicly available information to contribute to a "race to the top" in sustainability.[49] To that end, Gold Standard, a certification body, has launched a new scheme to certify business contributions to SDG targets, and by late 2017, a group of investors, including Aviva, will have launched an alliance to benchmark company performance.[50]

City and Local Governments

City and local governments are on the front lines of provision of basic services like clean drinking water and sanitation, education, electricity, transport, and public safety. This makes them important players in SDG implementation. Beyond Goal 11, which is specifically targeted at promoting sustainable cities, many of the SDGs need to be implemented at the municipal and local levels.

The Sustainable Development Solutions Network is tracking city-level initiatives in pursuit of the SDGs and has produced "Getting Started with the SDGs in Cities: A Guide for Local Stakeholders."[51] In the United States, the city of Baltimore is using the SDGs as a reference for improving access to justice and equitable development in the city, including by filling gaps in critical information on pretrial detention, poverty, and decent work.[52] In December 2015 the New York City Mayor's Office for International Affairs launched Global Vision | Urban Action, an initiative designed to highlight the synergies between the SDGs and New York City's local sustainability and development programs.[53] The International Cooperation Agency of the Association of Netherlands Municipalities (VNG) mounted a national awareness-raising campaign to educate local governments and citizens on the SDGs. In Spain the city of Valencia is mobilizing other municipalities in an SDG awareness-raising campaign.[54]

In Colombia the government is working closely with municipal and departmental authorities to disseminate the SDGs and to ensure their incorporation into subnational planning frameworks and budgets. The Ugandan government has developed and disseminated development planning guidelines for local governments to help integrate the SDGs into local government development plans. Sierra Leone has engaged nineteen local councils to integrate the SDGs into their district and municipal development plans.[55]

Academia

The SDGs span a wide range of sciences, social sciences, and other disciplines. Moreover, the SDGs are closely interconnected: progress towards one SDG affects and is affected by progress towards others. This suggests the need for an interdisciplinary approach in the scientific research informing policies to advance the 2030 Agenda. The scientific community has organized to bring together the many strands of sustainability science on a common platform. Future Earth, launched in 2015, is a ten-year initiative to advance global sustainability science, build research capacity, and provide an international research agenda to guide natural and social scientists working around the world, including a platform for international engagement with the SDGs.[56]

Another important piece of the sustainability puzzle is the economics of sustainable development. The New Climate Economy (NCE) initiative of the Global Commission on the Economy and Climate has published several reports making the case for the sizable net economic benefits of early action to reduce greenhouse gas emissions.[57] This initiative has also released a series of working papers on many aspects of the SDGs, including financing sustainable infrastructure development, green investment in developing countries, financing the transition to sustainable cities, and fossil-fuel subsidy reform.[58]

Universities also have key roles to play in implementing the 2030 Agenda. First, they can train students by embedding sustainable development principles and the SDGs across disciplines. Researchers will need to develop new conceptual frameworks to better understand the linkages and correlations among different goals, the costs of implementing the SDGs, and the opportunity costs of insufficient investment in the SDGs. Second, as a universal agenda, researchers should help address the SDGs at the global and local levels. Given that the 2030 Agenda is supposed to leave no one behind, collaboration among universities can also play a role in tackling the unequal distribution of universities and research centers around the world. Finally, universities are increasingly becoming actors in multi-stakeholder partnerships for the SDGs. Researchers and students are participating in hands-on projects, contributing to knowledge transfer and encouraging firsthand intervention. For example, Columbia University is collaborating in a joint program with UN agencies, the private sector, and the national government in Kono, Sierra Leone, to use geographical information system (GIS) technologies to better understand the territory and track its recovery after more than ten years of conflict and the Ebola outbreak in 2014.[59]

Moving Forward with Cautious Optimism

It is quite inspiring to see how the SDGs took hold in their first two years and were embraced by the world. In some places, governments are ahead of the public, and in other places people are ahead of their governments. In some countries, cities and municipalities have moved more rapidly than their national governments, and in others the private sector is taking the lead. There is a level of excitement about the SDGs that was unimaginable when negotiations began in March 2013. The successful launch and the initial global response bode well for implementation of the 2030 Agenda.

Despite the great energy and enthusiasm for the SDGs, a note of caution is in order. The multilateral system has been here before. In 1992 the UN Conference on Environment and Development (Earth Summit) in Brazil adopted Agenda 21, a sustainable development action plan, with much fanfare and excitement. The UN Commission on Sustainable Development was established to monitor implementation of Agenda 21 and systematically reviewed clusters of chapters during its first few years. Yet five years later, when the UN General Assembly convened a special session to review implementation of Agenda 21, the optimism and excitement had already turned to pessimism and despair. As then General Assembly President Razali Ismail stated in his closing remarks, "The overall results of the special session are sobering. They point to the enormous difficulties of

overcoming short-term and vested interests in order to bring about concrete commitments to specific targets and to global programmes. Our
words have not been matched by deeds."[60]

The 2030 Agenda could go the way of Agenda 21, and the HLPF could
go the way of its predecessor, the Commission on Sustainable Development, which was disbanded in 2012. In a scathing 2015 article titled "The
169 Commandments: The Proposed Sustainable Development Goals
Would Be Worse Than Useless," the *Economist* predicted that the SDGs
would be a disaster. Criticizing the number and breadth of the goals, the
authors said that the "efforts of the SDG drafting committees are so sprawling and misconceived that the entire enterprise is being set up to fail. That
would be not just a wasted opportunity, but also a betrayal of the world's
poorest people."[61]

Whether the SDGs and the 2030 Agenda will be a transformative success will not be known for a while, but there is cause for optimism. First,
unlike Agenda 21, this is not a lengthy agenda written in UN language. The
SDGs and targets, while more numerous than some people had wanted, are
more approachable than most UN action plans and declarations. The extensive marketing of the "global goals" has definitely helped. Furthermore,
the track record of the MDGs showed that governing through goals, targets, and indicators can be an effective tool to catalyze progress even if they
are no panacea.

Second, historically, many have thought of sustainable development as
a trade-off with economic growth. The 2030 Agenda starts from the recognition that this trade-off is not inevitable. Instead, it emphasizes the potential synergies across the goals and the economic, social, and environmental
dimensions of sustainable development. For example, reducing carbon di-
oxide emissions through development of new technologies and industries
can generate growth, profit, and employment opportunities. Will the huge
innovation and investment potential opened up by the SDGs be fully realized? This is still an open question, but the 2030 Agenda is arguably a big
step in the right direction.

Third, the 2030 Agenda is not just a UN agenda. The SDGs weren't precooked by UN technocrats. The ideas came from governments, citizens,
scientists, and practitioners around the world, and many of these ideas

went beyond typical UN thinking. It is a universal agenda to which all countries at all levels of development are committed. This is why there is such resonance. For example, the goal and targets on inequality were inspired in part by the global "Occupy" movement. The SDGs address issues that activists around the world have been advocating for decades. The OWG articulated these ideas and channeled the passion behind them into a global agenda and goal set. By channeling the power of the people, the SDGs just may have given the United Nations a new lease on life.

It is this power that will determine just how transformative the 2030 Agenda will be. Many people began to adopt the SDGs as their own even before the 2030 Agenda was formally adopted. Communities that care most about a particular goal or target, such as those promoting early childhood education, ending discrimination and violence against women, curtailing and treating communicable or noncommunicable diseases, or fighting land or ocean degradation, can be expected to work tirelessly for implementation. Communities and partnerships have coalesced around not just specific goals but even specific targets (such as halving food loss and waste). And, notably, for the first time UN member states recognize that a development agenda may just be too big to accomplish alone. To be successful, the SDGs need to continue to be a multi-stakeholder, global agenda, not just a UN or government agenda. And if these goals and targets are achieved, the potential for transforming lives is huge.

CONCLUSIONS AND LESSONS LEARNED

The inclusivity and transparency of the negotiation of the SDGs and the 2030 Sustainable Development Agenda paid off at the 2015 UN Sustainable Development Summit. Even though some countries may have still had problems with parts of the agenda (for example, sexual and reproductive health and rights, reference to the UN Convention on the Law of the Sea, people living under occupation), there was overwhelming support. No one had been left behind in the negotiations, and the numerous heads of state and government and other high-level officials, as well as heads of the UN agencies, programs, and funds, nongovernmental stakeholder groups, and even Pope Francis, welcomed the new agenda with open arms. Had the negotiations of the new agenda been held behind closed doors or had the agenda been developed by a small group of UN experts, it is unlikely that it would have been universally well-received.

However, it was not sufficient to merely adopt the 2030 Agenda. If this was to be a sustainable development agenda by the people for the people, it was even more important to spread the word around the world about the "Global Goals for Sustainable Development." The contributions of Richard Curtis, Global Citizen, and everyone else who helped launch the global public relations campaign succeeded in taking the SDGs and introducing them to the world with music, video, text messaging, engaging graphics, and colorful educational materials. These efforts have gone a long way to make the SDGs and the 2030 Agenda a truly global agenda.

Within the first two years of the SDG era, there were already numerous signs that the goals were being implemented at the global, regional, national, and local levels by national, state, and local governments, businesses, schools, and communities. It is too soon to understand what the true impact of the SDGs will be, but their successful launch and early momentum bode well for the future.

10

THE LEGACY OF
THE OPEN WORKING GROUP ON
SUSTAINABLE DEVELOPMENT GOALS

Our new development goals are ambitious. But thanks to the good work of many of you, they are achievalbe – if we work together[1]

—44TH PRESIDENT OF THE UNITED STATES – BARACK OBAMA

When Colombia's Paula Caballero Gómez first proposed the idea of the Sustainable Development Goals (SDGs) in May 2011 during the Rio+20 preparatory process, she was looking for something concrete that could come out of the 2012 conference: a result that could be compelling for a broad audience and could encourage the deep transformations so urgently needed on a planet facing increasing environmental, social, and economic threats. She did not think that the mandated outcomes—green economy and the institutional framework for sustainable development—would resonate with people beyond the United Nations. The SDGs were not originally on the agenda, but thanks to the vision of Caballero and the efforts of so many others, today they have become a reality and will guide the global sustainable development agenda until 2030.

This book has told the story of this monumental effort to develop a set of sustainable development goals and targets that were intergovernmentally negotiated but influenced by people from all over the world and all walks of life. History will judge the legacy of the 2030 Agenda and the SDGs. Yet it is important to recognize that the process through which the SDGs came to fruition is as monumental for multilateral diplomacy as the goals are for people, planet, prosperity, and peace. So looking back over the negotiations, it is worth recapping how the process not only led to an agreed-upon outcome but also led to the overwhelming acceptance of a universal sustainable development agenda.

LESSONS LEARNED

First, the language in the Rio+20 outcome, "The Future We Want," set the tone: "We resolve to establish an inclusive and transparent intergovernmental process on sustainable development goals that is open to all stakeholders, with a view to developing global sustainable development goals to be agreed by the General Assembly."[2] This language set the stage for an *intergovernmental* process to develop the SDGs. As described in Chapter 2, the Millennium Development Goals (MDGs) were the outcome of a drafting process led by the United Nations Development Programme, at the request of then UN Secretary-General Kofi Annan, who had been mandated to prepare a long-term road map towards implementation of the Millennium Declaration.[3] Many developing countries were initially skeptical of the MDGs in part because of the UN agency–dominated process by which they were drafted. This, in part, delayed their implementation, but over their fifteen-year life span, they did become the world's central reference point for development cooperation, made significant social progress possible, demonstrated the potential of governing through goals, and served as the starting point and inspiration for the SDGs.

By calling for an inclusive and transparent intergovernmental process to draft the SDGs, Rio+20 sent a clear message from the outset that not only would the views of all countries—developed and developing—be taken into account, but all stakeholders would be able to contribute as well. This helped immensely in getting countries and nongovernmental stakeholders to accept the goals from the beginning, and the early record of implementation can be credited, in part, to the open and inclusive nature of the process.

Second, leadership matters. The importance of the selection of co-chairs for both the Open Working Group (OWG) and the Intergovernmental Negotiations on the Post-2015 Development Agenda that followed cannot be underestimated. In Csaba Kőrösi and Macharia Kamau the OWG had the effective leadership it needed to succeed. The co-chairs worked hard to ensure that the membership had trust in their leadership as early as possible. As described in Chapter 3, Kőrösi and Kamau made it clear that even though their countries were members of the European Union and the Group of 77, respectively, they were "hired" for the process and would not represent any one group's position. The co-chairs also realized early on that the OWG could not agree on a set of universal SDGs if participation in the process was limited. To get a set of universal goals, they had to work with everyone—governments, nongovernmental organizations (NGOs), civil society, business, and international organizations—not just a slice of the international community.

Third, leadership also entails managing the process. Many were afraid that the OWG would collapse under its own weight. So convening eight stocktaking sessions effectively kept the discussions focused on the substance. Not every UN negotiating process has the luxury of time; however, these stocktaking sessions were essential to the success of the process. As described in Chapter 4, these sessions helped to build a common understanding of the issues and also gave delegations time to get to know one another and their priorities. This not only built trust and comfort among the delegates and between the delegates and the co-chairs but also strengthened the legitimacy of the process and the eventual outcome. Participants noticed that some of the most diametrically opposed and politically charged relationships mellowed over the eight stocktaking sessions. So by the time the OWG began actual negotiations in 2014, there was a high level of cohesion, a common sense of purpose, a shared understanding of the issues, and receptiveness to new ideas.

The stocktaking sessions also opened the door to greater participation from NGOs, the business community, and civil society. During these sessions, many member states developed a sense of comfort with observers in the room, and this opened the door for nongovernmental stakeholders to participate throughout the negotiations. The stocktaking process also allowed all participants to think much more critically because they were faced with concrete information about what they wanted to do and how they would have to do it. At the beginning, few had a deep understanding about the substance, relative importance, and interdependence of the issues. Towards the end there was a constant flow of ideas that opened people's eyes and built a common intellectual platform from which the negotiations could commence.

Fourth, the innovative seat-sharing system of the OWG leveled the playing field and allowed all countries to contribute. This seat-sharing system represented the first time such an arrangement has been used at the United Nations, and many agreed that it enriched the process tremendously. Under the traditional UN sustainable development coalition structure, one voice represented the 134 members of the Group of 77 and China, one voice represented the twenty-eight members of the European Union, and, unless speaking in coalitions, other member states spoke on their own behalf. This structure distorted the balance of interests, especially if only a handful of delegates spoke on each agenda item. The OWG structure democratized the process and allowed everyone to speak. In addition, many of the seat clusters of countries, or "troikas," crossed traditional interest or regional groups and enabled a more dynamic exchange both within and between troikas. Normally, delegates articulate their country's position only in closed meetings of their interest or regional groups. In the OWG they articulated their positions publicly with everyone, including civil society, present.

Fifth, it was important to look beyond the conference room where the negotiations took place. Unlike many UN General Assembly negotiations, the work of the OWG did not take place in a vacuum. The special events, high-level events, and side events and news of the day all played a role in educating delegates. The co-chairs and OWG members alike ensured that reports from these events and news from the outside world were all brought into the proceedings. These events and the global interest in poverty eradication, growing inequality, the economic crisis, and environmental degradation around the world gave real-world backing to the OWG's work. Furthermore, the OWG and the post-2015 negotiations that followed had to keep abreast of parallel negotiations under the UN Framework Convention on Climate Change and the Third International Conference on

Financing for Development to ensure that the SDG negotiations did not prejudge or prejudice their outcomes.

In addition, as exhausting as it was, the co-chairs also saw the importance of visiting national capitals around the world to bring high-level officials up to speed so they would become comfortable with the idea of the SDGs. As described in Chapter 5, the co-chairs had to learn the hopes, fears, strengths, and weaknesses of the different delegations. The co-chairs had to assure the Africans and the least-developed countries that the unfinished business of the MDGs would constitute the core of the new development agenda. They had to assure the Europeans and others that the new goals would put the world on an environmentally sustainable development path. They had to assure the UN programs, funds, and agencies, as well as NGOs and civil society, that even though this was a member-state–driven process, their participation, views, and concerns would be taken into account. These efforts and meetings, along with the countless meetings held by Amina Mohammed, the Secretary-General's special adviser on Post-2015 Development Planning, went a long way toward gaining worldwide acceptance of the new agenda.

Sixth, the co-chairs held the pen throughout the negotiations on both the SDGs and the 2030 Agenda. Rather than engaging in a lengthy group drafting exercise, which had become standard practice in the United Nations' sustainable development negotiations, the co-chairs used the strategy of a single negotiating text. As described in Chapter 6, this kept the drafting responsibilities with the co-chairs, simplified the process, and avoided turning the negotiations into a "zero-sum" game, played out on the screen in front of the room, where any gain achieved by one side is perceived to be a loss to the other side. By holding the pen, the co-chairs were also able to employ an iterative strategy aimed at convergence towards a consensus outcome. Another useful tool in this regard was the creation of Encyclopedia Groupinica. This document, which contained delegations' proposals and comments on the early focus area documents, reassured participants that their voices had been heard. This validated all of the participants and reinforced trust in the co-chairs.

Seventh, the co-chairs chose to limit the use of contact groups. These small negotiating groups, which often meet in parallel, are commonly used to reach agreement on sensitive issues that cannot be resolved by the plenary as a whole. However, contact groups can serve to disenfranchise governments whose delegates did not or could not participate. As a result, these excluded delegations can torpedo the outcome once it is brought back to the plenary. Furthermore, when co-chairs create contact groups, they risk losing control of the debate and the outcome. So when the co-chairs did create four contact groups in the final hours, the purpose was to show delegates that they had tried everything possible to reach agreement. And, in the event that consensus in the contact groups was elusive, the co-chairs were able to propose compromise text that allowed all seventeen goals and 169 targets to be accepted by consensus, as described in Chapter 7.

Eighth, once the OWG had completed its mandate, it was important to ensure that the next phase of the process, the Intergovernmental Negotiations (IGN) on the Post-2015 Development Agenda, reached agreement on a new agenda with the SDGs at its core. As described in Chapter 8, the president of the 69th session of the General Assembly, Sam K. Kutesa, saw the value of reappointing Kamau along with the permanent representative of Ireland to the United Nations, David Donoghue, to co-facilitate the IGN. Kamau brought continuity to the process, which allowed some of the practices from the OWG to seep in, including the participation of many nongovernmental observers. The IGN also continued to encourage individual member states, along with some of the OWG troikas that continued to work together informally, to convey their own views rather than hearing only from the larger regional groups.

As described in Chapter 8, some countries wanted to reopen the SDGs. Initially, some had hoped that the new co-facilitator, Ambassador Donoghue, would be receptive to this idea, but he quickly understood the consequences of reopening the goals and targets, and his diplomatic and drafting skills were a great addition to the process. As they shepherded the SDGs through the negotiations on the 2030 Agenda, Kamau and Donoghue had help from the Group of 77 and China, which argued against reopening the SDGs. Thus, they were able to keep the goals and targets together (albeit with some technical "tweaking") and ensured that the SDGs were the heart of the new *sustainable* development agenda.

NEGOTIATING PROCESSES MATTER

The OWG began its work at a time of frustration with multilateral sustainable development negotiations and long-standing mistrust between North and South. The experience of the OWG helped to rebuild this trust and improve multilateral negotiations in the UN system. Although not all of the techniques used by the OWG are replicable, such as the troika system, the notion that UN negotiations can experiment with new procedures and do not have to be wedded to the past is a major contribution of the OWG. The co-chairs and participants learned that if you build a sense of comfort and trust in the leadership, member states will allow innovation and even the bending or breaking of a few rules. The OWG may have been a once-in-a-lifetime event, but it has set a new precedent for efficient and inclusive negotiations.

Since the conclusion of the OWG, a number of negotiating processes at United Nations Headquarters have changed or adapted their working methods. Fewer negotiations have been creating long compilation texts through textual negotiations projected on screens at the front of the room. Fewer contact groups have been used. Instead, the entire General Assembly membership has been invited to participate, and more and more the co-chairs or chairs are holding the pen and reissuing drafts of decisions themselves. These changes did not spread as quickly from New York to conferences of the parties to the various multilateral environmental agreements or to the work of the United Nations Environment Assembly. However, the practices of these bodies are gradually evolving as well.

Receptiveness to the participation of nongovernmental stakeholders in sustainable development meetings and negotiations has also evolved. The High-Level Political Forum on Sustainable Development, like the OWG, has used panel discussions to educate delegates and has included NGOs and other stakeholders on the various panels. The annual Forum on Science, Technology and Innovation for the SDGs (STI Forum) has become a multi-stakeholder event involving scientists, entrepreneurs, NGOs, business and industry, and governments all participating as equals. The UN conference rooms are set up so that governments and other stakeholders alternate by rows, instead of the traditional practice of having NGOs and other stakeholders sit in the gallery or at the back of the room.

And in an unprecedented move, the United Nations General Assembly granted observer status to the International Chamber of Commerce (ICC) in December 2016. This marked the first time that a business organization has been admitted as a formal observer of the General Assembly. The list of UN observers is highly restricted and principally features intergovernmental organizations. The new role for the ICC means that business will for the first time have a direct voice in the UN system. The decision paved the way for ICC to contribute directly to the work of the General Assembly and reflects the important role the private sector is playing in implementing the 2030 Agenda for Sustainable Development.[4] Although not all UN processes have welcomed nongovernmental observers for many of the reasons described in Chapter 3, there has been a general acceptance of the role that these organizations are playing in the implementation of the 2030 Agenda and the idea that governments cannot do it alone.

The universal acceptance and early success of the SDGs demonstrate that negotiating processes do matter. Very few had faith that an intergovernmental negotiating process could result in a set of clear, concise goals that were both universal in their scope and extremely ambitious, aiming to leave no one behind. Many attributed the success of the MDGs to the fact that they were easy to understand by the public and had clear targets and timetables for their achievement. Some attributed these desirable attributes to the MDGs having been developed by a handful of UN technocrats, doubting whether the open intergovernmental negotiation process of the SDGs could replicate that success. They thought that government negotiators would inevitably revert to typical opaque UN language found in resolutions and treaties. But the OWG proved them wrong and in dramatic fashion. As *Transforming Our World: The 2030 Agenda for Sustainable Development* states at the outset,

> This Agenda is a plan of action for people, planet and prosperity. It also seeks to strengthen universal peace in larger freedom. We recognize that eradicating poverty in all its forms and dimensions, including extreme poverty, is the greatest global challenge and an indispensable requirement for sustainable development. All countries and all stakeholders, acting in collaborative partnership, will

implement this plan. We are resolved to free the human race from the tyranny of poverty and want and to heal and secure our planet. We are determined to take the bold and transformative steps which are urgently needed to shift the world onto a sustainable and resilient path. As we embark on this collective journey, we pledge that no one will be left behind. The 17 Sustainable Development Goals and 169 targets which we are announcing today demonstrate the scale and ambition of this new universal Agenda. They seek to build on the Millennium Development Goals and complete what these did not achieve. They seek to realize the human rights of all and to achieve gender equality and the empowerment of all women and girls. They are integrated and indivisible and balance the three dimensions of sustainable development: the economic, social and environmental.[5]

The 2030 Agenda, the seventeen SDGs, and the 169 targets are a direct reflection of the process used to create them. The process was universal, integrated, and represented the rich and the poor, governments and nongovernmental stakeholders, those concerned with each of the three dimensions of sustainable development (economic development, social development, and the environment), as well as peace and security. As the international community works collectively to implement these goals and targets at the international, national, and local levels, it is time to turn these words into action and create a more sustainable and equitable world for present and future generations.

APPENDIX I:
OWG Expert Presentations

OWG-1: MARCH 14–15, 2013
Interactive discussion on conceptualizing the SDGs

- Amina Mohammed, Secretary-General's special adviser on Post-2015 Development Planning
- Martin Khor, executive director, South Centre
- Manish Bapna, executive vice president and managing director, World Resources Institute
- David Steven, associate director, Center on International Cooperation, New York University

See https://sustainabledevelopment.un.org/processes/post2015/owg/session1.

OWG-2: APRIL 17–19, 2013
Conceptualizing the SDGs

- Claire Melamed, Overseas Development Institute
- Sakiko Fukuda-Parr, professor of international affairs, New School, New York
- Marc Levy, Columbia University Center for International Earth Science Information Network

Poverty eradication

- Abhijit Banerjee, international professor of economics, Massachusetts Institute of Technology
- Olav Kjørven, United Nations Development Programme
- Jomo Kwame Sundaram, Food and Agriculture Organization
- Sabina Alkire, director, Oxford University Poverty and Human Development Initiative
- Eva Jespersen, head of National Human Development Reports Unit, United Nations Development Programme

See https://sustainabledevelopment.un.org/processes/post2015/owg/session2.

OWG-3: MAY 22–24, 2013
Food security and nutrition; sustainable agriculture, desertification, land degradation and drought

- Maria Helena Semedo, deputy director-general, UN Food and Agriculture Organization
- Amir Abdulla, World Food Programme
- Carlos Seré, International Fund for Agricultural Development
- Luc Gnacadja, UN Convention to Combat Desertification executive secretary
- Hans Herren, president, Millennium Institute and Biovision Foundation
- Dennis Garrity, UN Drylands ambassador

Water and sanitation

- Michel Jarraud, secretary-general, World Meteorological Organization, and chair of UN-Water
- Rabi Mohtar, professor and executive director of Qatar Environment and Energy Research Institute
- Letitia Obeng, International Water Management Institute board member

See https://sustainabledevelopment.un.org/processes/post2015/owg/session3.

OWG-4: JUNE 17–19, 2013
Employment and decent work for all, social protection, youth, education and culture

- Greg Vines, deputy director-general, International Labour Organization
- Richard Morgan, United Nations Children's Fund (UNICEF)
- Jorge Sequeira, UN Educational, Scientific and Cultural Organization (UNESCO)
- Haroon Bhorat, University of Cape Town
- Karen Mundy, University of Toronto
- Fernando Filgueira, consultant, former collaborating researcher for the UN Research Institute for Social Development (UNRISD)

Health, population dynamics

- Anarfi Asamoa-Baah, deputy director-general, World Health Organization (WHO)
- Hans Rosling, Karolinska Institute and Gapminder Foundation
- Paulina K. Makinwa-Adebusoye, Nigerian Institute of Social and Economic Research
- Jeanette Vega, managing director, Rockefeller Foundation

See https://sustainabledevelopment.un.org/processes/post2015/owg/session4.

OWG-5: NOVEMBER 25–27, 2013

Sustained and inclusive economic growth, macroeconomic policy questions (including international trade, international financial system and external debt sustainability), infrastructure development and industrialization

- Jagdish Bhagwati, Columbia University
- Li Yong, director-general, UN Industrial Development Organization (UNIDO)
- Mukhisa Kituyi, UN Conference on Trade and Development (UNCTAD)
- Amadou Sy, Brookings Institution
- Amar Bhattacharya, Intergovernmental Group of Twenty-Four on International Monetary Affairs and Development (G-24)
- Jeffrey Sachs, director, Sustainable Development Solutions Network

Energy

- Adnan Amin, director-general, International Renewable Energy Agency (IRENA)
- Vijay Modi, Columbia University
- Daniel Kammen, University of California, Berkeley

See https://sustainabledevelopment.un.org/processes/post2015/owg/session5.

OWG-6: DECEMBER 9–13, 2013

Means of implementation (financing, science and technology, knowledge-sharing and capacity building)

- Erik Solheim, chair, Organization for Economic Cooperation and Development (OECD) Development Assistance Committee

- Rolf-Dieter Heuer, director-general of the European Organization for Nuclear Research (CERN)
- Martin Khor, executive director, South Centre
- Keith Maskus, University of Colorado
- Ambuj Sagar, Indian Institute of Technology

Global partnership for achieving sustainable development

- Paul Polman, CEO, Unilever
- Gargee Ghosh, Bill and Melinda Gates Foundation

Needs of countries in special situations: African countries, LDCs, LLDCs and SIDS as well as specific challenges facing middle-income countries

- Carlos Lopes, executive secretary of the UN Economic Commission for Africa (UNECA)
- Mahmoud Mohieldin, World Bank Group president's special envoy on MDGs and Financial Development
- Patrick Guillaumont, president, FERDI
- Selwin Hart, Caribbean Development Bank
- Debapriya Bhattacharya, distinguished fellow, Centre for Policy Dialogue

Human rights, the right to development, global governance

- Ivan Šimonović, assistant secretary-general for Human Rights, United Nations
- Bjorn Lomborg, director of the Copenhagen Consensus Center

See https://sustainabledevelopment.un.org/processes/post2015/owg/session6.

OWG-7: JANUARY 6–10, 2014
Sustainable cities and human settlements, sustainable transport

- Joan Clos, executive director, UN-HABITAT
- Adriana de Almeida Lobo, executive director of CTS Embarq Mexico
- Harriet Bulkeley, Durham University
- Ousmane Thiam, director-general, Conseil Exécutif des Transports Urbains de Dakar

- Aromar Revi, director, Indian Institute for Human Settlements, and Sustainable Development Solutions Network (SDSN)
- Lewis Fulton, Institute of Transportation Studies, University of California, Davis

Sustainable consumption and production (including chemicals and waste)
- Ernst Ulrich von Weizsäcker, co-chair of the International Resource Panel
- William McDonough, founder, McDonough and Partners
- Karti Sandilya, Blacksmith Institute
- Helio Mattar, president, Akatu Institute for Conscious Consumption

Climate change and disaster risk reduction
- Andrew Steer, president and CEO of the World Resources Institute (WRI)
- Pan Jiahua, director, Institute for Urban and Environmental Studies, Chinese Academy of Social Sciences
- Margareta Wahlström, special representative of the Secretary-General for Disaster Risk Reduction
- Debbra A. K. Johnson, DuPont Sustainable Solutions
- Peter deMenocal, Columbia University Earth Institute
- Ronald Jackson, executive director, Caribbean Disaster Emergency Management Agency

See https://sustainabledevelopment.un.org/processes/post2015/owg/session7.

OWG-8: FEBRUARY 3–7, 2014
Oceans and seas, forests, biodiversity
- Jane Lubchenco, Oregon State University
- Sylvia Earle, oceanographer, explorer-in-residence, National Geographic
- Braulio Ferreira de Souza Dias, Convention on Biological Diversity executive secretary
- Alfred Oteng-Yeboah, University of Ghana
- Virgilio Viana, Amazonas Sustainable Foundation
- Mark Smith, director, International Union for Conservation of Nature (IUCN) Global Water Programme
- Marie Haga, executive director, Global Crop Diversity Trust

- Daju Resosudarmo, scientist, Forests and Livelihoods Programme, Center for International Forestry Research (CIFOR)

Promoting equality, including social equity, gender equality and women's empowerment

- Phumzile Mlambo-Ngcuka, executive director, UN Women
- Babatunde Osotimehin, executive director, UN Population Fund (UNFPA)
- José Antonio Ocampo, Columbia University
- Lenín Moreno, UN Secretary-General's special envoy on Disability and Accessibility
- Nicole Ameline, chair of the Committee on the Elimination of Discrimination Against Women

Conflict prevention, post-conflict peacebuilding and the promotion of durable peace, rule of law and governance

- Mary Robinson, chair, the Mary Robinson Foundation, UN special envoy for the Great Lakes Region of Africa
- Cassam Uteem, former president of Mauritius
- Irene Khan, director-general, International Development Law Organization
- William O'Neill, Conflict Prevention and Peace Forum

See https://sustainabledevelopment.un.org/processes/post2015/owg/session8.

APPENDIX II:
Technical Support Team Issue Briefs

The Technical Support Team (TST) was co-chaired by the UN Department of Economic and Social Affairs and the United Nations Development Programme. The agencies listed contributed to each issue brief. The acronyms are spelled out at the end of this appendix. The TST issue briefs can be found at https://sustainabledevelopment.un.org/index.php?page=view&type=400 &nr=1554&menu=1561.

1. **Conceptual Issues:** DESA, ESCAP, FAO, IFAD, ILO, ITU, OHCHR, OHRLLS, UNDP, UNEP, UNESCO, UNFPA, UN-Habitat, UNICEF, UNOOSA,UNV, UN-Women, PBSO, WIPO, World Bank, and WTO.

2. **Poverty:** DESA, ESCAP, FAO, IFAD, ILO, OHCHR, OHRLLS, PBSO, UNAIDS, UNDP, UNEP, UNESCO, UNFPA, UNICEF, UNV, UN-Women, WFP, WMO, and World Bank.

3. **Desertification, Land Degradation, and Drought:** Led by UNCCD. Contributors include FAO, UNFPA, WMO, ESCAP, World Bank, UN-Women, UNEP, UNDP, CBD, UNOOSA, and ITU.

4. **Food Security and Nutrition:** Co-led by WFP, FAO, and IFAD, with contributions from ESCAP, ILO, UNEP, UNICEF, UNV, and UN-Women.

5. **Sustainable Agriculture:** Co-led by FAO and IFAD, with contributions from UN-Women, WMO, ESCWA, WB, UNIDO, WTO Secretariat, UNOOSA, UNCCD/CBD, UNDP, UNESCO, OHCHR, UNFPA, and ESCAP.

6. **Water and Sanitation:** Led by UN-Water. Contributors to this brief include DESA, FAO, ILO, OHCHR, PBSO, CBD, UNCCD, UNDP, ECE, ECLAC, UNEP, ESCAP, UNESCO, UNFPA, UNICEF, UNOOSA, UNU, UN-Women, WHO, World Bank, and WTO, as well as numerous UN-Water Partners.

7. **Education and Culture:** UNESCO, UNICEF, UNFPA, WFP, ILO, ITU, UNV, OHCHR, PBSO, UNDP, and IFAD.

8. **Employment and Decent Work:** ILO, DESA, ESCAP, IFAD, IOM, UNDP, UNFPA, UNIDO, and UN-Women.

9. **Health and Sustainable Development:** WHO, UNFPA, UNAIDS, UN-Women, UNICEF, WMO, UNDP, ILO, PBSO, and CBD.

10. **Population Dynamics:** UNFPA, DESA, UN-Habitat, IOM, ILO, OHCHR, UN-Women, UNAIDS, UNDP, ECLAC, UNEP, ESCAP, UNICEF, WFP, and WMO.

11. **Social Protection:** ILO, UNICEF, ESCAP, FAO, IFAD, OHCHR, UNAIDS, DESA, UNDP, UNFPA, UN-Women, WFP, WMO, and with contributions from members of the Social Protection Interagency Cooperation Board (SPIAC-B).

12. **Energy:** UNEP, UN-Women, UNDP, ESCAP, World Bank, DESA, UN-Habitat, OHRLLS, UNIDO, FAO, CBD, IFAD, UNFF, WMO, WHO, ESCWA, UNESCO, and UN-Energy.

13. **Macroeconomic policy questions (including international trade, international financial system, and external debt sustainability):** Co-led by DESA and UNDP, with contributions from ILO, OHCHR, ESCAP, UNFPA, UN-Habitat, UNIDO, UN-Women, WFP, and WTO.

14. **Sustained and Inclusive Economic Growth, Infrastructure Development, and Industrialization:** Co-led by UNIDO, UNDP, UN-Habitat, and UNEP, with contributions from ESCAP, WFP, UNFPA, UN-Women, ITU, ILO, OSAA, OHRLLS, OHCHR, IFAD, ECE, and UNICEF.

15. **Global Governance:** Led by UNDP and DESA, drawing on comments provided by members of the TST.

16. **Human Rights, including the right to development:** OHCHR, UNICEF, UN-Women, UNDP, and UNEP, with comments from the following agencies: UNESCO, UNAIDS, World Bank, EOSG Rule of Law Unit, PBSO, ILO, DESA, UNFPA, and OSAA.

17. **Means of Implementation; Global Partnership for achieving sustainable development:** Led by UNDP, UNEP, and DESA. Contributors to this brief include ESCAP, FAO, ILO, IOM, ITU, OHCHR, OHRLLS, OOSA, UN-Women, UNAIDS, UNESCO, UNFPA, UNIDO, UNV, WFP, WIPO, WMO, the World Bank, and WTO.

18. **Needs of Countries in Special Situations—African Countries, Least Developed Countries, Landlocked Developing Countries, and Small Island Developing States, as well as the specific challenges facing Middle-Income Countries:** Co-led by OSAA and OHRLLS, with contributions from ECA, ECLAC, FAO, IFAD, OCHA, UNCCD, UNEP, UNFF, UNFPA, UNIDO, UNISDR, UN-Women, and WFP.

19. **Science, Technology, and Innovation, Knowledge-Sharing, and Capacity-Building:** Led by UNESCO, with contributions from IFAD, ITU, UNAIDS, UN-Women, UNDP, UNEP, UNISDR, UNOOSA, WFP, WIPO, and WMO.

20. **Climate Change and Disaster Risk Reduction:** UNDP, UNEP, ESCAP, UNFCCC, UNISDR, and WMO, with contributions from FAO, IFAD, ITU, OCHA, PBSO, UNCCD, DESA, ESCWA, UNFF, UNFPA, UN-Habitat, UNIDO, UNOOSA, UN-Women, WFP, WHO, and the World Bank.

21. **Sustainable Cities and Human Settlements:** Co-led by UN-Habitat and UNEP, with the participation of ECLAC, ESCAP, IFAD, ILO, UNDP, UNFPA, UNICEF, UNISDR, UN-Women, WHO, WMO, and the World Bank.

22. **Sustainable Consumption and Production (SCP), including Chemicals and Waste:** TST drafting group on SCP with inputs from the 10YFP Inter-Agency Coordination Group (IACG).

23. **Sustainable Transport:** Led by UNEP, with contributions from ECE, ESCAP, FAO, WFP, and WMO.

24. **Biodiversity:** Co-led by the CBD, FAO, UNEP, UNDP, and the World Bank, with contributions from ESCAP, UNFF, UNESCO, UN-Women, WMO, and other biodiversity-related conventions (CITES, CMS, ITPGR, and Ramsar).

25. **Conflict Prevention, Post-conflict Peacebuilding and the Promotion of Durable Peace, Rule of Law and Governance:** PBSO, EOSG, and UNDP, and including inputs and comments from DPA, DPKO, ESCAP, ILO, ITU, OCHA, OHCHR, UNAIDS, UNDEF, UNEP, UNESCO, UNFPA, UNHCR, UNICEF, UNODC, UNV, UN-Habitat, UN-Women, WFP, and the World Bank.

26. **Forests:** CBD, DESA, ECLAC, ESCAP, FAO, GEF, ICRAF, ITTO, IUCN, IUFRO, UNCCD, UNDP, UNECE, UNEP, UNFCCC, UN-Habitat, UNOOSA, UN-Women, World Bank, and WMO.

27. **Gender Equality and Women's Empowerment:** UN-Women, UNDP, and UNFPA, with contributions from DSPD/DESA, FAO, IFAD, ITU, OHCHR, PBSO, UNAIDS, UNESCO, UNICEF, World Bank, WFP, and WMO.

28. **Oceans and Seas:** Co-led by DESA, ESCAP, FAO, UNDP, UNEP, UNESCO-IOC, and World Bank, with contributions from CBD, IAEA, ILO, IMO, DOALOS, OSAA, UNOOSA, UN-Women, WMO, and WTO.

29. **Promoting Equality, including Social Equity:** UNICEF, UN-Women, UNDP, and OHCHR, with contributions from UNEP, PBSO, DESA, ESCAP, IFAD, UN-Habitat, IOM, UNESCO, ILO, World Bank, UNAIDS, UNV, WFP, UNFPA, ITU, UNV, DPA, OHRLLS, WTO, and other agencies of the TST.

LIST OF TECHNICAL SUPPORT TEAM MEMBERS

1. CBD — Convention on Biological Diversity
2. CITES — Convention on International Trade in Endangered Species of Fauna and Flora
3. CMS — Convention on Migratory Species
4. DESA — UN Department of Economic and Social Affairs
5. DPA — UN Department of Political Affairs
6. DPKO — UN Department of Peacekeeping Operations
7. DSPD — UN Division for Social Policy and Development
8. ECE — UN Economic Commission for Europe
9. ECLAC — UN Economic Commission for Latin America and the Caribbean
10. EOSG — Executive Office of the Secretary General Rule of Law Unit
11. ESCAP — UN Economic and Social Commission for Asia and the Pacific
12. ESCWA — UN Economic and Social Commission for Western Asia

13. FAO   Food and Agriculture Organization

14. GEF   Global Environment Facility

15. IACG   10 Year Framework of Programmes on Sustainable Consumption and Production Inter-Agency Coordination Group

16. IAEA   International Atomic Energy Agency

17. ICRAF   International Council for Research in Agroforestry

18. IFAD   International Fund for Agricultural Development

19. ILO   International Labor Organization

20. IOM   International Organization for Migration

21. ITPGR   International Treaty on Plant Genetic Resources for Food and Agriculture

22. ITTO   International Tropical Timber Organization

23. ITU   International Telecommunications Union

24. IUCN   International Union for Conservation of Nature and Natural Resources

25. IUFRO   International Union of Forest Research Organizations

26. OCHA   UN Office for the Coordination of Humanitarian Affairs

27. OHCHR   UN Office of the High Commissioner for Human Rights

28. OHRLLS   UN Office of the High Representative for the Least Developed Countries, Landlocked Developing Countries and Small Island Developing States

29. DOALOS   UN Office of Legal Affairs Department of Ocean Affairs and the Law of the Sea

30. OSAA   UN Office of the Special Adviser on Africa

31. PBSO   UN Peacebuilding Support Office

32. Ramsar   Ramsar Convention on Wetlands of International Importance

33. SPIAC-B   UN Social Protection Interagency Cooperation Board

34. UNAIDS   Joint United Nations Programme on HIV/AIDS

35. UNCCD   UN Convention to Combat Desertification
36. UNDEF   UN Democracy Fund
37. UNDP   UN Development Programme
38. UN-Energy   Inter-agency group on energy
39. UNEP   UN Environment Programme
40. UNESCO   UN Educational, Scientific and Cultural
                   Organization
41. UNESCO-IOC   UNESCO Intergovernmental Oceanographic
                   Commission
42. UNFCCC   UN Framework Convention on Climate Change
43. UNFF   UN Forum on Forests
44. UNFPA   UN Population Fund
45. UN-Habitat   UN Human Settlements Programme
46. UNICEF   UN Children's Fund
47. UNIDO   UN Industrial Development Organization
48. UNISDR   UN Office for Disaster Risk Reduction
49. UNODC   UN Office on Drugs and Crime
50. UNOOSA   UN Office for Outer Space Affairs
51. UNU   UN University
52. UNV   UN Volunteers programme
53. UN-Water   Inter-agency group on water
54. UN-Women   UN Entity for Gender Equality and the
                   Empowerment of Women
55. WFP   World Food Programme
56. WHO   World Health Organization
57. WIPO   World Intellectual Property Organization
58. WMO   World Meteorological Organization
59. World Bank   The World Bank Group
60. WTO   World Trade Organization

NOTES

1: SETTING THE STAGE

1. Ban Ki-moon, "Secretary-General's Remarks at Summit for the Adoption of the Post-2015 Development Agenda," United Nations Sustainable Development Summit, New York, September 25, 2015, https://www.un.org/sg/en/content/sg/statement/2015-09-25/secretary-generals-remarks-summit-adoption-post-2015-development.

2. Uhuru Kenyatta, "Statement to the Plenary for the Adoption of the Post-2015 Development Agenda," United Nations General Assembly, New York, September 25, 2015, https://sustainabledevelopment.un.org/content/documents/20305kenya.pdf.

3. Liz Ford, "Global Goals Received with Rapture in New York—Now Comes the Hard Part," *Guardian*, September 25, 2015, www.theguardian.com/global-development/2015/sep/25/global-goals-summit-2015-new-york-un-pope-shakira-malala-yousafzai.

4. Adam Russell Taylor, "Caring for Our Common Home, Pope Francis and the SDGs," World Bank blog, October 1, 2015, http://blogs.worldbank.org/climatechange/caring-our-common-home-pope-francis-and-sdgs-0.

5. UN General Assembly, "The Future We Want," A/RES.66/288, September 11, 2012, www.un.org/ga/search/view_doc.asp?symbol=A/RES/66/288&Lang=E.

6. Ministry of Foreign Affairs, Republic of Colombia, "Rio+20: Sustainable Development Goals (SDGs): A Proposal from the Governments of Colombia and Guatemala," November 2011.

7. See United Nations, "Transforming Our World: The 2030 Agenda for Sustainable Development," A.69/L.85, August 15, 2015, www.un.org/ga/search/view_doc.asp?symbol=A/69/L.85&Lang=E.

8. Andrew Simms, "The Current Economic Development Model Is Defunct—We Need to Ditch It," *Guardian*, March 11, 2015, www.theguardian.com/environment/2015/mar/11/the-current-economic-development-model-is-defunct-we-need-to-ditch-it.

9. Ibid.

10. Michael Redclift, *Sustainable Development: Exploring the Contradictions* (New York: Methuen, 1987).

11. Pamela Chasek, "Achieving Sustainable Development," in *Introducing Global Issues,* eds. Michael Snarr and D. Neil Snarr, 6th ed. (Boulder: Lynne Rienner, 2016), 292.

12. World Commission on Environment and Development, *Our Common Future* (New York: Oxford University Press, 1987), 8.

13. Chasek, "Achieving Sustainable Development," 293.

14. Joanna Depledge and Pamela Chasek, "Raising the Tempo: The Escalating Pace and Intensity of Environmental Negotiations," in *The Roads from Rio: Lessons Learned from Twenty Years of Multilateral Environmental Negotiations,* eds. Pamela Chasek and Lynn Wagner (New York: RFF/Routledge, 2012), 31–32.

15. Saadia Touval, "Multilateral Negotiation: An Analytic Approach," in *Negotiation Theory and Practice,* eds. J. William Breslin and Jeffrey Z. Rubin (Cambridge, MA: Program on Negotiation at Harvard Law School, 1991).

16. This paragraph has been adapted from Non-Governmental Liaison Service (NGLS), *Intergovernmental Negotiations and Decision Making at the United Nations: A Guide,* 2nd ed. (New York: United Nations, 2007), 19.

17. Ibid., 22.

18. Ibid., 23.

19. Ibid., 24.

20. Ibid., 20–21.

21. Ibid., 21.

2: MULTILATERALISM: COMPLEXITY AND INTRIGUES

1. James Muldoon, "Return to Multilateralism (1992–)," in *Oxford Bibliographies in International Relations,* ed. Cathal Nolan (New York: Oxford University Press, 2012).

2. Margaret P. Karns and Karen A. Mingst, *International Organizations: The Politics and Processes of Global Governance* (Boulder, Colorado: Lynne Rienner, 2004), 27.

3. George H. W. Bush, Address Before a Joint Session of Congress, September 11, 1990, http://millercenter.org/president/bush/speeches/speech-3425.

4. United Nations press release, "Secretary-General Names High-Level Panel to Study Global Security and Reform of the International System," November 4, 2003, as cited in Edward Newman, Ramesh Thakur, and John Tirman, eds., *Multilateralism Under Challenge* (Tokyo, Japan: United Nations University Press, 2006), 1.

5. Carlos Lopes, "Challenges to Multilateralism," United Nations

Economic Commission for Africa, 20 March 2015, www.uneca.org/es-blog
/challenges-multilateralism.

6. Muzaffer Ercan Yilmas, "'The New World Order': An Outline of the
Post-Cold War Era," *Alternatives: Turkish Journal of International Relations* 7,
no. 4 (2008): 52.

7. James Sebenius, "Negotiating a Regime to Control Global Warming,"
in *Greenhouse Warming: Negotiating a Global Regime,* ed. Jessica Tuchman
Mathews (Washington, DC: World Resources Institute, 1991), 87.

8. South Commission, *The Challenge to the South: The Report of the South
Commission* (Oxford: Oxford University Press, 1990); Mohammed Ayoob,
"The New-Old Disorder in the Third World," *Global Governance* 1, no. 1
(1995): 59–77; Adil Najam, "An Environmental Negotiation Strategy for the
South," *International Environmental Affairs* 7, no. 3 (1995): 249–287; Najam,
"The View from the South," 224–243.

9. This was part of a longer-term decline in the real prices of primary
products in the world market caused by slow growth in demand, the development of cheaper substitutes, and overproduction. See UNDP, *Human
Development Report 1992* (New York: UNDP, 1992), 59.

10. UNDP, "Financial Inflows and Outflows," *Human Development Report
1998* (New York: Oxford University Press, 1998). The term *least-developed
countries* (LDCs) was originally used by the United Nations in 1971 to describe the "poorest and most economically weak of the developing countries,
with formidable economic, institutional and human resources problems,
which are often compounded by geographical handicaps and natural and
man-made disasters." There are currently 47 LDCs.

11. See International Monetary Fund, "Debt Relief Under the Heavily Indebted Poor Countries (HIPC) Initiative," September 20, 2016, www.imf.org
/en/About/Factsheets/Sheets/2016/08/01/16/11/Debt-Relief-Under-the
-Heavily-Indebted-Poor-Countries-Initiative.

12. World Commission on Environment and Development, *Our Common
Future* (New York: Oxford University Press, 1987), 5.

13. Ibid., 43.

14. Lars-Göran Engfeldt, *From Stockholm to Johannesburg and Beyond*
(Stockholm: Government Offices of Sweden, 2009), 111.

15. Ibid., 143.

16. Organization for Economic Cooperation and Development, Net ODA
(indicator), doi 10.1787/33346549-en, 2017. http://data.oecd.org/oda/net-
oda.htm

17. World Bank, "World Development Indicators and Global Development Finance," 2015, databank.worldbank.org/data/home.aspx.

18. Ibid.

19. Ibid.

20. M. Ayhan Kose and Eswar Prasad, *Emerging Markets: Resilience and Growth Amid Global Turmoil* (Washington, DC: Brookings Institution Press, 2010), 1.

21. John W. McArthur, "The Origins of the Millennium Development Goals," *SAIS Review* 34, no. 2 (2014): 6.

22. For the text of the Millennium Declaration, see www.un.org /millennium/declaration/ares552e.htm.

23. McArthur, "Origins," 7.

24. Ibid., 5.

25. UN General Assembly, "Follow-Up to the Outcome of the Millennium Summit, Resolution 55/162," December 18, 2000.

26. United Nations, "Road Map Towards the Implementation of the United Nations Millennium Declaration: Report of the Secretary-General," UN General Assembly A/56/326 (2001).

27. Bilyana Lilly, "Global Development Baton Passes from MDGs to SDGs," *Washington Diplomat,* August 27, 2015, www.washdiplomat.com /index.php?option=com_content&view=article&id=12291:global -development-baton-passes-from-mdgs-to-sdgs&catid=1535:september -2015&Itemid=561.

28. Organization for Economic Cooperation and Development, 2017.

29. For more information about the accomplishments and shortcomings of the Millennium Development Goals, see United Nations, *The Millennium Development Goals Report: 2015* (New York: United Nations, 2015), www .un.org/millenniumgoals/reports.shtml.

30. Lopes, "Challenges."

31. Joel Havemann, "The Financial Crisis of 2008," *Encyclopaedia Brittanica,* www.britannica.com/topic/Financial-Crisis-of-2008-The-1484264.

32. "The Origins of the Financial Crisis," *Economist,* September 7, 2013, www.economist.com/news/schoolsbrief/21584534-effects-financial-crisis -are-still-being-felt-five-years-article.

33. Ibid.

34. Lopes, "Challenges."

35. Ricardo Meléndez-Ortiz, Christophe Bellmann, and Shuaihua Cheng, eds., *A Decade in the WTO: Implications for China and Global Trade*

Governance (Geneva: International Centre for Trade and Sustainable Development, 2011), 1, www19.iadb.org/intal/intalcdi/PE/2012/10006.pdf.

36. Ibid.

37. United Nations, *Millennium Development Goals Report: 2015,* 4–7.

38. Ibid., 8–9.

39. Mark Tran, "Mark Malloch-Brown: Developing the MDGs Was a Bit Like Nuclear Fusion," *Guardian,* November 16, 2012, www.theguardian.com /global-development/2012/nov/16/mark-malloch-brown-mdgs-nuclear.

40. Dan Smith, "So What's Wrong with the MDGs?" Dan Smith's Blog, September 20, 2010, https://dansmithsblog.com/2010/09/20/so-whats-wrong -with-the-mdgs.

41. Intergovernmental Panel on Climate Change, *Fourth Assessment Report: Climate Change 2007* (Geneva: IPCC, 2007).

42. United Nations Environment Programme, *Global Chemicals Outlook* (Nairobi: UNEP, 2012).

43. Millennium Ecosystem Assessment, *Ecosystems and Human Well -Being: Biodiversity Synthesis* (Washington, DC: World Resources Institute, 2005).

44. World Health Organization, "Deaths from NCDs," Global Health Observatory Data, www.who.int/gho/ncd/mortality_morbidity/ncd_total_text /en.

45. United Nations, "Delivering as One: Report of the Secretary-General's High-Level Panel on UN System-Wide Coherence in the Areas of Development, Humanitarian Assistance, and the Environment," document A/61/583, November 2006, 18–19, www.un.org/en/ga/search/view_doc.asp?symbol =A/61/583.

46. Ibid., 10.

47. "Statement of H.E. Luiz Inácio Lula da Silva, President of the Federative Republic of Brazil, at the General Debate of the 62nd Session of the United Nations General Assembly," New York, September 25, 2007, www .un.org/webcast/ga/62/2007/pdfs/brazil-en.pdf.

48. United Nations, "Global Crises Offer Chances to Use Sustainable Development as Engine for Common Purposes, Meeting International Development Goals, Second Committee Told," Press Release GA/EF/3223, October 27, 2008, www.un.org/press/en/2008/gaef3223.doc.htm.

49. United Nations General Assembly, "Implementation of Agenda 21, the Programme for the Further Implementation of Agenda 21 and the Outcomes of the World Summit on Sustainable Development," Resolution 64/236,

March 31, 2010, www.un.org/en/ga/search/view_doc.asp?symbol=A/RES /64/236.

50. Xinhua News Agency, "UNEP Chief Urges World to Invest in Green Economy," July 24, 2009, www.china.org.cn/environment/news/2009–07/24 /content_18194869.htm.

51. International Institute for Sustainable Development (IISD), "Summary of the Copenhagen Climate Change Conference: 7–19 December 2009," *Earth Negotiations Bulletin,* December 22, 2009, www.iisd.ca/download/pdf /enb12459e.pdf.

52. Ibid.

53. UNFCCC, "Copenhagen Accord," decision 2/CP.15, in "Report of the Conference of the Parties on Its Fifteenth Session, Held in Copenhagen from 7 to 19 December 2009, Addendum, Part Two: Action Taken by the Conference of the Parties at Its Fifteenth Session," FCCC/CP/2009/11/Add.1, March 30, 2010, http://unfccc.int/resource/docs/2009/cop15/eng/11a01.pdf.

54. UNEP, *Towards a Green Economy: Pathways to Sustainable Development and Poverty Eradication* (Nairobi: UNEP, 2011), web.unep.org/green economy/sites/unep.org.greeneconomy/files/field/image/green_economy report_final_dec2011.pdf.

55. The Bolivarian Alliance for the Americas (ALBA) was founded by Cuba and Venezuela. Members also include Antigua and Barbuda, Bolivia, Dominica, Ecuador, Grenada, Nicaragua, Saint Kitts and Nevis, Saint Lucia, and Saint Vincent and the Grenadines.

56. "ALBA Nations Declare: Nature Has No Price!" *Climate and Capitalism,* November 15, 2010, http://climateandcapitalism.com/2010/11/15 /alba-nations-declare-nature-has-no-price.

57. John Scanlon, "Enhancing Environmental Governance for Sustainable Development: Function-Oriented Options," Governance and Sustainability Issue Brief Series (Boston: University of Massachusetts Boston, March 2012), hqweb.unep.org/delc/Portals/24151/JohnScanlonEnhancingEnvironmental-GovernanceSustainablDevelopment.pdf.

58. Jacques Chirac, Speech on the occasion of the "Citizens of the Earth" conference for global ecological governance, Paris, February 2, 2007, www .jacqueschirac-asso.fr/archives-elysee.fr/elysee/elysee.fr/anglais/speeches _and_documents/2007/fi001295.html.

59. IISD, "Summary of the UNCSD Informal Informal Consultations and Third Intersessional Meeting: 19–27 March 2012," *Earth Negotiations Bulletin,* March 30, 2012, www.iisd.ca/download/pdf/enb2724e.pdf.

60. IISD, "Summary of the Third Round of UNCSD Informal Informal Consultations: 29 May–2 June 2012," *Earth Negotiations Bulletin,* June 5, 2012, www.iisd.ca/download/pdf/enb2740e.pdf.

61. Ibid. See also Lynn M. Wagner, "A Forty-Year Search for a Single-Negotiating Text: Rio+20 as a Post-Agreement Negotiation," *International Negotiation* 18 (2013): 333–356.

62. Paula Caballero Gómez, "A Short History of the SDGs," informal paper, April 2016, http://deliver2030.org/wp-content/uploads/2016/04/A-short -history-of-the-SDGs-Paula-Caballero.pdf .

63. Colombian Ministry of Foreign Affairs, "Inputs of the Government of Colombia to Draft Zero of the Outcome Document," November 30, 2011, www.uncsd2012.org/content/documents/372Colombia.pdf.

64. Caballero Gómez, "Short History," 7.

65. Caballero Gómez, "Short History," 12–13.

66. Ibid., 13.

67. Ibid., 15. Farrukh Khan, who represented Pakistan in the discussions, said he believed that the group could consist of no more than thirty members or it wouldn't be effective. They both used as a model the Green Climate Fund Board, which has twenty-four members—equally drawn from developed and developing countries—and is seen as effective. See also Farrukh Khan, "The SDG Story: An Insider Account of How It All Came About," *Impakter,* December 13, 2016, http://impakter.com/sdg-story-insider-account -came.

68. UN General Assembly, "The Future We Want," A/RES.66/288, September 11, 2012, www.un.org/ga/search/view_doc.asp?symbol=A/RES/66/288 &Lang=E.

69. Ibid.

70. IISD, "UNCSD PrepCom III: Friday, 15 June 2012," *Earth Negotiations Bulletin,* June 16, 2012, www.iisd.ca/download/pdf/enb2744e.pdf.

71. Wagner, "A Forty-Year Search for a Single-Negotiating Text"; IISD, "Summary of the United Nations Conference on Sustainable Development: 13–22 June 2012," *Earth Negotiations Bulletin,* June 25, 2012, www.iisd.ca /download/pdf/enb2751e.pdf.

72. Felix Dodds, Jorge Laguna-Celis, and Liz Thompson, *From Rio+20 to a New Development Agenda: Building a Bridge to a Sustainable Future* (London: Routledge, 2014), 163.

Nikhil Seth, e-mail correspondence, July 25, 2017.

73. IISD, "Summary of the United Nations Conference on Sustainable Development:13–22 June 2012."

74. Ibid.

3: GETTING STARTED: CREATING THE OPEN

1. Farrukh Khan, "The SDG Story: An Insider Account of How It All Came About," *Impakter,* December 13, 2016, http://impakter.com/sdg -story-insider-account-came.

2. United Nations General Assembly, "The Future We Want," Resolution 66/288, September 11, 2012, www.un.org/en/ga/search/view_doc. asp?symbol=%20A/RES/66/288.

3. United Nations General Assembly, "123rd Plenary Meeting, Friday, 27 July 2012, 10 A.M. New York," document A/66/PV.123, 5, www.un.org/en/ga /search/view_doc.asp?symbol=A/66/PV.123.

4. United Nations General Assembly, "Agenda of the 67th Session of the General Assembly," document A/67/251, September 21, 2012, www.un.org /en/ga/search/view_doc.asp?symbol=A/67/251.

5. See United Nations General Assembly, "The Future We Want," paragraphs 84–86, and United Nations General Assembly, "Format and Organizational Aspects of the High-Level Political Forum on Sustainable Development," Resolution 67/290, August 23, 2013, www.un.org/en/ga/search /view_doc.asp?symbol=A/RES/67/290.

6. See United Nations General Assembly, "The Future We Want," paragraph 88, and United Nations General Assembly, "Report of the Governing Council of the United Nations Environment Programme on Its Twelfth Special Session and the Implementation of Section IV.C, Entitled 'Environmental Pillar in the Context of Sustainable Development' of the Outcome Document of the United Nations Conference on Sustainable Development," Resolution 67/213, March 15, 2013, www.un.org/en/ga/search/view_doc.asp?symbol=A /RES/67/213.

7. See United Nations General Assembly, "The Future We Want," paragraph 180, and United Nations General Assembly, "Follow-Up to and Implementation of the Mauritius Strategy for the Further Implementation of the Programme of Action for the Sustainable Development of Small Island Developing States," Resolution 67/207, March 5, 2013, www.un.org/en/ga /search/view_doc.asp?symbol=A/RES/67/207.

8. United Nations General Assembly, "Implementation of Agenda 21, the Programme for the Further Implementation of Agenda 21 and the

Outcomes of the World Summit on Sustainable Development and of the United Nations Conference on Sustainable Development," Resolution 67/203, February 27, 2013, www.un.org/en/ga/search/view_doc.asp?symbol=A/RES/67/203.

9. Ibid.

10. United Nations General Assembly, "The Future We Want," paragraph 248.

11. For a list of members of the Secretary-General's high-level panel and outputs, see www.un.org/sg/en/management/hlppost2015.shtml.

12. For more information about the Green Climate Fund Board, see www.greenclimate.fund/boardroom/the-board.

13. Permanent Mission of Switzerland to the United Nations, *The PGA Handbook: A Practical Guide to the United Nations General Assembly* (New York: Permanent Mission of Switzerland to the United Nations, 2011), 19.

14. United Nations Department for Public Information, "General Assembly Concludes Main Part of Session Following Consensus in Fifth Committee on Member State Contributions to Regular, Peacekeeping Budgets," General Assembly Meetings Coverage GA/11335, December 24, 2012, www.un.org/press/en/2012/ga11335.doc.htm.

15. Interview with Csaba Kőrösi, former permanent representative of Hungary to the United Nations, September 18, 2014.

16. There are fifty-four members in the African Group, fifty-four in the Asia-Pacific Group, twenty-three in Eastern Europe, thirty-three in Latin America and the Caribbean, and twenty-eight in Western European and Others (WEOG, plus one observer, Israel). In May 2000 Israel became a WEOG full member on a temporary basis (subject to renewal) in WEOG's headquarters in the United States, thereby enabling it to put forward candidates for election to various UN General Assembly bodies. In 2004 Israel obtained a permanent renewal to its membership. As of 2010, Kiribati (geographically in Oceania) is not a member of any regional group, despite other Oceania nations belonging to the Asian group. Despite its membership in the United Nations, Kiribati has never delegated a permanent representative. Turkey participates fully in both WEOG and the Asian Group, but for electoral purposes it is considered a member of WEOG only. The United States is not a member of any regional group but attends meetings of WEOG as an observer and is considered to be a member of that group for electoral purposes. See www.un.org/depts/DGACM/RegionalGroups.shtml.

17. Interview with Nikhil Seth, former director, UN Division for Sustainable Development, UN Department for Economic and Social Affairs, September 9, 2014.

18. Interview with Farrukh Khan, formerly with the Mission of Pakistan to the United Nations, July 11, 2016.

19. Ibid.

20. United Nations General Assembly, "Decision 67/555. Open Working Group of the General Assembly on Sustainable Development Goals," *Resolutions and Decisions Adopted by the General Assembly During Its Sixty-Seventh Session Volume III 25 December 2012–16 September 2013*, A/67/49 (New York: United Nations, 2013), 176, www.un.org/ga/search/view_doc.asp? symbol=a/67/49(Vol.III).

21. President of the General Assembly, "Letter to All Permanent Representatives of the Members of the Open Working Group on Sustainable Development Goals," February 20, 2013, www.un.org/en/ga/president/67/letters/pdf /Open%20Woking%20Group%20on%20Sustainable%20Development%20 Facilitators%20appointed%20-%2020%20February%202013.pdf.

22. "Open Working Group on Sustainable Development Goals: Provisional Agenda," document A/AC.280/2013/1, March 8, 2013, www.un.org/ga/search /view_doc.asp?symbol=A/AC.280/2013/1&Lang=E.

23. United Nations, "General Assembly Open Working Group on Sustainable Development Goals: Methods of Work," https://sustainablede velopment.un.org/content/documents/1692OWG_methods_work_adopted_ 1403.pdf.

24. United Nations, *Charter of the United Nations*, available at www.un.org /en/charter-united-nations.

25. Mori Satoko, "Institutionalization of NGO Involvement in Policy Functions for Global Environmental Governance," in *Emerging Forces in Environmental Governance*, eds. Norichika Kanie and Peter M. Haas (Tokyo: UNU Press, 2004), 158–160.

26. Ibid.

27. Tobias Ogweno, e-mail correspondence, 2016.

28. Ibid.

29. Ibid.

30. Ibid.

31. Ibid.

32. UN News Centre, "Azerbaijan Wins Final Vacancy on Security

Council," October 24, 2011, www.un.org/apps/news/story.asp?News-ID=40174&Cr=security+council&Cr1=#.V6ntyrgrJaQ.

33. United Nations News Centre, "New Permanent Representative of Hungary Presents Credentials," September 9, 2010, www.un.org/press/en/2010/bio4234.doc.htm.

34. Ibid.

35. United Nations News Centre, "New Permanent Representative of Kenya Presents Credentials," December 16, 2010, www.un.org/press/en/2010/bio4257.doc.htm.

36. Ibid.

37. Ibid.

38. Bo Kjellén, "The New Diplomacy from the Perspective of a Diplomat: Facilitation of the Post-Kyoto Climate Talks," in *Climate Change Negotiations: A Guide to Resolving Disputes and Facilitating Multilateral Cooperation*, eds. Gunnar Sjostedt and Ariel Macaspac Penetrante (New York: Routledge, 2013), 52.

39. Ibid.

40. P. Terrence Hopmann, *The Negotiation Process and the Resolution of International Conflicts* (Columbia, SC: University of South Carolina Press, 1996), 265.

41. Oran Young, "The Politics of International Regime Formation," *International Organization* 43, no. 3 (1989): 355.

42. Steiner Andresen, "Leadership and Climate Talks: Historical Lessons in Agenda Setting," in *Climate Change Negotiations: A Guide to Resolving Disputes and Facilitating Multilateral Cooperation,* eds. Gunnar Sjostedt and Ariel Macaspac Penetrante (New York: Routledge, 2013), 150.

43. Ibid.

44. Kjellén, "The New Diplomacy," 60.

45. Guy-Olivier Faure, "International Negotiation: The Cultural Dimension," in *International Negotiation: Analysis, Approaches, Issues,* 2nd ed., ed. Victor A. Kremenyuk (San Francisco: Jossey-Bass, 2002), 396.

46. Ibid., 412.

47. Ibid., 413.

48. Bradley C. Parks and J. Timmons Roberts, "Inequality and the Global Climate Regime: Breaking the North-South Impasse," *Cambridge Review of International Affairs* 21, no. 4 (2008): 636–637.

49. Kőrösi interview.

4: UNCERTAIN BEGINNINGS

1. Vuk Jeremić, "Remarks on the Opening of the First Meeting of the Open Working Group of the General Assembly on Sustainable Development Goals," March 14, 2013, https://sustainabledevelopment.un.org/content /documents/3435pga.pdf.

2. Ibid.

3. United Nations General Assembly, "Initial Input of the Secretary-General to the Open Working Group on Sustainable Development Goals," A/67/634, December 17, 2012, www.un.org/ga/search/view_doc.asp?symbol =A/67/634&Lang=E.

4. See the full survey at "Questionnaire Related to the Development of Sustainable Development Goals to Seek Input from National Governments in Preparation for the Secretary-General's Initial Input to the Open Working Group," September 28, 2012, https://sustainabledevelopment.un.org/content /documents/14421360Questionnaire%20SDGs_final_2809-1.pdf.

5. Ibid., 5.

6. International Institute for Sustainable Development (IISD), "Summary of the First Session of the UN General Assembly Open Working Group on Sustainable Development Goals: 14–15 March 2013," *Earth Negotiations Bulletin,* March 18, 2013, www.iisd.ca/download/pdf/enb3201e.pdf.

7. Ibid.

8. The United Nations Development Group (UNDG) unites the thirty-two UN funds, programs, specialized agencies, departments, and offices that play a role in development. See https://undg.org.

9. UN System Task Team on the Post-2015 UN Development Agenda, *Realizing the Future We Want for All* (New York: United Nations, 2012), 25–32, www.un.org/en/development/desa/policy/untaskteam_undf/untt_report.pdf.

10. Ibid., 7.

11. Ibid.

12. Ibid.

13. Nikhil Seth, e-mail correspondence, July 25, 2017.

14. See International Council for Science, "Health and the Sustainable Development Goals: An Urban Systems Perspective," June 5, 2013, https:// sustainabledevelopment.un.org/index.php?page=view&type=400&nr =894&menu=35.

15. 2014 Development Cooperation Forum Switzerland High-Level Symposium, "Development Cooperation in a Post-2015 Era: Sustainable Development for All," 2014, https://sustainabledevelopment.un.org/content /documents/2519dcf_switzerland_aide_memoire.pdf.

16. Submission by Rashida Manjoo, UN special rapporteur on Violence Against Women, Its Causes and Consequences, Open Working Group on Sustainable Development Goals, 2014, https://sustainabledevelopment.un-.org/content/documents/3337RM%20submission%20to%20OWG%20on%20post%202015%20SDGs.pdf.

17. Pamela Chasek and Lynn Wagner, "Breaking the Mold: A New Type of Multilateral Sustainable Development Negotiation," *International Environmental Agreements: Politics, Law and Economics* 16, no. 3 (2016): 405.

18. Lynn M. Wagner, Reem Hajjar, and Asheline Appleton, "Global Alliances to Strange Bedfellows: The Ebb and Flow of Negotiating Coalitions," in *The Roads from Rio: Lessons Learned from Twenty Years of Multilateral Environmental Negotiations,* eds. Pamela S. Chasek and Lynn M. Wagner (New York: RFF Press/Routledge, 2012).

19. Chasek and Wagner, "Breaking the Mold," 402–403.

20. Wagner, Hajjar, and Appleton, "Global Alliances," 89.

21. Chasek and Wagner, "Breaking the Mold," 404.

22. United Nations, "The Threat of Growing Inequalities: Building More Just and Equitable Societies to Support Growth and Sustainable Development," press release, January 20, 2014, www.un.org/webcast/pdfs/stiglitz140120pm.pdf.

23. Joseph Stiglitz, "The Threat of Growing Inequalities: Building More Just and Equitable Societies to Support Growth and Sustainable Development," roundtable presentation, UN Headquarters, New York, January 20, 2014, http://webtv.un.org/watch/the-threat-of-growing-inequalities-roundtable-with-prof.-joseph-stiglitz-nobel-laureate-for-economic-sciences-2001/3086046375001. See also Michael W. Doyle and Joseph E. Stiglitz, "Eliminating Extreme Inequality: A Sustainable Development Goal, 2015–2030," Carnegie Council for Ethics and International Affairs, March 20, 2014, www.ethicsandinternationalaffairs.org/2014/eliminating-extreme-inequality-a-sustainable-development-goal-2015–2030.

24. Stiglitz, "Threat of Growing Inequalities."

25. Doyle and Stiglitz, "Eliminating Extreme Inequality."

26. Michael Shear and Peter Baker, "Obama Focuses on Economy, Vowing to Help Middle Class," *New York Times,* July 24, 2013, www.nytimes.com/2013/07/25/us/politics/obama-to-restate-economic-vision-at-knox-college.html?_r=0.

27. Pope Francis, "WYD 2013: Full Text of Pope Francis's Address in Rio Slum," *Catholic Herald*, July 25, 2013, www.catholicherald.co.uk/news/2013 /07/25/wyd-2013-full-text-of-pope-franciss-address-in-rio-slum.

28. Oxfam, "The Cost of Inequality: How Wealth and Income Extremes Hurt Us All," Media Briefing 2/2013, January 18, 2013, www.oxfam.org/sites /www.oxfam.org/files/cost-of-inequality-oxfam-mb180113.pdf.

29. See Thomas Picketty, *Capital in the Twenty-First Century* (Cambridge: Harvard University Press, 2014).

30. Sally Goldenberg, "At Midterm, de Blasio Reflects on Accomplishments, Mistakes," *Politico*, December 21, 2015, www.politico.com/states /new-york/albany/story/2015/12/at-midterm-de-blasio-reflects-on -accomplishments-mistakes-000000.

31. "Statement on behalf of the African Group by H.E. Ahmad Allam-Mi, permanent representative of the Republic of Chad to the United Nations on the occasion of the first meeting of the Open Working Group on Sustainable Development," United Nations, New York, March 14, 2013, https:// sustainabledevelopment.un.org/content/documents/3423africangroup.pdf.

32. European Union and Its Member States, "Speaking Points on 'Conceptualizing the SDGs and the SDG Process,'" meeting of the General Assembly Open Working Group on Sustainable Development Goals, United Nations, New York, April 17–19, 2013, https://sustainabledevelopment.un.org /content/documents/3522euconcept.pdf.

33. Secretary-General's remarks at opening of Open Working Group on the Sustainable Development Goals, United Nations, New York, March 14, 2013, https://sustainabledevelopment.un.org/content/documents/3483sg.pdf.

34. Jeremić, "Remarks."

35. Paul Polman, "Global Partnership for Achieving Sustainable Development," speech to the 6th session of the UN Open Working Group on Sustainable Development Goals, December 10, 2013, www.unilever.com/Images /paul_polman_un_open_working_group_sdgoals_tcm13-379200_tcm 244-420733_en.pdf.

36. See paragraph 79 of UN General Assembly, "Keeping the Promise: United to Achieve the Millennium Development Goals," Resolution 65/1, www.un.org/en/mdg/summit2010/pdf/outcome_documentN1051260.pdf.

37. Nicole Rippin, "Post 2015: Special Event on Post-2015—Stuck in the Process?" Briefing Paper 19/2013, German Development Institute, www.die-gdi.de/en/briefing-paper/article/post-2015-special-event-on-post -2015-stuck-in-the-process.

38. UN General Assembly, "Outcome Document of the Special Event to Follow Up Efforts Made Towards Achieving the Millennium Development Goals," Resolution 68/6, www.un.org/en/ga/search/view_doc.asp?symbol=A /RES/68/6.

39. Ibid.

40. Ibid.

41. Chasek and Wagner, "Breaking the Mold," 406.

42. Ibid., 407.

43. Ibid., 405.

5: THE CAST OF CHARACTERS

1. Csaba Kőrösi, "OWG8 Concluding Remarks of Co-Chairs," eighth session of the Opening Working Group on the SDGs, New York, February 7, 2014, https://sustainabledevelopment.un.org/content/documents/3195 cochairconcluding.pdf.

2. Deborah M. Kolb and Guy-Olivier Faure, "Organization Theory: The Interface of Structure, Culture, Procedures, and Negotiation Processes," in *International Multilateral Negotiation: Approaches to the Management of Complexity*, ed. I. William Zartman (San Francisco: Jossey-Bass, 1994), 113–131.

3. Saadia Touval, "Multilateral Negotiation: An Analytical Approach," *Negotiation Journal* 5 (1989): 165–167.

4. Ibid.; André Auer and Jérôme Racine, "Multilateral Negotiations: From Strategic Considerations to Tactical Recommendations," *Sumbiosis*, 2001, www.sumbiosis.com/fileadmin/downloads/tools/d/multilateral_negotiations _e.pdf.

5. Fred Charles Iklé, *How Nations Negotiate* (New York: Harper & Row, 1964), 159.

6. Auer and Racine, "Multilateral Negotiations."

7. The ideas in this paragraph are derived from Arild Underdal, "Leadership Theory—Rediscovering the Arts of Management," in *International Multilateral Negotiation: Approaches to the Management of Complexity*, ed. I. William Zartman (San Francisco: Jossey-Bass, 1994), 188.

8. "Statement by H.E. Ambassador Dr. Peter Wittig, Permanent Representative of Germany to the United Nations," first formal meeting of the Open Working Group on Sustainable Development Goals, New York, March 14, 2013, https://sustainabledevelopment.un.org/content/documents/345 0germany.pdf.

9. "Intervention de M. Pascal Canfin, Ministre Delegue Charge du Developpement," Reunion du Groupe de Travail sur les Objectifs du Developpement Durable, New York, March 14, 2013, https://sustainabledevelopment.un.org/content/documents/3420France.pdf.

10. "Insights on the Post-2015 Process and the SDGs: A Contribution from the Governments of Colombia and Guatemala to Start a Substantive Discussion," Open Working Group on the SDGs, New York, March 14–15, 2013, https://sustainabledevelopment.un.org/content/documents/3445 colombia.pdf.

11. Ibid.

12. Anne Anderson, "Statement on Behalf of Denmark, Ireland and Norway on the Occasion of the First Meeting of the Open Working Group on Sustainable Development Goals," first meeting of the Open Working Group on Sustainable Development Goals, New York, March 14, 2013, https:// sustainabledevelopment.un.org/content/documents/3461denmark.pdf.

13. See Rio Declaration Principle 7 in United Nations, *Agenda 21* (New York: United Nations Department of Public Information, 1993), 9, https:// sustainabledevelopment.un.org/content/documents/Agenda21.pdf.

14. Centre for International Sustainable Development Law, "The Principle of Common but Differentiated Responsibilities: Origins and Scope," *CISDL Legal Brief,* August 2002, http://cisdl.org/public/docs/news/brief_common .pdf.

15. "Statement by Ambassador Manjeev Singh Puri, Acting Permanent Representative on Behalf of the Asian-Pacific Troika of India, Pakistan & Sri Lanka," first meeting of the Open Working Group on Sustainable Development Goals, New York, March 14, 2013, https://sustainabledevelopment .un.org/content/documents/3428india.pdf.

16. International Institute for Sustainable Development (IISD), "Summary of the First Session of the UN General Assembly Open Working Group on Sustainable Development Goals: 14–15 March 2013," *Earth Negotiations Bulletin,* March 18, 2013, www.iisd.ca/download/pdf/enb3201e.pdf.

17. "Statement by Ambassador Wang Min at the First Meeting of the Sustainable Development Goals Open Working Group," first meeting of the Open Working Group on Sustainable Development Goals, New York, March 14, 2013, https://sustainabledevelopment.un.org/content/documents/3424 china.pdf.

18. Ibid.

19. "Statement on Behalf of the African Group by H.E. Ahmad Allam-Mi, Permanent Representative of the Republic of Chad to the United Nations on the Occasion of the First Meeting of the Open Working Group on Sustainable Development," New York, March 14, 2013, https://sustainable development.un.org/content/documents/3423africangroup.pdf.

20. "Intervención a Cargo del Secretario General de Cooperación Internacional para el Desarrollo Don Gonzalo Robles Orozco," Primera Sesión del Grupo de Trabajo de Composición Abierta sobre los Objectivos de Desarrollo Sostenible de la Asemblea General, Nueva York, Marzo 14–15, 2013, https://sustainabledevelopment.un.org/content/documents/3434spain.pdf.

21. "Remarks by Ambassador Elizabeth Cousens, U.S. Representative to ECOSOC, for the US/Canada/Israel Team," second session of the SDG Open Working Group on a Proposal for SDGs, New York, April 17, 2013, https://sustainabledevelopment.un.org/content/documents/7522us3.pdf.

22. See "Statement by Ambassador Sul Kyung-hoon, Deputy Permanent Representative of the Republic of Korea," first formal meeting of SDGs Working Group, New York, March 14, 2013, https://sustainabledevelopment .un.org/content/documents/3624korea3.pdf; and Anne Anderson, "Statement on Behalf of Denmark, Ireland and Norway on the Occasion of the First Meeting of the Open Working Group on Sustainable Development Goals," New York, March 14, 2013, https://sustainabledevelopment.un.org /content/documents/3461denmark.pdf.

23. Australia-Netherlands-United Kingdom of Great Britain and Northern Ireland, "Guiding Principles for the Post-2015 Development Agenda," first meeting of the Open Working Group on Sustainable Development Goals, New York, March 15, 2013, https://sustainabledevelopment.un.org/content /documents/3484130315%20Team%20Australia-Netherlands-UK%20SDGs %20Guiding%20Principles.pdf.

24. High-Level Panel on the Post-2015 Development Agenda, *A New Global Partnership: Eradicate Poverty and Transform Economies Through Sustainable Development* (New York: United Nations, 2013), www.post2015hlp .org/the-report.

25. Interview with Csaba Kőrösi, September 18, 2014.

26. International Institute for Sustainable Development (IISD), "Summary of the Fourth Session of the UN General Assembly Open Working Group on Sustainable Development Goals: 17–19 June 2013," *Earth Negotiations Bulletin,* June 21, 2013, www.iisd.ca/download/pdf/enb3204e.pdf.

27. Saudi Arabia Intervention: Open Working Group on Sustainable Development Goals, March 3, 2014, https://sustainabledevelopment.un.org /content/documents/7202saudiarabia.pdf.

28. International Institute for Sustainable Development (IISD), "Summary of the Eighth Session of the UN General Assembly Open Working Group on Sustainable Development Goals: 3–7 February 2014," *Earth Negotiations Bulletin,* February 10, 2014, www.iisd.ca/download/pdf/enb3208e.pdf.

29. The Holy See is the universal government of the Catholic Church and operates from Vatican City State, a sovereign, independent territory. The Pope is the ruler of both Vatican City State and the Holy See.

30. IISD, "Summary of the Fourth Session."

31. "Statement by Mr. Bernard Charles Mifsud, First Secretary, Permanent Mission of the Republic of Malta to the United Nations," fourth session of the Open Working Group on Sustainable Development Goals, New York, June 19, 2013, https://sustainabledevelopment.un.org/content/documents/3675 malta.pdf.

32. "U.S. Cuts Aid to Uganda, Cancels Military Exercise over Anti-gay Law," *Reuters,* June 19, 2014, www.reuters.com/article/us-usa-uganda -gay-announcement-idUSKBN0EU26N20140619.

33. Martin Plaut, "Uganda Donors Cut Aid After President Passes Anti-gay Law," *Guardian,* February 25, 2014, www.theguardian.com/global -development/2014/feb/25/uganda-donors-cut-aid-anti-gay-law.

34. "U.S. Cuts Aid to Uganda."

35. Interview with Tobias Ogweno, former first secretary, Mission of Kenya to the United Nations, November 8, 2016.

36. Abdullah Khalid Tawlah, e-mail correspondence, June 1, 2017.

37. Saudi Arabia Intervention.

38. Ogweno interview.

39. Ibid.

40. Ambassador Martin Sajdik on behalf of members of the Group of Friends of the Rule of Law, "8th Session of the Open Working Group on Sustainable Development Goals: Conflict Prevention, Post-conflict Peacebuilding and the Promotion of Durable Peace, Rule of Law and Governance," New York, February 6–7, 2014, https://sustainabledevelopment.un.org/content /documents/6565austria.pdf.

41. "Elements of an Irish/Danish/Norwegian Intervention on the Topic of 'Promoting Equality Including Social Equity, Gender Equality and Women's Empowerment,'" eighth session of the Open Working Group on Sustainable

Development Goals, February 3–7, 2014, https://sustainabledevelopment
.un.org/content/documents/6155ireland.pdf.

42. UN General Assembly, "Keeping the Promise: United to Achieve the
Millennium Development Goals," Resolution 65/1, www.un.org/en/mdg
/summit2010/pdf/outcome_documentN1051260.pdf.

43. United Nations, "Secretary-General Appoints Amina J. Mohammed of
Nigeria as Special Adviser on Post-2015 Development Planning," document
SG/A/1349-BIO/4373-DEV/2944, June 7, 2012, www.un.org/press/en/2012
/sga1349.doc.htm.

44. High-Level Panel on the Post-2015 Development Agenda, "A New
Global Partnership: Eradicate Poverty and Transform Economies Through
Sustainable Development," www.post2015hlp.org/the-report.

45. Ibid.

46. Secretary-General Ban Ki-moon, "Remarks at Opening of the Open
Working Group on the Sustainable Development Goals," New York, March
14, 2013, https://sustainabledevelopment.un.org/content/documents/3483sg
.pdf.

47. Ogweno interview.

48. Nikhil Seth, e-mail correspondence, July 25, 2017.

49. World Bank, "IMF/World Bank Spring Meetings 2014: Development
Committee Communique," press release, April 12, 2014, www.worldbank
.org/en/news/press-release/2014/04/12/imf-world-bank-spring-meetings
-2014-development-committee-communique.

50. Olav Kjørven, "The Unlikely Journey to the 2030 Agenda for Sustainable Development," *Impakter,* December 8, 2016, http://impakter.com
/impakter-essay-unlikely-journey-2030-agenda-sustainable-development.

51. Ibid.

52. United Nations, *Agenda 21* (New York: United Nations Department
of Public Information, 1993), 219, https://sustainabledevelopment.un.org
/content/documents/Agenda21.pdf.

53. UN Sustainable Development Knowledge Platform, "About Major
Groups and Other Stakeholders," https://sustainabledevelopment.un.org
/majorgroups/about.

54. Interview with representative of the International Chamber of Commerce, October 25, 2016.

55. Interview with Ambassador Elizabeth Cousens, former US Representative to the Economic and Social Council, November 8, 2016.

56. Ibid.

57. United Nations Foundation, "Post-2015 Development and the UN Foundation's Role," January 1, 2015, www.unfoundation.org/assets/pdf/post-2015-one-pager-1.pdf.

58. Maruxa Cardama, "Beyond 2015 Campaign Final Evaluation," December 2015, 13, www.beyond2015.org/sites/default/files/Beyond2015final evaluation_LongEN_final_10Feb2016.pdf.

59. Ibid., 18.

60. Beyond 2015, "Review of Beyond 2015 Advocacy Positions and the Final Outcome Document of the Post-2015 Agenda," August 2015, 1, www.beyond2015.org/sites/default/files/Review%20of%20Final%20Post-2015%20outcome%20doc%20and%20Beyond%202015%20positions%5B2%5D.pdf. Since 2015, Beyond 2015 has been renamed Together 2030.

61. Louise Kantrow, "Intervention Delivered by Louise Kantrow, Permanent Representative of the International Chamber of Commerce to the United Nations on Behalf of Business and Industry," second session of the General Assembly Open Working Group on Sustainable Development Goals, April 17–19, 2013, https://sustainabledevelopment.un.org/content/documents/3539business.pdf.

62. Körösi interview.

63. Winfried Lang, "Multilateral Negotiations: The Role of Presiding Officers," in *Process of International Negotiations,* ed. Frances Mautner-Markhof (Laxenburg, Austria: International Institute for Applied Systems Analysis, 1989), 37.

64. John McArthur, "Own the Goals: What the Millennium Development Goals Have Accomplished," Brookings Institution, February 21, 2013, www.brookings.edu/articles/own-the-goals-what-the-millennium-development-goals-have-accomplished.

65. Ibid.

6: THE USE OF PROCESS AND DRAMA

1. Paula Caballero Gómez, "A Short History of the SDGs," April 19, 2016, http://deliver2030.org/?p=6874.

2. International Institute for Sustainable Development (IISD), "Summary of the Ninth Session of the UN General Assembly Open Working Group on Sustainable Development Goals: 3–5 March 2014," *Earth Negotiations Bulletin,* March 8, 2014, www.iisd.ca/download/pdf/enb3209e.pdf.

3. "Briefing of the Co-Chairs," fifth session of the Open Working Group on Sustainable Development Goals, New York, November 25, 2013, https://

sustainabledevelopment.un.org/content/documents/2663Brifing%20OWG
.pdf.

4. Open Working Group on Sustainable Development Goals, "SDG
Focus Areas," informal document, February 24, 2014, https://sustainable
development.un.org/content/documents/3276focusareas.pdf.

5. IISD, "Summary of the Ninth Session," 2.

6. See Open Working Group on Sustainable Development Goals, "Annex
1: Interlinkages," informal document, March 19, 2014, https://sustainable
development.un.org/content/documents/3387Annex_interlinkages_1903
.pdf.

7. IISD, "Summary of the Ninth Session," 2.

8. International Institute for Sustainable Development (IISD), "Summary
of the Tenth Session of the UN General Assembly Open Working Group on
Sustainable Development Goals: 31 March–4 April 2014," *Earth Negotiations
Bulletin,* April 7, 2014, 3, www.iisd.ca/download/pdf/enb3210e.pdf.

9. Open Working Group on Sustainable Development Goals, "SDG Focus
Areas," informal document, March 19, 2014, https://sustainabledevelopment.
un.org/content/documents/3402Focus%20areas_20140319.pdf.

10. Open Working Group on Sustainable Development Goals, "Working
Document for 5–9 May Session of Open Working Group," informal document, April 17, 2014, https://sustainabledevelopment.un.org/content
/documents/3686WorkingDoc_0205_additionalsupporters.pdf.

11. International Institute for Sustainable Development (IISD), "Summary
of the Eleventh Session of the UN General Assembly Open Working Group
on Sustainable Development Goals: 5–9 May 2014," *Earth Negotiations Bulletin,* May 12, 2014, 3, www.iisd.ca/download/pdf/enb3211e.pdf.

12. IISD, "Summary of the Eleventh Session," 1.

13. See Open Working Group on Sustainable Development Goals,
"Introduction and Proposed Goals and Targets on Sustainable Development
for the Post-2015 Development Agenda," June 2, 2014, https://sustainable
development.un.org/content/documents/4528zerodraft12OWG.pdf.

14. International Institute for Sustainable Development (IISD), "Summary
of the Twelfth Session of the UN General Assembly Open Working Group on
Sustainable Development Goals: 16–20 June 2014," *Earth Negotiations Bulletin,* June 23, 2014, 7, www.iisd.ca/download/pdf/enb3212e.pdf.

15. Ibid., 16.

16. Ibid., 1.

17. See Open Working Group on Sustainable Development Goals, "Final Compilation of Amendments to Goals and Targets by Major Groups and Other Stakeholders Including Citizens' Responses to My World 6 Priorities," June 30, 2017, https://sustainabledevelopment.un.org/content/documents /4438mgscompilationowg13.pdf.

18. Macharia Kamau and Csaba Kőrösi, letter dated June 30, 2014, https:// sustainabledevelopment.un.org/content/documents/4324lettercochairs30 june14.pdf.

19. The UN Statistical Commission, established in 1947, brings together the chief statisticians from member states from around the world. It is the highest decision-making body for international statistical activities, especially the setting of statistical standards, the development of concepts and methods, and their implementation at the national and international level. See https://unstats.un.org/unsd/statcom.

20. IISD, "Summary of the Twelfth Session," 4.

21. Sustainable Development Solutions Network, "An Action Agenda for Sustainable Development: Report for the UN Secretary-General," May 5, 2014, x, unsdsn.org/wp-content/uploads/2013/06/140505-An-Action -Agenda-for-Sustainable-Development.pdf.

22. Ibid., 28–31.

23. United Nations, "A New Global Partnership: Eradicate Poverty and Transform Economies Through Sustainable Development," in *The Report of the High-Level Panel of Eminent Persons on the Post-2015 Development Agenda* (New York: United Nations, 2013).

24. John McArthur, "Why 17 Is a Beautiful Number," Future Development, a Brookings Institution blog, September 28, 2015, www.brookings.edu/blog /future-development/2015/09/28/why-17-is-a-beautiful-number.

25. See Lynn M. Wagner, "A Forty-Year Search for a Single-Negotiating Text: Rio+20 as a Post-Agreement Negotiation," *International Negotiation* 18 (2013): 333–356.

26. See Howard Raiffa, *The Art and Science of Negotiation* (Cambridge, MA: Harvard University Press, 1982), and Roger Fisher, William Ury, and Bruce Patton, *Getting to Yes: Negotiating Agreement Without Giving In* (New York: Penguin, 1991).

27. Interview with Stephan Contius, Federal Ministry for the Environment, Nature Conservation, Building and Nuclear Safety, September 23, 2014.

28. Interview with Nikhil Seth, director, Division for Sustainable Development, UN Department of Economic and Social Affairs, September 9, 2014.

29. International Institute for Sustainable Development (IISD), "Summary of the Thirteenth Session of the UN General Assembly Open Working Group on Sustainable Development Goals: 14–19 July 2014," *Earth Negotiations Bulletin*, July 22, 2014, 25, www.iisd.ca/download/pdf/enb3213e.pdf.

30. Interview with Csaba Kőrösi, former permanent representative of Hungary to the United Nations, September 18, 2014.

31. "Encyclopedia Groupinica: A Compilation of Goals and Targets Suggestions from OWG-10 in response to Co-Chairs' Focus Area Document Dated 19 March, 2014," is available at https://sustainabledevelopment.un.org/content/documents/3698EncyclopediaGroupinica.pdf.

32. IISD, "Summary of the Tenth Session," 19.

33. IISD, "Summary of the Thirteenth Session," 4.

34. Ibid.

35. Kamau did apologize to one delegation whose compromise text in Goal 16 was erroneously left out of the current text (Ogweno interview).

36. Ogweno interview.

37. Ibid.

38. Author's notes from the July 19, 2014, meeting of the Open Working Group on Sustainable Development Goals.

39. IISD, "Summary of the Thirteenth Session," 23.

40. Ibid., 25.

7: THE BIRTH OF THE GOALS

1. UN-OHRLLS (UN Office of the High Representative for the Least Developed Countries, Landlocked Developing Countries and Small Island Developing States), "A Blueprint for the Sustainable Development Goals," interview with Amina J. Mohammed, Secretary-General's special adviser on Post-2015 Development Planning, *Commitment*, Spring 2015, 19–20, https://unohrlls.org/custom-content/uploads/2015/03/FINAL-VERSION-The-Commitment-Spring-2015.pdf.

2. Claire Provost, "Future Development Goals: 'The Tough Work Is About to Begin,'" *Guardian*, October 21, 2013, www.theguardian.com/global-development/2013/oct/21/united-nations-sustainable-development-goals.

3. UN General Assembly, "The Future We Want," A/RES.66/288, September 11, 2012, www.un.org/ga/search/view_doc.asp?symbol=A/RES/66/288&Lang=E.

4. Simon Rogers, "Occupy Protests Around the World: Full List Visualized," *Guardian,* November 14, 2011, www.theguardian.com/news/datablog/2011/oct/17/occupy-protests-world-list-map.

5. World Health Organization, "Non-Communicable Diseases Fact Sheet," updated April 2017, www.who.int/mediacentre/factsheets/fs355/en.

6. Marie-Paule Kieny, "Universal Health Coverage: Unique Challenges, Bold Solutions," World Health Organization Commentary, August 3, 2016, www.who.int/mediacentre/commentaries/2016/universal-health-coverage-challenges-solutions/en.

7. United Nations, *The Millennium Development Goals Report 2015* (New York: United Nations, 2015), 4, www.un.org/millenniumgoals/2015_MDG_Report/pdf/MDG%202015%20rev%20(July%201).pdf.

8. Maya Fehling, Brett D. Nelson, and Sridhar Venkatapuramd, "Limitations of the Millennium Development Goals: A Literature Review," *Global Public Health* 8, no. 10 (2013): 1109–1122.

9. United Nations, *Millennium Development Goals Report,* 5.

10. International Institute for Sustainable Development (IISD), "Summary of the Eleventh Session of the UN General Assembly Open Working Group on Sustainable Development Goals: 5–9 May 2014," *Earth Negotiations Bulletin,* May 12, 2014, 8–10, www.iisd.ca/download/pdf/enb3211e.pdf.

11. World Health Organization, *Unsafe Abortion: Global and Regional Estimates of the Incidence of Unsafe Abortion and Associated mortality,* 5th ed. (Geneva: World Health Organization, 2007).

12. Open Working Group on Sustainable Development Goals, "Working Document for 5–9 May Session of the Open Working Group," May 2016, https://sustainabledevelopment.un.org/content/documents/3686 WorkingDoc_0205_additionalsupporters.pdf.

13. IISD, "Summary of the Eleventh Session," 8–10.

14. Interview with Amit Narang, Permanent Mission of India to the United Nations, July 21, 2016.

15. United Nations, "Goal 7," *Sustainable Development Goals,* www.un.org/sustainabledevelopment/energy.

16. Interview with Abdullah Tawlah, senior Saudi climate change negotiator and representative to the Open Working Group on Sustainable Development Goals, May 30, 2017.

17. See Ahmed Sareer, permanent representative of Maldives to the United Nations, "Energy," Eleventh Session of the Open Working Group on Sustainable Development Goals, New York, May 5–9, 2014, https://

sustainabledevelopment.un.org/content/documents/10007maldives4.pdf; and Alliance of Small Island States, "Statement on Energy, Economic Growth, Employment, and Infrastructure," Eleventh Session of Open Working Group on Sustainable Development Goals, New York, May 7, 2014, https://sustainable development.un.org/content/documents/9967aosis5.pdf.

18. For more about the Sustainable Energy for All initiative, see www.se4all.org.

19. See, for example, Slovenia and Montenegro, "(Sustainable) Energy, Economic Growth, Employment and Infrastructure: SI and MNE Elements," eleventh session of the Open Working Group on Sustainable Development Goals, New York, May 6, 2014, https://sustainabledevelopment.un.org /content/documents/10092slovenia4.pdf; and France, Germany, and Switzerland, "Statement," eleventh session of Open Working Group on Sustainable Development Goals, New York, May 5–9, 2014, https://sustainable development.un.org/content/documents/9590france2.pdf.

20. See "Intervention by Md. Mustafizur Rahman, Deputy Permanent Representative of Bangladesh to the UN at the Eleventh Session of the OWG on SDGs Under Focus Area 7: Energy & 8: Economic Growth, Employment and Decent Jobs," May 8, 2014, https://sustainabledevelopment.un.org /content/documents/9446bangladesh.pdf; "Intervention by Viet Nam on Behalf of Troika Bhutan/Thailand/Viet Nam on Focus Area 7: 'Energy' and 8: 'Economic Growth, Employment and Infrastructure,'" eleventh session of the Open Working Group on Sustainable Development Goals, New York, May 5–9, 2014, https://sustainabledevelopment.un.org/content/documents/9158 vietnam5.pdf.

21. "Statement by the Troika of China, Indonesia and Kazakhstan, Focus Area 7: Energy and Focus Area 8: Economic Growth, Employment and Infrastructure," eleventh session of the Open Working Group on Sustainable Development Goals, New York, May 5–9, 2014, https://sustainable development.un.org/content/documents/9218indonesia2.pdf.

22. Ambassador Guillermo Rishchynski, on behalf of United States, Israel, and Canada, "Economic Growth, Employment and Infrastructure: Energy," eleventh session of the Open Working Group on Sustainable Development Goals, New York, May 5–9, 2014, https://sustainabledevelopment.un.org /content/documents/9178canada2.pdf; and Norway, Denmark, Ireland, "Statement on FA 7–Energy," eleventh session of the Open Working Group on Sustainable Development Goals, New York, May 5–9, 2014, https:// sustainabledevelopment.un.org/content/documents/9542norway2.pdf.

23. "Intervention by Viet Nam."

24. Norway, Denmark, Ireland, "Statement on FA 8—Economic growth, employment and infrastructure," eleventh session of the Open Working Group on Sustainable Development Goals, New York, May 5–9, 2014, https://sustainabledevelopment.un.org/content/documents/9230ireland3.pdf.

25. Ibid.

26. International Labor Organization, "ILO's Decent Work Agenda," www.ilo.org/global/topics/decent-work/lang—en/index.htm.

27. Troika of Argentina, Bolivia, and Ecuador, "Comentarios al documento de áreas focales en temas: empleo, igualdad de género y empoderamiento de la mujer, salud y educación," tenth session of the Open Working Group on Sustainable Development Goals, New York, March 31–April 4, 2014, https://sustainabledevelopment.un.org/content/documents/7662bolivia.pdf.

28. Brazil and Nicaragua, "Cluster 2—Education; Health and Population Dynamics; Gender Equality and Women's Empowerment; Employment and Decent Work for All," tenth session of the Open Working Group on Sustainable Development Goals, New York, March 31–April 4, 2014, https://sustainabledevelopment.un.org/content/documents/7737brazil3.pdf.

29. See Ireland, Norway, and Denmark, "Statement on the Focus Areas: Economic Growth, Industrialization and Infrastructure," tenth session of the Open Working Group on Sustainable Development Goals, New York, March 31–April 4, 2014, https://sustainabledevelopment.un.org/content/documents/7972ireland4.pdf; and Jakub Wejchert, European Commission, "Sustained and Inclusive Economic Growth, Macroeconomic Policy Questions (Including International Trade, International Financial System and External Debt Sustainability), Infrastructure Development and Industrialization," statement on behalf of the European Union and Its Member States, Open Working Group on Sustainable Development Goals, New York, November 25, 2013, https://sustainabledevelopment.un.org/content/documents/4438eu1.pdf.

30. Interview with Louise Kantrow, International Chamber of Commerce, October 25, 2016.

31. Compilation of statements by major groups, eleventh session of the Open Working Group on Sustainable Development Goals, New York, May 5–9, 2014, https://sustainabledevelopment.un.org/content/documents/3678Compilation%20Summary-%20April%2011-%20final.pdf.

32. Brazil and Nicaragua, "Statement on Cluster 1: Poverty Eradication and Promoting Equality," tenth session of the Open Working Group on

Sustainable Development Goals, New York, March 31–April 4, 2014, https://sustainabledevelopment.un.org/content/documents/7732brazil2.pdf.

33. Elizabeth Cousens, "US/Canada/Israel Statement on Methodology and Consolidation of Focus Areas: Poverty Eradication and Promoting Equality," tenth session of the Open Working Group on SDGs, March 31-April 4, 2014, New York, https://sustainabledevelopment.un.org/content/documents/8457 us.pdf.

34. Jason Hickel, Joe Brewer, and Martin Kirk, "4 Things You Probably Know About Poverty That Bill and Melinda Gates Don't," *Fast Company*, February 3, 2016, www.fastcompany.com/3041841/4-things-you-probably -know-about-poverty-that-bill-and-melinda-gates-dont.

35. Third World Network, "SDGs: The Disappearing Act of the 'Inequality' Goal," *Global Policy Forum*, June 26, 2014, www.globalpolicy.org/component /content/article/252-the-millenium-development-goals/52649-sdgs-the -disappearing-act-of-the-inequality-goal.html.

36. Sustainable Development Solutions Network, *An Action Agenda for Sustainable Development: Report for the UN Secretary-General*, May 5, 2014, 41, http://unsdsn.org/wp-content/uploads/2013/06/140505-An-Action -Agenda-for-Sustainable-Development.pdf.

37. Ibid.

38. Major Group on Local Authorities, "Statement on Sustainable Cities and Urbanization," eleventh session of the Open Working Group on Sustainable Development Goals, New York, May 5-9, 2014, https://sustainable development.un.org/content/documents/9490authorities.pdf.

39. See relevant statements at https://sustainabledevelopment.un.org /processes/post2015/owg/session10 and https://sustainabledevelopment .un.org/processes/post2015/owg/session11.

40. Amit Narang, Permanent Mission of India to the United Nations, "Statement on Focus Areas 9 and 10," eleventh session of the Open Working Group on Sustainable Development Goals, New York, May 7, 2014, https:// sustainabledevelopment.un.org/content/documents/9202india3.pdf.

41. Amit Narang, Permanent Mission of India to the United Nations, "Cluster 5—Sustainable Cities and Human Settlements, Promoting Sustainable Consumption and Production, and Climate," tenth session of the Open Working Group on SDGs, March 31-April 4, 2014, New York, https:// sustainabledevelopment.un.org/content/documents/8498india5.pdf.

42. United Nations, "Responsible Consumption and Production: Why It Matters," www.un.org/sustainabledevelopment/wp-content/uploads /2016/08/16–00055L_Why-it-Matters_Goal-12_Consumption_2p.pdf.

43. MDG Monitor, "SDG 12—Ensure Sustainable Consumption and Production," September 6, 2016, www.mdgmonitor.org/sdg12 -ensure-sustainable-consumption-and-production.

44. Women and NGO Major Group, Feminist Task Force, Mining Working Group, "Focus Area 15: Climate," tenth session of the Open Working Group on Sustainable Development Goals, March 31-April 4, 2014, https:// sustainabledevelopment.un.org/content/documents/8212women2.pdf.

45. David O'Connor, "Potential and Limits of the UN in International Environmental Negotiations," presentation at Princeton University Woodrow Wilson School Class on Mainstreaming Environment in Asia, Princeton, New Jersey, March 3, 2016.

46. Author's notes, thirteenth session of the Open Working Group on Sustainable Development Goals, July 17, 2014.

47. Ibid.

48. Tommy Remengesau Jr., president of the Republic of Palau, statement for the eighth session of the United Nations Open Working Group on Sustainable Development Goals, New York, February 3, 2014, https://sustainable development.un.org/content/documents/6040PSIDS%20SDG%20OWG%20 8%20Statement%20with%20Oceans%20and%20Seas%20Draft%20SDG%20 Annex%20(1).pdf.

49. New Zealand, "Extended Views on Focus Area 13 Oceans and Seas," eleventh session of the Open Working Group on Sustainable Development Goals, New York, May 8, 2014, https://sustainabledevelopment.un.org /content/documents/9790newz2.pdf.

50. Interview with Ambassador Elizabeth Cousens, former US Representative to the Economic and Social Council, November 8, 2016.

51. IISD, "Summary of the Thirteenth Session," 17.

52. Letter from Cristiane Engelbrecht, counselor, Permanent Mission of the Bolivarian Republic of Venezuela to the United Nations, to the OWG co-chairs, n.d., https://sustainabledevelopment.un.org/content/documents /11122venezuela2.pdf.

53. See Convention on Biological Diversity, "Aichi Biodiversity Targets," https://www.cbd.int/sp/targets, and IUCN, *Building the Sustainable Development Goals on the Aichi Biodiversity Targets,* Sustainable Development Goals Policy Brief Series-1 (Gland, Switzerland: IUCN, 2013).

54. There were a few other targets that had either 2020 or 2025 deadlines throughout the OWGs because they were also taken from existing targets in other forums.

55. Luc Gnacadja, "Statement on the Occasion of the Introduction of the Issues Brief on DLDD," third session of the United Nations General Assembly Open Working Group on Sustainable Development Goals, New York, May 22, 2013, https://sustainabledevelopment.un.org/content/documents/3583 UNCCD.pdf.

56. UNCCD/Science-Policy Interface, "Land in Balance: The Scientific Conceptual Framework for Land Degradation Neutrality (LDN)," Science-Policy Brief 02 (Bonn, Germany: UNCCD, 2016), www2.unccd.int/sites /default/files/documents/18102016_Spi_pb_multipage_ENG_1.pdf.

57. Brazil and Nicaragua, "Statement on Cluster 6—Conservation and Sustainable Use of Marine Resources, Oceans and Seas; Ecoystems and Biodiversity," tenth session of the Open Working Group on Sustainable Development Goals, New York, April 3, 2014, https://sustainabledevelopment.un.org /content/documents/8534brazil6.pdf.

58. IISD, "Summary of the Thirteenth Session," 17.

59. Elizabeth Cousens, US representative to the Economic and Social Council, "Closing Statement and Explanation of Position," thirteenth session of the Open Working Group on Sustainable Development Goals, New York, July 19, 2014, https://sustainabledevelopment.un.org/content/documents /11117United%20States.pdf.

60. UN System Task Team on the Post-2015 UN Development Agenda, *Realizing the Future We Want for All* (New York: United Nations, 2012), 31, www.un.org/en/development/desa/policy/untaskteam_undf/untt_report.pdf.

61. Amit Narang, "Intervention by Amit Narang, Counsellor, Permanent Mission of India During Discussions on Cluster 8—Peaceful and Non-violent societies, Rule of Law and Capable Institutions," tenth session of the Open Working Group on Sustainable Development Goals, New York, March 31–April 4, 2014, https://sustainabledevelopment.un.org/content/documents /8506india6.pdf.

62. Nicaragua, on behalf of Brazil and Nicaragua, "Statement on Focus Area 19: Peaceful and Non-violent Societies, Rule of Law and Capable Institutions," tenth session of the Open Working Group on Sustainable Development Goals, New York, April 4, 2014, https://sustainabledevelopment.un.org /content/documents/8132nicaragua.pdf.

63. For reference to all of these statements, see UN Sustainable Development Knowledge Platform, tenth session of the Open Working Group on Sustainable Development Goals, Statements and Presentations, https://sustainabledevelopment.un.org/processes/post2015/owg/session10; and International Institute for Sustainable Development (IISD), "Summary of the Tenth Session of the UN General Assembly Open Working Group on Sustainable Development Goals: 31 March–4 April 2014," *Earth Negotiations Bulletin,* April 7, 2014, 19–21, www.iisd.ca/download/pdf/enb3208e.pdf.

64. Martin Sajdik, "Remarks on Conflict Prevention, Post-conflict Peacebuilding and the Promotion of Durable Peace, Rule of Law and Governance, on Behalf of Members of the Group of Friends of the Rule of Law," eighth session of the Open Working Group on Sustainable Development Goals, New York, February 6–7, 2014, https://sustainabledevelopment.un.org/content/documents/6565austria.pdf.

65. Sofia Borges, ambassador of Timor-Leste to the United Nations, "Statement on Conflict Prevention, Post-conflict Peacebuilding and the Promotion of Durable Peace, Rule of Law and Governance," eighth session of the Open Working Group on Sustainable Development Goals, New York, February 6, 2014, https://sustainabledevelopment.un.org/content/documents/6540timor.pdf.

66. Author's notes, thirteenth session of the Open Working Group on Sustainable Development Goals, July 18, 2014.

67. Ibid.

68. Cousens interview.

69. IISD, "Summary of the Twelfth Session," 15.

70. Ibid.; author's notes, twelfth session of the Open Working Group on Sustainable Development Goals, June 20, 2014.

71. Author's notes, thirteenth session, July 15, 2014.

8: PULLING IT ALL TOGETHER:
THE SDGS AND THE POST-2015 DEVELOPMENT AGENDA

1. Sam K. Kutesa, president of the 69th session of the UN General Assembly, "Statement at the Stocktaking Session of the Intergovernmental Negotiations on the Post-2015 Development Agenda," New York, January 19, 2015, https://sustainabledevelopment.un.org/content/documents/12402kutesa.pdf.

2. United Nations General Assembly, "Report of the Open Working Group on Sustainable Development Goals Established Pursuant to General

Assembly Resolution 66/288," A/RES/68/309, September 12, 2014, www
.un.org/en/ga/search/view_doc.asp?symbol=A/RES/68/309.

3. United Nations General Assembly, "Sixty-Eighth Session, 108th Plenary
Meeting," Official Records, A/68/PV.108, September 10, 2014, 6–7, www
.un.org/en/ga/search/view_doc.asp?symbol=A/68/PV.108.

4. Irish Mission to the UN, "Ambassador David Donoghue, Curriculum
Vitae," www.dfa.ie/pmun/newyork/about-us/welcome-message.

5. Sam K. Kutesa, president of the 69th session of the UN General
Assembly, "Letter to All Permanent Representatives and Permanent
Observers to the United Nations," October 17, 2014, www.un.org/pga/
wp-content/uploads/sites/3/2014/10/171014_post-2015-development-
agenda.pdf.

6. Nikhil Seth, e-mail correspondence, July 25, 2017.

7. United Nations General Assembly, "Modalities for the Process of
Intergovernmental Negotiations on the Post-2015 Development Agenda,"
A/69/L.46, January 14, 2015, www.un.org/ga/search/view_doc.asp?symbol
=A/69/L.46&Lang=E.

8. Olav Kjørven, "The Unlikely Journey to the 2030 Agenda for Sustainable
Development," February 15, 2016, http://deliver2030.org/?p=6767.

9. United Nations General Assembly, "The Road to Dignity by 2030:
Ending Poverty, Transforming All Lives and Protecting the Planet: Synthesis
Report of the Secretary-General on the Post-2015 Development Agenda,"
document A/69/700, December 4, 2014, www.un.org/en/development/desa
/publications/files/2015/01/SynthesisReportENG.pdf.

10. United Nations General Assembly, "The Road to Dignity," 28–29.

11. Tony Pipa, "U.S. Statement, Goals and Targets and Political Declaration, Post-2015 Intergovernmental Negotiation Process," New York, January
19, 2015, https://sustainabledevelopment.un.org/content/documents/12394
usa2.pdf.

12. Ambassador Michael Grant, "Statement on Combined Session on the
Declaration and the Goals/Targets, Post-2015 Intergovernmental Negotiation
Process," New York, January 20, 2015, https://sustainabledevelopment.un.org
/content/documents/12408canada1.pdf.

13. "UK Opening Statement, Post-2015 Intergovernmental Negotiation
Process," New York, January 19–21, 2015, https://sustainabledevelopment.un-
.org/content/documents/12203opening%20statement%20final.pdf; Takeshi
Osuga, "Statement of Japan, Post-2015 Intergovernmental Negotiation

Process," New York, January 19–21, 2015, https://sustainabledevelopment
.un.org/content/documents/12998japan4.pdf.

14. See statements by the Group of 77 and China, India, Brazil, among
others, at https://sustainabledevelopment.un.org/post2015/stock-taking.

15. David Donoghue, "My Perspective on the SDG Negotiations," De-
liver2030.org, May 2016, http://deliver2030.org/wp-content/uploads/2016
/05/DAVID-DONOGHUE-sdgs-history.pdf.

16. Ibid.

17. Ibid.

18. Ambassador Kingsley Mamabolo, permanent representative of the Republic of South Africa to the United Nations and Chairman of the Group of
77, "Statement on the Occasion of the Third Session for the Intergovernmental Negotiations on the Post-2015 Development Agenda," New York, March
23, 2015, https://sustainabledevelopment.un.org/content/documents/13289
g77.pdf.

19. United Nations, "History of the FfD Process," www.un.org/esa/ffd/ffd3
/conference/history.html.

20. Ibid.

21. Ambassador Kingsley Mamabolo, permanent representative of the Republic of South Africa to the United Nations and Chairman of the Group of
77, "Statement on the Occasion of the Stock-Taking Session for the Intergovernmental Negotiations on the Post-2015 Development Agenda," New York,
January 20, 2015, https://sustainabledevelopment.un.org/content/documents
/123762group77.pdf.

22. European Union, "Speaking Points, Post-2015 Intergovernmental Negotiations," New York, February 19, 2015, https://sustainabledevelopment
.un.org/content/documents/13034eu2.pdf.

23. Macharia Kamau and David Donoghue, "Discussion Document for
Declaration, Intergovernmental Negotiations on the Post-2015 Development
Agenda," New York, February 20, 2017, https://sustainabledevelopment.un
.org/content/documents/6155Discussion%20Document%20for%20for%20
Declaration%2019%20Feb.pdf.

24. Macharia Kamau and David Donoghue, "Elements Paper for a Declaration Discussion, Intergovernmental Negotiations on the Post-2015 Development Agenda," New York, February 5, 2017, https://sustainable
development.un.org/content/documents/5977Intergovernmental%20
Negotiations%20Post-2015%20Dev.Agenda%20-%206%20February%
202015.pdf.

25. International Institute for Sustainable Development (IISD), "Summary of the Second Session of the Intergovernmental Negotiation Process on the Post-2015 Development Agenda: 17–20 February 2015," *Earth Negotiations Bulletin,* February 23, 2015, 13, http://enb.iisd.org/download/pdf/enb3215e.pdf.

26. Kingdom of the Netherlands, "Statement on the Declaration, Post-2015 Intergovernmental Negotiations," New York, February 17, 2015, https://sustainabledevelopment.un.org/content/documents/12773netherlands.pdf.

27. Maldives on behalf of the Alliance of Small Island States, "Statement at the Second Session of Intergovernmental Negotiations on the Post-2015 Development Agenda," New York, February 17–20, 2015, https://sustainable development.un.org/content/documents/13130aosis.pdf.

28. Amit Narang, Permanent Mission of India, "Statement at the Second Session of Intergovernmental Negotiations on the Post-2015 Development Agenda," New York, February 17–20, 2015, https://sustainabledevelopment.un.org/content/documents/12935india2.pdf.

29. "Post 2015 Agenda Declaration Discussion Draft Paper Comments by Brazil, Second Session of Intergovernmental Negotiations on the Post-2015 Development Agenda," New York, February 17–20, 2015, https://sustainable development.un.org/content/documents/13055brazil2.pdf.

30. IISD, "Summary of the Sixth Session of the Intergovernmental Negotiation Process on the Post-2015 Development Agenda: 22–25 June 2015," *Earth Negotiations Bulletin,* June 28, 2015, 3, http://enb.iisd.org/download/pdf/enb3219e.pdf.

31. Delegation of Brazil, "Statement on the Political Declaration, Seventh Session of Intergovernmental Negotiations on the Post-2015 Development Agenda," New York, July 21, 2015, https://sustainabledevelopment.un.org/content/documents/15802brazil2.pdf.

32. IISD, "Summary of the Seventh and Eighth Sessions of the Intergovernmental Negotiation Process on the Post-2015 Development Agenda: 20 July–2 August 2015," *Earth Negotiations Bulletin,* August 5, 2015, 13, http://enb.iisd.org/download/pdf/enb3220e.pdf.

33. See United Nations, *Transforming Our World: The 2030 Agenda for Sustainable Development,* A/RES/70/1 (New York: United Nations, 2015), https://sustainabledevelopment.un.org/content/documents/21252030%20Agenda%20for%20Sustainable%20Development%20web.pdf.

34. Donoghue, "My Perspective."

35. See United Nations, "Report of the Open Working Group of the General Assembly on Sustainable Development Goals," A/68/970, August 12, 2014, http://undocs.org/A/68/970. The targets in question include 4.4, 4.6, 4.b, 4.c, 6.3, 9.5, 11.5, 11.b, and 15.2.

36. For more information on the UN System Task Team on the post-2015 development agenda, see www.un.org/en/development/desa/policy /untaskteam_undf.

37. Donoghue, "My Perspective."

38. See "Targets in the Proposed SDGs Framework," n.d., https:// sustainabledevelopment.un.org/content/documents/6769Targets%20 document__March.pdf.

39. Kingsley Mamabolo, "Statement on Behalf of the Group of 77 and China, Third Session of the Intergovernmental Process on the Post-2015 Development Agenda," New York, March 23, 2015, https://sustainable development.un.org/content/documents/13289g77.pdf.

40. He proposed deletion of the x's and inclusion of "substantially" in Targets 4.4 (skills for employment), 4.6 (literacy and numeracy), 4.b (scholarships), 4.c (qualified teachers), 6.3 (water quality), 9.5 (scientific research and technological capabilities in industrial sectors), 11.5 (disasters), 11.b (cities and human settlements adopting integrated policies and plans), and 15.2 (sustainable management of forests). See Group of 77 and China, "Statement on Goals and Targets, Eighth Session of the Intergovernmental Process on the Post-2015 Development Agenda," New York, July 28, 2015, https:// sustainabledevelopment.un.org/content/documents/16399g77sdgs.pdf.

41. For a full set of the "tweaked" targets, see IISD, "Summary of the Seventh and Eighth Sessions," 13–14.

42. Donoghue, "My Perspective."

43. Ibid.

44. Thembela Ngculu, "Statement on Behalf of the Group of 77 and China on the Relationship Between the FfD and the Post-2015 Processes (Global Partnership and Possible Key Deliverables), Fourth Session of the Intergovernmental Process on the Post-2015 Development Agenda," New York, April 23, 2015, https://sustainabledevelopment.un.org/content/documents/13946g 77.pdf.

45. Gaspar Frontini, "EU Speaking Points on the Relationship Between FfD and Post-2015 Processes, Including Coherence Between Respective Outcome Documents, Fourth Session of the Intergovernmental Process on the

Post-2015 Development Agenda," New York, April 24, 2015, https://
sustainabledevelopment.un.org/content/documents/14279eu5.pdf.

46. IISD, "Summary of the Fourth Session of the Intergovernmental Negotiation Process on the Post-2015 Development Agenda: 21–24 April 2015,"
Earth Negotiations Bulletin, April 27, 2015, 16, http://enb.iisd.org/download
/pdf/enb3217e.pdf.

47. Ibid.

48. Ibid.

49. United Nations, "Food for Thought Paper on a Possible Technology
Facilitation Mechanism," informal paper, May 2015, https://sustainable
development.un.org/content/documents/7167TFM%20Food%20for%20
Thought%20Paper.pdf.

50. Donoghue, "My Perspective."

51. IISD, "Summary of the Seventh and Eighth Sessions,"14.

52. Closing statement on behalf of the Group of 77 and China by Ambassador Kingsley Mamabolo, permanent representative of the Republic of
South Africa to the United Nations, chair of the Group of 77 and China, at
the Third International Conference on Financing for Development, Addis
Ababa, Ethiopia, July 16, 2015, http://undocs.org/A/CONF.227/11.

53. IISD, "Summary of the Seventh and Eighth Sessions," 15.

54. United Nations, *Addis Ababa Action Agenda of the Third International
Conference on Financing for Development* (New York: United Nations, 2015),
paragraph 123, www.un.org/esa/ffd/wp-content/uploads/2015/08/AAAA
_Outcome.pdf.

55. Americo Beviglia Zampetti, "Statement on Behalf of the European
Union and Its Member States on Follow-Up and Review," fifth session of the
Intergovernmental Process on the Post-2015 Development Agenda, New
York, May 18, 2015, https://sustainabledevelopment.un.org/content
/documents/14566eu.pdf.

56. Donoghue, "My Perspective."

57. Mahlatse Mminele, "Statement on Behalf of the Group of 77 and China
on Follow-Up and Review," fifth session of the Intergovernmental Process on
the Post-2015 Development Agenda, New York, May 18, 2015, https://
sustainabledevelopment.un.org/content/documents/14330g77.pdf.

58. Donoghue, "My Perspective."

59. United Nations, *Transforming Our World,* paragraphs 72–91.

60. Donoghue, "My Perspective."

61. IISD, "Summary of the Seventh and Eighth Sessions," 21.

62. See the least-developed countries' proposed amendments in their annotated version of the outcome document: https://sustainabledevelopment.un.org/content/documents/16573ldcs7.pdf.

63. IISD, "Summary of the Seventh and Eighth Sessions," 22–23.

64. Donoghue, "My Perspective."

9: TRANSFORMING OUR WORLD

1. Malala Yousafzai, "Speech at the UN Sustainable Development Summit," New York, September 25, 2015, https://blog.malala.org/transcript-malalas-speech-at-un-sustainable-development-summit-2015-c8d6ece5c600.

2. Ban Ki-moon, "Remarks at the Summit for the Adoption of the Post-2015 Development Agenda," New York, September 25, 2015, https://sustainabledevelopment.un.org/content/documents/20229sg.pdf.

3. International Institute for Sustainable Development (IISD), "Summary of the UN Sustainable Development Summit: 25–27 September 2015," *Earth Negotiations Bulletin,* September 30, 2015, 15, www.iisd.ca/download/pdf/enb3224e.pdf.

4. Ellen Johnson Sirleaf, "Statement at the UN Sustainable Development Summit," New York, September 25, 2015, https://sustainabledevelopment.un.org/content/documents/20309liberia.pdf.

5. IISD, "Summary of the UN Sustainable Development Summit," 15.

6. Sheikh Hasina, "Statement at the UN Sustainable Development Summit," New York, September 27, 2015, https://sustainabledevelopment.un.org/content/documents/20878bangladesh.pdf.

7. IISD, "Summary of the UN Sustainable Development Summit," 15.

8. Arnold J. Nicholson, "Statement at the UN Sustainable Development Summit," New York, September 25, 2015, https://sustainabledevelopment.un.org/content/documents/20269jamaica.pdf.

9. Simonetta Sommaruga, "Statement at the UN Sustainable Development Summit," New York, September 25, 2015, https://sustainabledevelopment.un.org/content/documents/20337switzerland-eng-pdf.

10. United Nations, "United Nations Summit on Sustainable Development: Informal Summary," 2015, https://sustainabledevelopment.un.org/content/documents/8521Informal%20Summary%20-%20UN%20Summit%20on%20Sustainable%20Development%202015.pdf.

11. IISD, "Summary of the UN Sustainable Development Summit," 16.

12. For more about Global Citizen, see www.globalcitizen.org.

13. United Nations News Centre, "Spotlighting Sustainable Development, 'Global Goals' Campaign Launched at UN," September 3, 2015, www.un.org /apps/news/story.asp?NewsID=51791#.WUV_F2grJaQ.

14. Ibid.

15. For more information on The New Division, see www.thenewdivision .world.

16. See the World's Largest Lesson website at http://worldslargestlesson .globalgoals.org.

17. See the ad at www.youtube.com/watch?v=Ob-K-dECobE.

18. See "We the People" for the Global Goals at www.youtube.com/watch ?v=RpqVmvMCmp0.

19. See Project Everyone, www.project-everyone.org.

20. IISD, "Summary of the 2016 Meeting of the High-Level Political Forum on Sustainable Development: 11–20 July 2016," *Earth Negotiations Bulletin,* July 23, 2016, 16, http://enb.iisd.org/download/pdf/enb3327e.pdf.

21. David O'Connor, "Sustainable Development Goals: How to Sustain Momentum Towards Their Achievement in All Countries?" Lecture at Pace University, Pleasantville, New York, April 19, 2017.

22. United Nations, *Transforming Our World: The 2030 Agenda for Sustainable Development,* A/RES/70/1 (New York: United Nations, 2015), https://sustainabledevelopment.un.org/content/documents/21252030%20 Agenda%20for%20Sustainable%20Development%20web.pdf.

23. United Nations, "Voluntary National Reviews," United Nations Sustainable Development Knowledge Platform, https://sustainabledevelopment .un.org/hlpf.

24. The twenty-two countries that participated in the 2016 voluntary national reviews (in alphabetical order) were China, Colombia, Egypt, Estonia, Finland, France, Georgia, Germany, Madagascar, Mexico, Montenegro, Morocco, Norway, Philippines, Republic of Korea, Samoa, Sierra Leone, Switzerland, Togo, Turkey, Uganda, and Venezuela.

25. IISD, "Summary of the 2016 Meeting of the High-Level Political Forum," 16.

26. David O'Connor et al., "Universality, Integration, and Policy Coherence for Sustainable Development: Early SDG Implementation in Selected OECD Countries," World Resources Institute Working Paper, August 2016, www.wri.org/sites/default/files/Universality_Integration_and_Policy _Coherence_for_Sustainable_Development_Early_SDG_Implementation _in_Selected_OECD_Countries.pdf.

27. Ibid.

28. United Nations, Voluntary National Reviews, 2017, https://sustainable development.un.org/hlpf/2017#vnrs.

29. O'Connor, "Sustainable Development Goals."

30. O'Connor, "Sustainable Development Goals"; United Nations Division for Sustainable Development, *2016 Synthesis of Voluntary National Reviews* (New York: United Nations, 2016), 31–32.

31. United Nations News Centre, "Despite Slow Progress on World Development Goals, Still Reason for Optimism: UN Adviser," December 20, 2006, www.un.org/apps/news/story.asp?NewsID=21066.

32. O'Connor, "Sustainable Development Goals."

33. Ibid.

34. See SDG Funders Philanthropy Platform, http://sdgfunders.org.

35. Karolina Mzykcallias, "Brazilian Foundations Embrace the SDGs," *Medium,* April 5, 2017, https://medium.com/@karolinamzyk/brazilian -foundations-embrace-the-sdgs-fb05ab9b377a.

36. See Alliance Sud, www.alliancesud.ch/en.

37. See SDG Watch Europe, www.sdgwatcheurope.org.

38. See African Monitor, www.africanmonitor.org/what-we-do/2030 -agenda-for-sustainable-development.

39. Elizabeth Hege, "SDGs Need NGOs, NGOs Need SDGs," IDDRI Blog, February 8, 2017, http://blog.iddri.org/en/2017/02/08/sdgs-need-ngos-ngos -need-sdgs.

40. Gillian Tett, "The UN Has Started to Talk Business," *Financial Times,* September 22, 2017, www.swissinfo.ch/eng/sustainable-development-goals _the-un-has-started-to-talk-business/43539974.

41. Ibid.

42. Ibid.

43. KPMG, "Integrating the Sustainable Development Goals into Safaricom's Corporate Strategy," KPMG Case Study, 2016, https://home.kpmg .com/content/dam/kpmg/pdf/2016/07/za-safaricom-case-study.pdf.

44. BSR and Globescan, "The State of Sustainable Business 2016: Results of the 8th Annual Survey of Sustainable Business Leaders," October 2016, www.bsr.org/reports/BSR_GlobeScan_State_of_Sustainable_Business_Survey _2016.pdf.

45. International Copper Association, "The Copper Industry: Our Contribution to Sustainable Development," September 20, 2016, https://issuu.com /copperalliance/docs/ica-sustainable-dev-goals-web.

46. UNCTAD, "International Chamber of Commerce and UNCTAD Pledge to Work Together on 2030 Development Agenda," January 22, 2016, http://unctad.org/en/pages/newsdetails.aspx?OriginalVersionID=1192.

47. O'Connor, "Sustainable Development Goals"; Business and Sustainable Development Commission, *Better Business, Better World*, 2017, http://report .businesscommission.org/uploads/BetterBiz-BetterWorld_170215_012417 .pdf.

48. WBCSD, "UN India Business Forum Launched to Bring Business Solutions to the SDGs," news release, March 22, 2017, www.wbcsd.org /Overview/About-us/India/News/UN-India-Business-Forum-launched-to -bring-business-solutions-to-the-SDGs.

49. O'Connor, "Sustainable Development Goals"; "United Nations, Speakers in General Assembly Event Urge 'Dramatic' Increase in Private Investment, Pooled Resources to Meet $6 Trillion Annual Cost of Sustainable Development Goals," GA/11905, April 18, 2017, www.un.org/press/en/2017 /ga11905.doc.htm.

50. Mike Scott, "Engaging with the UN's Sustainable Development Goals," *Telegraph,* July 31, 2017, www.telegraph.co.uk/connect/better-business /business-sustainability/business-engaging-un-sustainable-development-goals.

51. Sustainable Development Solutions Network, "Getting Started with the SDGs in Cities: A Guide for Stakeholders," July 2016, http://unsdsn.org /wp-content/uploads/2016/07/9.1.8.-Cities-SDG-Guide.pdf.

52. Cary L. Biron, "How Baltimore Is Using the Sustainable Development Goals to Make a More Just City," *Citiscope,* March 9, 2017, http://citiscope .org/story/2017/how-baltimore-using-sustainable-development-goals-make -more-just-city.

53. New York City Mayor's Office for International Affairs, "Global Vision Urban Action," www1.nyc.gov/site/international/programs/global-vision -urban-action.page.

54. Letty Reimerink, "First Step for Cities on the Sustainable Development Goals: Making People Aware of Them," *Citiscope,* September 2, 2016, http:// citiscope.org/story/2016/first-step-cities-sustainable-development -goals-making-people-aware-them.

55. O'Connor, "Sustainable Development Goals."

56. See Future Earth, www.futureearth.org.

57. O'Connor, "Sustainable Development Goals."

58. See a list and links to the New Climate Economy working papers here: http://newclimateeconomy.report/workingpapers.

59. Paloma Duran, "Universities: Getting Ready for the SDGs," United Nations Academic Impact Blog, June 15, 2017, https://academicimpact.un.org/content/universities-getting-ready-sdgs.

60. UN General Assembly, 11th Meeting of the 19th Special Session of the General Assembly, Official Records, A/S-19/PV.11, June 27, 1997, 7, https://documents-dds-ny.un.org/doc/UNDOC/GEN/N97/857/92/PDF/N9785792.pdf?OpenElement.

61. "The 169 Commandments: The Proposed Sustainable Development Goals Would Be Worse Than Useless," *Economist,* March 25, 2015, www.economist.com/news/leaders/21647286-proposed-sustainable-development-goals-would-be-worse-useless-169-commandments.

10: THE LEGACY OF THE OPEN WORKING GROUP
ON SUSTAINABLE DEVELOPMENT GOALS

1. Barack Obama, "Remarks by the President on Sustainable Development Goals, "General Assembly Hall, United Nations, New York, September 27, 2015.

2. UN General Assembly, "The Future We Want," A/RES.66/288, September 11, 2012, paragraph 248, www.un.org/ga/search/view_doc.asp?symbol=A/RES/66/288&Lang=E.

3. UN General Assembly, "Follow-Up to the Outcome of the Millennium Summit, Resolution 55/162," December 18, 2000.

4. International Chamber of Commerce, "ICC Granted UN Observer Status," press release, December 13, 2016, https://iccwbo.org/media-wall/news-speeches/un-general-assembly-grants-observer-status-international-chamber-commerce-historic-decision. For a complete list of organizations with UN observer status, see www.un.org/ga/search/view_doc.asp?symbol=A/INF/71/5.

5. UN General Assembly, "Follow-Up."

INDEX

321